MW01331149

PRAISE FOR

Downriver

"*Downriver: Memoir of a Warrior Poet* is a very moving, deeply introspective, and exceedingly forthright book. Ryan McDermott brings an exceptional voice to the post-9/11 literary landscape, blending the harrowing realities of combat with the raw reflections of a gifted poet. His journey—from leading soldiers during the fight to Baghdad to navigating the financial world, enduring personal loss, and, ultimately, finding self-discovery—offers an unflinching look at the sacrifices of service and the often-overlooked challenges of reintegration after that service. Few war memoirs achieve the level of literary depth and emotional resonance of *Downriver*. And even fewer help us understand the enduring impact of war, the burden of leadership in combat, and the resilience required to forge a new path beyond the battlefield."

—**GENERAL DAVID PETRAEUS**, US Army (Ret.), Former Commander of the Surge in Iraq, US Central Command, and NATO/US Forces in Afghanistan; Former Director of the CIA; Co-Author of the Bestselling *Conflict: The Evolution of Warfare from 1945 to Gaza*

"*Downriver: Memoir of a Warrior Poet* is a powerful story of our generation of veterans. Ryan provides a moving and thoughtful account of his personal experience as a son, father, and husband during war, peace, and the time in between. It is an important lens into the life of a multigenerational modern American military family."

—**ERIC CHEWNING**, Operation Iraqi Freedom Veteran and Former Chief of Staff to the US Secretary of Defense

"*Downriver: Memoir of a Warrior Poet* is a powerful testament to the character, courage, and sacrifice of those who served—including my son, Captain Travis Patriquin, whose leadership was instrumental in the Anbar Awakening in Iraq and who gave his life in service to our country. Ryan McDermott brings to life the journey of becoming a leader, weaving in lessons he learned from Travis along the way. Through his vivid storytelling, I saw the same spirit that so many have described in Travis—the selflessness, the humor, and the unwavering commitment to a purpose greater than oneself. This book not only honors the memory of those we have lost but also ensures their legacy endures, capturing the essence of who they were—not just as soldiers, but as extraordinary individuals whose impact continues to inspire."

—**GARY PATRIQUIN**, Gold Star Parent of Captain Travis Patriquin, US Army, killed in action in Ramadi, Iraq on December 6, 2006

"Ryan embodies the American spirit of resilience, opportunity, and hope. From challenging beginnings, he navigates a path marked by diverse hardships and opportunities, ultimately arriving at a place of understanding and peace after decades of struggle. His time in the Army was transformative, shaping his outlook on leadership and purpose. Through poems written in the moment, we witness the journey of his soul. Most importantly, Ryan captures his quest for meaning—a story rooted in the profound question, 'Why?'"

—**LIEUTENANT GENERAL ED CARDON**, US Army (Ret.)

"During Operation Iraqi Freedom, Task Force 3-69 Armor was the advance guard for the 1st Brigade and the 3rd Infantry Division, leading the charge toward Baghdad in one of the most intense and decisive armored offensives in modern warfare—truly embodying our motto, 'Speed & Power.' Ryan McDermott's platoon played a crucial role in this historic operation, functioning within a company under my command as we engaged determined enemy resistance, captured key objectives, and advanced with relentless momentum. Ryan exemplified the grit, initiative, and battlefield leadership vital to our success. *Downriver: Memoir of a Warrior Poet* is not only a personal account; it is a tribute to the warriors who led from the front in one of the most significant campaigns of our time."

—**LIEUTENANT COLONEL ROCK MARCONE**, US Army (Ret.), Former Commander, Task Force 3-69 Armor in Iraq

"A heartwarming memoir that will help with life's struggles."

—**R. EDWARD FREEMAN**, Stephen E. Bachand University Professor of Business Administration and Olsson Professor of Business Administration, the Darden Business School, University of Virginia

"Ryan McDermott gives us an intimate and detailed account of what it is like to be part of a modern American military family—from childhood trauma and being on the tip of the spear going into Baghdad to marital separation, home invasion, encouraging sons to go to West Point, and rebuilding his life. His account is patriotic, emotional, telling, and, like life, often chaotic and messy. All Americans owe a big debt of gratitude to families like McDermott's for their service, sacrifice, and utter commitment to American ideals. His style engaged me to the point I could feel the tingling tension leading armor into harm's way, the gut-wrenching pain of losing the love of his life, the shock of violent burglary, and the pride over his developing son. His account made me proud again to be an American with fellow citizens like him."

—**JAMES G. CLAWSON**, Professor Emeritus of Leadership and Organizational Behavior, the Darden Business School, University of Virginia

DOWNRIVER

Downriver: Memoir of a Warrior Poet

by Ryan McDermott

ISBN 979-8-88824-708-2

Cover art and design by Lauren Sheldon

Published by

köehlerbooks™

3705 Shore Drive
Virginia Beach, VA 23455
800-435-4811
www.koehlerbooks.com

Downriver

Memoir of a Warrior Poet

Ryan McDermott

VIRGINIA BEACH
CAPE CHARLES

To the men and women who have served overseas, along
with the family, friends, and communities who supported
our warfighters during the Global War on Terror,
I dedicate this to you.

CONTENTS

AUTHOR'S NOTE

As I sit to write this note, I feel a sense of privilege, humility, and obligation to share my story as honestly as possible—a story that belongs to countless others who've journeyed through the same treacherous waters. *Downriver: Memoir of a Warrior Poet* is, at its core, a search for meaning and sense of self through transformation before, during, and after war. It is a story that explores the meaning of the American dream and how the choices we make as individuals can take us on unintended paths with profound consequences. It represents a search for a common denominator to what makes us all human and the values that define us as Americans.

Some scenes within the story are dramatized to simplify the narrative from much more complicated realities. For example, the chapters regarding the counseling sessions, while based on my actual therapy process, are completely dramatized. The lessons I took from them are real, though. My writing, revised from catharsis to coherence, also incorporates another layer of development, taking creative liberties in some cases, to make the overall story a poem in itself with the river as a central theme.

The river, which flows as memories in prose and poems through the pages that follow, has both symbolic and literal meaning. Our perspective along the river of life often reflects the confines of the immediate terrain in which we find ourselves. At some points along the river, the future seems certain, and at others we can't see beyond the bend or sense the calm waters beyond the rapids. The river reminds us that life rarely offers a straightforward path, and that healing is not a destination but a journey that demands courage, persistence, and the willingness to keep going, even when we can't see the way ahead.

The term "warrior poet" has a specific meaning within the context of this book. It represents both a symbolic and literal term. A warrior poet is a person who commits to mastering the art of war through both physical and intellectual rigor. But I also believe it represents anyone who has endured trauma and has journeyed to process that experience into personal growth. As a veteran with post-traumatic stress disorder, I reject the notion that any of us are any less because of our wounds. Rather, those experiences make us warriors, and our ability to translate our experiences for others—whether that is through poetry, prose, or other artistic avenues—makes us warrior poets.

To my fellow veterans, especially my West Point classmates and the Dog-Faced Soldiers of the 3rd Infantry Division: this book is for you. I hope it reminds you of your path to become a warrior and the bonds you formed on the battlefield. May it remind you that you are not alone, that your service remains valued, your warrior heart is seen, and the sun always rises on the horizon after the night.

To the families who support our soldiers: I hope your story is adequately honored and revered within these pages. To civilians who seek to understand: I hope this story provides insight into the heart of our warriors and their families who sacrifice so much for our country. To young Americans who have answered the call to serve: May God bless you on your journey and grant you protection as you become warriors and defend our nation. You represent the pride of America, and the commitment you demonstrate each day binds you to the legacy of heroes that precede you. Your country is forever proud of you and grateful for your service.

Thank you for reading and joining me for my journey downriver. May it inspire you to reflect on your unique journey and influence your path forward.

INTRODUCTION

Remains of the Night

The secret to happiness is freedom,
and the secret to freedom is courage.

—THUCYDIDES

The evening was cool and damp in the early spring of 2011. Clouds drooped over the nation's capital, creating the faintest fog as I walked along the Potomac River trail from Georgetown toward the Lincoln Memorial. My mind replayed the battles I thought I'd left behind, between the deserts of Iraq in 2003 and the trading floors of Lehman Brothers in 2008. I now had to fight to save myself and cope with losing my marriage. I ruminated on memories that, in Lucy's absence, held painful meaning. Our love story, one for the ages, was over. After I got home, I wrote a poem.

Throughout my adult life, I've written poetry whenever I feel intense emotions that demand expression. Each poem represents a cathartic journey inspired by an emotion or experience, iterated countless times until it finally translates into art. I search for the rhythm and tempo to reach a climax and conclusion—and when it is completed, I gain a sense of closure.

"Remains of the Night"

As I lie here still, awaiting the light, I wonder how to fill the remains of the night.

Another dream fills my mind, that we come to find our love again shining bright.

But now, each day we become strangers, while regret in my heart lingers.

As the sun rises, I awake with the light. Realizing there is nothing of life in sight.

Only cold soot and ash remains. As lightning is bound to the rains,

So too, the fire that burned bright, now extinguished, leaving nothing but charred stains,

Remains of the night.

WASHINGTON, DC

April 1, 2011

Failure can be a great teacher if one has the humility to admit their mistakes and courage to see personal flaws. For years, my pride put me on a slow downward spiral in my marriage, which accelerated with my inability to cope with the pressures of the 2008 financial crisis. An inability that stemmed in part from my combat experience in Iraq in 2003.

War is a strange experience. I'd always been able to fight another day and maintain a front of stability. In my youth, I lost my home on my journey to West Point. Yet I persevered to graduate and receive a commission as an infantry officer. War shows you the moral ambiguity in others—and in yourself. It strips away the illusions of invincibility, leaving you to face your mortality. I learned a lot in 2003, as I waited to cross the bridge over the Euphrates River, explosions echoing in the distance and the weight of leadership pressing on my shoulders. It wasn't until years later, as I lay on a stretcher in the emergency room on that chilly night in April 2011, that I truly appreciated the impact of the war.

I lay on a stretcher in Howard University Hospital's ER, waiting for stitches in my chin and thinking life couldn't get any worse. One might assume that at rock bottom, there is nowhere to go but up, but you can spend a lot of time going sideways, neither up nor down but stagnant. It takes a concerted effort to ascend from the abyss when there's no ray of light to follow—when there is no hope.

Hours before, the home where I lived in the Shaw district just south of U Street and east of 14th Street had been invaded. I'd never felt more defeated than when one of the two intruders, a man built like an NFL linebacker, stood above me after landing a right cross to my chin. He demanded money, but I had nothing to give. I think he relented because he saw the desperation in my eyes. When the police arrived and began to question me about what happened, I broke down.

Neither the attack nor having my computer and phone taken caused me this grief. Everything from the past twelve months just seemed to hit me in the moments after the home invaders ran away: losing my wife, Lucy; career disappointment; and missing my children, who were a thousand miles away.

As I waited for the doctor, my tears dried, leaving a salty residue on my face, and my mind spiraled into the past.

A year before, I was working at a Wall Street job and living with my family in a nice apartment in northern Manhattan. On the surface, everything seemed well enough, and we did a lot together as a family. But the marriage had deteriorated during my time in business school. At the time, I was blind to the roots of failures that grew in the aftermath of my deployment to Iraq. I did not yet realize that I had come home with post-traumatic stress disorder (PTSD). Combat left a mark on me that I was too proud to deal with. Plus, Lucy and I were busy growing our family.

By 2006, Lucy and I had three children, and then I started an MBA program at the University of Virginia. The financial stress, combined with the need to pass my classes and find a job, was too much for me to handle on top of trying to manage a family of five. I pulled away, into myself and into my work. Lucy pulled away in response. She came to view my ambition in my career as a path toward leaving her behind. I did not see it that way, of course. Plunging into my work provided escape from the trauma of war. I also saw it as necessary in order for her to stay at home with the kids.

Lucy and I tried to reconcile for the sake of the children, but our arguing was not good for them. And it wasn't good for us. We argued about money and how we spent our time. I was frustrated with the way Lucy managed our finances in my absence. Lucy hated that I was emotionally and physically unavailable because of my long work hours. I got annoyed that she called me in the middle of the day when I was trying to work on important projects. She resented that my ambition took me into a career where I'd have to work such long hours and not be interrupted.

I felt like I didn't have a choice, with the financial crisis driving record unemployment. It was a great job that paid extraordinarily well, but I could not meet my potential at work due to distractions at home. Lucy felt isolated and overwhelmed raising three children on her own. In the end, our resentments were too deep and marked a point of no return; we stopped trying, or at least I did. I still loved her and felt an obligation to her for supporting me through the war; I just didn't feel we could be together any longer.

As the last days of Lehman Brothers unfolded, I watched dreams I'd built crumble, not unlike the destruction I saw in Iraq. The stock market crashed, and with it the deliberately constructed facade of my life. I had been a soldier turned banker, trading a rifle for a set of golden handcuffs, only to find the enemy within was more daunting.

I had felt a connection with Lucy from the moment we met. Our whirlwind romance began as the United States entered a war footing, with Savannah as the backdrop. We cherished our moments together and shared similar dreams. She wrote me letters every day I was deployed to Iraq, and that carried me through. Without her support, I don't see how I would have made it. That was 2003. By late 2009, though, we were different people.

When it became clear that investment banking wasn't viable for a father of three young children, I sought a new position in New York City but eventually accepted a job in Washington, DC. Although it required fewer hours, it came with a significant pay cut. Lucy and the kids moved to Florida, a decision I later regretted. At the time, though, I was consumed by self-loathing and feared that my presence might continue to harm my children. Florida seemed like a safer option, with Lucy's parents and my mother, Patty, nearby. I could provide a better life for Lucy and the kids there while I endured my self-imposed isolation.

In my new DC life, a self-inflicted purgatory in the months preceding the home invasion, I lived off cereal, Subway sandwiches, and canned tuna and slept on an inflatable bed. My job paid well, but I needed to make sure Lucy and the kids were well taken care of. I also wanted a minimal footprint so I could move if necessary. Living out of a suitcase was like being in Ranger School or combat all over again. I enjoyed the simplicity and began to understand the homeless veteran epidemic. There are only a few degrees of separation between those experiences.

I lived in five different apartments in the year prior to the home invasion—two in NYC and three in DC. I had no less than six roommates, not including my wife and kids. When I first moved to DC, I stayed in a temporary hotel in Foggy Bottom that was paid for by my employer. From there, I moved to the eastern part of the Shaw district to live with two young professionals relatively early in their careers. They gave me a three-month deal to get comfortable in the area and find another place more suitable for the long run.

After that, I found a spot closer to the subway, which allowed me to commute around the city as I did not have a car. The apartment was just five blocks from the metro. Scott worked as a government civilian employed by the Environmental Protection Agency while Robert worked as a public affairs specialist at the Department of Commerce. The home, which was tightly bunched among other homes, had two floors with three bedrooms. The front door opened into the living room, with the stairs to the second floor in plain sight. The kitchen was behind the living room. Each room had a window, with the living room window facing an alley where people passing by could peep in. Scott had the master bedroom at the top of the stairs and was outfitted with his own bathroom. Robert and I shared a bathroom at the opposite end of the hall from Scott's room. Robert's room was closest to our bathroom, and I was in the middle, which meant I was the only one who had to endure his late-night rendezvous with guests.

At approximately 9 p.m. on the night of the home invasion, Scott had a friend over for a visit. I was upstairs taking a break from work on my laptop in the living room and heard them talking downstairs but didn't pay attention to the conversation. As I returned to my project, Scott walked back up to his room. About two minutes later, I heard three loud knocks on the front door. I tried the peephole but could not see anything in the dark. Assuming it was Scott's friend, who had just left the house, I made the fateful mistake of opening the door, which dramatically changed the course of my life.

On the other side of the door stood two large men who clearly were not the same guy who had just left. Not wanting to dismiss them outright, I asked, "Hi, can I help you?"

One man responded, "Yeah, we need to come in."

At that moment, I knew something was terribly wrong. They pressed against the door. I attempted to push them back with the door itself, but they blocked it and shoved me inside. With the door still ajar, I tried to run past them and outside. This was not a fight I could win, regardless of my combat training; fighting increased the risk of ending up dead because they could have a gun. That's when the larger of the two men decked me in the cheek just below my eye. I absorbed the first punch without getting disoriented and yelled out to warn my roommate.

"Scott, we got company!" Then I yelled at the intruder, "Let me out!"

I heard Scott scrambling around upstairs, and the second man, who was skinnier and nimble, raced to grab my laptop and cell phone from the table. The bigger dude stood me down in a boxer stance to block me from the door. When I tried to run around him again, he hit me with a right cross to the chin. I hit the ground. Disoriented, I curled into a seated defensive posture, my Army training taking over. He kicked at me while I was down but backed away as I shoved him back with my foot. The intruder just wanted me to stay put.

The irony is that I never got into hand-to-hand fighting in Iraq when I led troops at the tip of the spear. I got home without a scratch. Instead, my first injury came from a fight in the heart of the nation's capital.

That Scott locked himself in his room may have saved my life. The intruders knew someone else was there to call the police and that their time was limited. In fact, several police officers arrived on the scene within minutes of the men running from the apartment. The speed of action was so fast that for a moment, I wondered if they'd caught them.

A police officer pointed out that I was bleeding profusely from my chin and helped me find a rag to compress my wound. He asked me questions, but I could hardly recount what had just transpired.

I handled the situation without much emotion—until I went to my room to collect my wallet and saw my West Point class ring, which might have been stolen had I been wearing it.

I broke down into tears. I felt like a complete failure. Life had kicked me when I was at my lowest, showing me new depths of despair.

The police officers were professional in their investigation and quickly loaded me into an ambulance. The hospital was less than three minutes away.

Waiting in the emergency room offered time to recover in a safe environment. I composed myself as people who dealt with these situations daily bustled around me. They had bigger problems. As I waited, I avoided eye contact with anyone besides the nurses or doctors, who treated their job like a factory line. Once it was my turn, the doctor stitched me up quickly and put a bandage over my wound. It was approximately 2 a.m. when I was released from the hospital. The city felt more dangerous than ever, my paranoia making the short walk home seem impossible. I hailed a taxi. When I got home, sleep evaded me as my mind sought a way out of the mess my life had become.

In the midst of it all, I was looking for meaning and rationality. Searching for a way to reconcile the man I had become with the boy who once believed in duty, honor, country, and the American dream. Searching for the light in the darkness, clarity in the fog.

I realized that my American dream was not material; it was not about attaining a house, car, job, or making the most money. No, it was defined by the general well-being of my family. Certainly, material things help us enjoy our family lives, but they mean nothing without the relationships that comprise a family and, more broadly, our American communities. I had not been focused on those things. I was living to work, whereas I should have been working to live.

When I was a child, imagining my life as an adult, I hoped to have a decent home, a family, and a fulfilling job. I wanted memorable holidays. I hoped to provide my children a better life than my own. Back in the 1990s, that did not seem like an improbable goal. The stock market was booming, and opportunity seemed boundless. I first aspired to become a professional athlete or a scientist, but my experiences gradually steered me toward a different, higher calling.

Coming from a working-class family, I planned to serve my country as a down payment for my dreams. And I embarked on that path successfully, my idealism continuously nourished—until I ventured off to war and later the trading floor of a Wall Street investment bank. Then the carnage of war and the disconnected corporate culture and excesses on Wall Street left me disillusioned and broken. Now I stood at a crossroads, wondering what direction to go. I looked further back in time. I saw my mom—her struggle to sustain her dreams and the impact of her journey upon my own. Were there lessons I might learn from her?

Before I went to sleep, I wrote a letter to my estranged wife, Lucy. I imagined our journey together as a stroll along a river. Where we had once walked side by side, we now found ourselves separated by treacherous waters. I couldn't imagine what the future might hold for us but knew we had to repair our relationship, if for no other reason than to become the parents our children deserved.

April 2011

"Conflux"

I reach the conflux walking downstream. A decision has to be made.

Which path leads to my dream? With distance, certainty begins to fade.

I ask a stranger for the way. For a while, I walk with the crowd,

Deaf to my own heart's say. For the penitent path, I was too proud,

Ignorant of being led astray. I come to realize my mistake.

We must choose our own way, paved by the decisions we make.

This memoir is of my quest—a quest to find love, build a family, and reconcile my past, developed through fifteen years of catharsis and countless iterations. It is a journey through losing a childhood home, the deserts of Iraq, the financial corridors of power, and the harsh realities of life. It is a story of loss and redemption, of battles fought on enemy territory and in the heart, mind, and soul. And it begins with a step into the unknown, requiring courage and a leap of faith.

I realized that I was a broken man and needed help. The next morning, I sought out a counselor to assist me. The counselor's name was Paul Rubin.

PART I

An American Dream

CHAPTER 1

Counseling—Session 1

WASHINGTON, DC

April 20, 2011

Sitting in my office at Booz Allen's downtown DC location, the weight of everything bore down on me—years of pushing myself harder than I knew was possible. In Iraq, I had led men in combat, fighting through the deserts of Iraq into Baghdad, and returned to accolades from my family and community. But now the pride I once carried had eroded, exposing wounds I could no longer ignore.

It had been months since I felt any sense of normalcy. Each night, I lay awake, replaying the events of my past. I thought about my children—and the tears in their eyes when they hugged me goodbye. Every moment felt like a battle to keep going. I poured myself into work and avoided the challenging issues with distractions.

When I finally realized I needed help, I found Paul Rubin's contact information in a search for local counselors specializing in relationships and trauma. I was barely holding it together at work and inside. As I approached Paul's office on K Street, I felt a faint sense of hope that he could lift me up. I ventured into his small office and took a seat on his couch.

Paul was of modest physical stature with gray hair and a puffy gray beard. He was a Jewish chaplain and counselor. After several minutes of pleasantries, Paul explained his process: "I'm not sure what you know about what I do, but I want to caution you that this will be hard work."

He then merely regarded me with his wise eyes, and after a moment of reflection, I decided to lay it all out for him.

"Paul, I am just overwhelmed by everything," I began. "I feel out of breath and can't process what is happening. I had everything. And now, nothing. There is this weight on my shoulders. I was an infantry officer some years ago, and I could carry any weight—fight on to any battle. This is a battle I cannot win. I can't see the future. It is an abyss. I am barely treading water." I looked at Paul, praying for answers.

What he gave me was compassion but also firmness. "What we are going to do is peel back some layers. I can be your guide, but you are going to have to make this journey."

"Where do we start? What can I do to begin moving forward?" My breathing grew heavy as I felt all my problems bearing down on me.

"Ryan, just breathe, nice and slow," Paul said. "Breathing is one of the most basic forms of freedom we have as human beings. Remember that. No matter what, you can control your breathing. Use it to calm yourself and find your center."

Paul waited as I steadied my breath and relaxed.

"Let's start at the beginning. Tell me about your life."

We spent the next hour going over aspects of my childhood that provided initial clues to my blind spots and opportunities for post-traumatic growth. Leaving Paul's office, I felt both heavier and lighter. I hadn't expected him to have answers, but he offered me something important: clarity. For the first time, I realized that the journey ahead wasn't about fixing external circumstances of my life. I had to journey within and confront the truths lurking there. The strategies I used to survive as a child—burying my emotions, pushing through the pain—were not working as an adult. As I walked back to my office, I realized that this would be the hardest challenge I had ever faced.

CHAPTER 2

Great Expectations

> Now, I return to this young fellow. And the communication I have to make is, that he has great expectations.
>
> —CHARLES DICKENS, *GREAT EXPECTATIONS*

ORLANDO, FL

May 1978–September 1995

Our lives are constructed on the foundation of expectations—those we set for ourselves and those set by others. From the moment I was born in May 1978, my path was being shaped by those who came before me. My mother, Patty, was only twenty-three when she brought me into the world as a single parent. She had high hopes for me, as I would later have for myself, and like most parents, she did everything she could to ensure my future was bright. But as I grew older and began to craft my own ambitions, I learned dreams couldn't shield me from the inequities of life. But they gave me hope.

Patty broke up with my biological father, Bill Carder Jr., before realizing she was pregnant. By the time I was born, Bill was engaged to another woman, leaving me with little knowledge of my parents' relationship.

As a fatherless child, I fantasized about being a Jedi like Luke Skywalker, rising from humble beginnings to become something more. I imagined becoming strong enough to confront my father. But the truth was, I didn't know Bill Carder; whether he was good or bad, he wasn't in my life.

As time passed, I continued searching for my Obi Wan Kenobi. But the most important figure in my life was my mother. Patty was eccentric and vulnerable but also wise and empathetic. And she was a loving and optimistic role model. For the first years of my life, I hardly noticed that I didn't have a dad.

Mom and I lived in a small apartment on the south side of Orlando, near my grandmother's house, surrounded by suburban homes and remnants of old orange groves. My world was small, defined by this familiar landscape until I entered elementary school.

The McDermott family has a history of moving around the country. My maternal grandfather, Bill McDermott, served in Air Force Strategic Air Command units, flying classified missions over the Pacific. He and my grandmother, Maryanne, were high school sweethearts from Butte, Montana, and spent their lives going from one assignment to another, including a tour in Japan. For his last assignment, in the mid-1960s, my grandfather was stationed at McCoy Air Force Base in Orlando and stayed there after he retired.

Patty described her father as a man with an enormous heart and compassion but who also resorted to physical violence under the influence of alcohol. Yet my mother loved him more than any person in her childhood. There were five McDermott siblings: Karen, Patty, Billy, Peggy, and Danny.

Growing up, I knew nothing of the Carder family, my paternal side. Only members of the McDermott clan and friends of the family were around to welcome me into the world. My grandfather wanted to take me as another son after Bill Carder denied paternity. Eventually, tests confirmed paternity, but as a child all I would know of my biological father were the $130 checks that came every month until I was eighteen years old.

My grandfather unexpectedly died of cardiac arrest due to acute pancreatitis before I turned one. Bill McDermott was a mentor to young men, and I'm told many showed up at his funeral. With his loss, life looked different.

Both of my uncles, Billy and Danny, served somewhat as role models growing up. Danny existed in my daily life, since he lived with my grandmother, though our relationship gradually drifted apart as he became a man and I followed Mom to a new life. Billy remained a more distant role model, since he had joined the Army and started his own family.

Still in high school when I was born, Danny was a bit like an older brother; he was not exactly responsible and got into a lot of trouble.

My mother worked the night shift at a local 7-Eleven when I was a baby and lived with my grandparents for a short while before moving into a nearby apartment complex. She used my grandmother as a sitter on many occasions. Danny cared for me once in a while but did not set the best example in terms of right and wrong. For example, he once gave me chewing tobacco and offered me dog food to eat. But Danny had a compassionate side. One day when I was five, I was watching a kung fu movie with him.

"You like that fighting, Ryan?" Danny asked as he stood to retrieve the mail for my grandmother. "I'll be right back, and I'll show you some moves."

Highly entertained by watching guys kicking each other, I decided to impress Danny with a kick I had watched on TV. I ran outside, and he was on his way back in. He smiled and swooped in closer as if to pick me up.

Flawlessly executing the kung fu move I'd seen, I kicked him right between the legs. He fell to his knees gasping and cursing. I ran like I've never run before and hid in a closet inside.

Danny never retaliated. He loved me too much to do that. However, he would remind me of that incident for years to come.

"I'm sorry, Uncle Danny," I would say with remorse.

"It's alright, Ryan," he told me with some pride. "You have a strong kick. I wouldn't have thought that out of a little runt like you."

On another occasion, Danny reinforced my belief in Christmas by leaving a small deer antler for me to find on the front lawn on Christmas Eve. My cousins and I were playing in the front yard when Danny got my attention.

"Hey, Ryan. Go over there and get that ball." As I grabbed the ball, I saw the small deer antler and picked it up.

"Uncle Danny, come look at this," I said with excitement. "It looks like a deer antler."

"Yeah, it does," Danny said. "That must be from one of Santa's reindeer. That's very special." He might not have been teaching me much about the true meaning of Christmas, but it was a special moment that reinforced the magic of the holiday. Danny showed me love and something to believe in.

The absence of my biological father growing up created a void that I have wrestled with all my life. My self-esteem was shaped by his absence and how it was explained to me. My mother told me Bill Carder held me only once after the paternity test confirmed our genetic relationship. Yet despite his not seeking to be involved in my life, she always reaffirmed my father's positive qualities.

"When your father walked into a room, he just lit it up," she would say as I listened in awe. "He is very smart, and people really like him." Or "He was a great guitar player and musician but was even better with people." These words painted an idealistic picture of this man, and I never questioned why I was not in his life until later in adolescence. I just accepted my position in life. I was born a bastard, but I didn't know the term or understand the implications.

This image of my biological father became a powerful force in my development. I learned from the mistakes of those men present in my life while I aspired to become more like a man who existed only in my imagination.

When I entered elementary school, Mom began to consider the need for a more normal family structure. She dated throughout my early childhood but was careful to introduce me only to those she was serious about. And Mom ended relationships if there was an issue between me and the boyfriend.

She met Rick Hardwicke when I was in kindergarten. They dated and later married when I was in first grade. I was the ring bearer at the beachside wedding ceremony. Soon after Mom and I moved in with Rick in the new apartment, I learned that life would be different. At six years old, I was still accustomed to crawling into bed with Mom. Rick set new boundaries, forbidding this. However, I had my own room, a slight expansion in my small world. And my mother and Rick together became "my parents."

We lived in that small apartment north of Orlando for about a year before moving into a suburban home in nearby Casselberry during the summer of 1986. My parents financed the purchase of the home with a mortgage that provided a low teaser rate, leaving them with more home than they could afford when the rate increased later. I wouldn't understand this until I was much older, but the balloon note could never be refinanced. For the working class, good credit is hard to come by in a volatile economy. Rick's unstable work as a construction worker meant loan officers never trusted his wages. Somehow, my parents managed each year despite the rising payments, though there was nothing left for savings.

I spent the remainder of my childhood, from 1986 to 1996, in that home on Sandpiper Drive. There were three bedrooms, a kitchen, a living room, and an office. Behind the house was a spacious backyard with trees I could climb and space to run around with our black Labrador, Hawk. It was in that home that my dreams developed and where, for the first time, I gained a sense of a family life. For Mom, I imagine this was something she had only dreamed of. Except for the absence of my biological father, I had a relatively normal childhood.

Rick had a rough edge and a deep appreciation for the simple things. His hands, always calloused and swollen from swinging a hammer, told the story of a man who worked hard. He worked construction during the week and fished on the weekends. We went fishing together occasionally, but we never bonded on the water. I hated fishing and was too impatient to appreciate the connection with nature.

Rick spent part of his early adult years in Alaska, where he first picked up the construction trade. He was a good man but had not fully matured before taking on the role of stepfather. In retrospect, Rick pushed me to grow in ways that I would not have with only Mom. Patty inspired me to dream about what is possible, but she coddled me. Rick got me involved in youth football and instilled in me discipline and a work ethic.

Household chores were the cornerstone of my development under Rick. In the spring and summer, I mowed the lawn on a weekly basis for a $5 weekly allowance. In the fall, I had to rake leaves. But there was more to our family life. Rick and Mom shared a passion for living in the moment. We enjoyed many outings on the boat in nearby lakes, exploring the open water, and spent weekends camping, usually near the ocean.

After my sister Jessica was born when I was nine, my parents settled down. Increased childcare expenses forced them to sacrifice more in the present so that there would be a future. Our roles in the household evolved, and Mom often worked nights to help pay the bills. She accomplished a great deal in building a family with Rick. Their life gave them purpose in raising their children and afforded them years of wonderful memories—the wonder years of my childhood.

In the fifth grade, one of my teachers recommended me for intelligence testing. My IQ score placed me in the gifted program. I had previously been an average student because I was ignorant that I had more to offer or accomplish. From that point on, I allowed myself to dream of going to college, which no one in my family had done.

There is a trap that many in lower socioeconomic circles face: low expectations and feeling powerless. This vision of going to college inspired me to strive for goals I wouldn't otherwise have attempted, such as involvement with varsity athletics and clubs. Without that dream, I might have drifted along with the crowd and ended up nowhere.

For my parents, college was merely a dream to sustain me through high school before I moved on to something more practical. The reality was that college might be unattainable even if I did everything right. For my mom, though, an unattainable dream was still worth pursuing. She would catch me when I fell. Meanwhile, Rick encouraged me to learn a trade, such as carpentry. I helped him reroof our house one summer with money received from our insurance company for hail damage.

My middle school years were the best of my childhood. I developed friendships and continued to perform well in school. I had a reasonably normal and happy home life, despite the constant concern of losing our home. Mom took a supporting role in her career and gave up her office job so she could have more children. She had my sister Laura when I was eleven.

Mom eventually returned to work, catering at a restaurant that allowed her flexible hours so that she could accommodate Rick's construction career. When times were tough, Patty stepped up to the plate. We lived the American dream. Three kids, a dog, a home with a big backyard, and good friends. These were the few years that all the McDermotts—Karen, Bill, Peggy, and Danny—seemed to have it together.

On Christmas Eve 1988, everyone met at my grandmother's house for a great celebration. It was one of the only times when someone did not get into an argument and everyone left happy, looking forward to the next year's celebration. I talked to Aunt Peggy on the living room couch about her recent bout with breast cancer. She had spent the previous year in chemotherapy and was supposedly cleared. Her husband, though, failed to keep up with insurance, and she never followed up with additional doctor visits. But we mostly chatted about small things that occupy a middle school boy's time.

I remember hearing her cough as we said goodbye that night.

"It's just a bad cold, Ryan," Peggy said with a smile. "Keep it up in school."

"I will. I love you and hope you feel better."

I left with my family and thought nothing of it. A month later, Peggy was in a coma, dying of cancer-caused pneumonia in the same hospital where I was born. Cancer had aggressively reappeared in her lungs, taking over her body. The diagnosis came too late to save her life. Two weeks after that last goodbye, I came to understand the finality of death at her funeral.

By the time I entered high school, the lives of Mom's family members had deteriorated. Alcohol derailed my uncles' trajectories. Danny spent time in jail on at least three separate occasions. Billy lost his job with a defense contractor in Orlando, his wife left him, and he became a stranger to his own children. He moved in with my grandmother and died of liver failure years later. With their downfalls, I had no positive male role models left other than Rick. But my relationship with him came under increasing strain as I grew into a man.

During my first months in high school, I realized that I would end up like most of my family if I did not focus on school. The trends were clear in my family: underachievement, alcoholism, failure, and a vicious cycle of codependency. The dream of attending college kept me on the straight and narrow. Choosing good friends who shared my ideals would make me more likely to succeed. Joining the track team helped on both fronts. I tried distance running and came to find a great group of friends. I then decided to do cross-country running, even though I lacked the body for such endurance racing.

Joining the team introduced me to Cory Frank. Cory seemed to have everything figured out and was well liked on the team. He maintained excellent grades and lived a structured life. His parents attended every track meet and offered him great support. It caused me to evaluate the strengths and weaknesses of my own family.

I was also increasingly seeking to understand myself as I entered adolescence. Mom would comment on how much I looked and sounded like Bill Carder as I matured. We had the same eyes, the feature my mother most adored in Bill and now saw in me. In my mother, I saw where I got many of my qualities, but I struggled to understand other differences. I found myself seeking to redeem my birthright as Bill's son. If I allowed myself to fall to temptation as my uncles had done, then I would deserve the abandonment by my father. It was my mission to make something of myself.

But I also wondered why Bill never tried to be a part of my life. These questions grew to compete with my mother's idealistic portrayal.

Throughout my teenage years, my mother was my best friend, even if I couldn't fully appreciate it at the time. Her unwavering support and understanding were constants, providing a sense of security amid the chaos. The larger dynamic between myself, my mom, and Rick, though, grew strained partly because of that close bond.

Rick and I argued constantly as I sought more independence. He unleashed a verbal storm meant to put me in my place whenever I expressed anything he perceived as disrespect. I grew to resent him. I probably was disrespectful, but there was a general lack of understanding between us. Rick seemed to assume the worst of me, perhaps because he had been a wayward teen. People naturally apply their experience of the world in their parenting. Rick did drugs and was a poor student in school but found a new life in Alaska. That was why he always emphasized hard work and labor.

Rick did not always provide moral support. On one occasion, his close friend mocked my desire to become a military officer. "You'll never make it in the military, Ryan. You're too much of a momma's boy," he laughed. It hurt deeply that Rick didn't stand up for my dreams.

As my relationship with him frayed, so did Mom's. During my junior year of high school, they grew apart, with Rick working and living in a different city.

Mom remained strongly in my corner. "Don't listen to that loser," she ordered. "If you want to go to West Point, then you're going to go."

When I turned sixteen, I took a part-time job flipping burgers at a Checkers. Based on Mom's recommendation, I bought my first car, a 1986 Chevy Chevette hatchback, for $400. The car was a lemon, and I had to immediately put in another $1,000 to replace the clutch. It often stalled out on me even after I got the clutch replaced. Lesson learned: Do your own research before an important purchase. Driving that car was a humbling experience and made me want more in life. I turned to sport to give me a path to achievement.

During my sophomore year, I met a coach who, in addition to teaching me how to pole-vault, helped me build my self-esteem. In short, I found my Obi Wan Kenobi—Coach Bill Cashman. Cashman was the son of a career Army officer and had grown up in Maryland. He was a respected pole-vault coach in Maryland for years before moving to Florida in the late 1980s. He was married and working as a financial adviser when he turned back to the pole vault as a freelance coach in Central Florida in 1991.

After my first practice, Cashman shook my hand, looked me in the eye, and told me with the utmost confidence, "You are going to be a state champion." It was a total surprise to me. *Someone believes in me?* I was in awe of his confidence and dedicated myself to the event for the duration of my high school years. Cashman exuded energy and optimism and demonstrated that he cared about his athletes.

A technically complex event, pole-vaulting requires a combination of speed, agility, and kinesthetic awareness. Cashman knew how to teach all aspects and viewed the process of developing a pole-vaulter as an art.

The process consists of an approach run, planting of the pole, jump, and physical inversion of the body, culminating in the pole-vaulter clearing a crossbar many feet in the air. To learn how to pole-vault, one must break down the event into several phases and train them individually. At a personal level, that's what I tried to achieve in developing my self-esteem, one part at a time, so I would eventually become a man. As I entered my junior year of high school, I aspired to an eventual state championship in the pole vault and more in my future.

The United States Military Academy first came to my attention during my junior year when I began considering a career in the military as a rite of passage to manhood. I took the PSAT and listed Reserve Officer Training Corps (ROTC) as an option. Sometime after that, I received a mailer from West Point, presumably identifying me as a competitive candidate for an appointment. It was an attractive option.

To gain admission, a candidate must qualify medically, academically, and physically. The most important admissions hurdle at any service academy, though, is the congressional nomination. Academy candidates must apply for a nomination from an elected official overseeing their area: either the senator of their state or their own congressman. Senators Bob Graham and Connie Mack and Congressman John Mica served as my representatives at the time. Most candidates apply to all three.

Senator Bob Graham's interview board took place in the Tampa area, roughly a ninety-minute drive from where I was living at the time. I made the trip in my run-down Chevette, which could barely make it around town, let alone a long trip. Every time the car stopped for a light, it stalled, and I had to turn the ignition to get it running again. Between my home and school, there were probably eight stops. On occasion, when the traffic lights were timed right, I completed the trip without stalling at all.

On the drive to Tampa for my interview, my car barely got up to the minimum speed limit. At top speed, it vibrated so violently that it seemed like the engine would fall out. Fortunately, there were only a few stops en route to the interview location. The drive took approximately three hours, which was as far and long as my car ever drove.

At the interview, a panel composed of business leaders and a uniformed officer asked me why I wanted to be a cadet at West Point.

"I want to serve my country," I told the panel.

"What would you want to do after graduation?" the officer asked me.

"Well, I'm not sure yet, but I hope to learn more about Special Forces," I said. "I'm a pole-vaulter, which is an intense sport, so I think I would do well in that type of environment."

I did not know enough about the Army to speak coherently about where I wanted to serve other than the jobs I saw on TV. I wanted to jump out of airplanes and experience what I saw in Army commercials. It looked intense and exciting.

On the way home from the interview, the Chevette teetered on the verge of falling apart. Somehow, it completed the trip, and I eventually received an alternate nomination from Senator Bob Graham. I completed my two other interviews, with panels serving Senator Mack and Congressman Mica, and several months later I would get a final answer.

Great expectations had filled my heart and mind as I embarked on my senior year in 1995, but storms and obstacles lurked on the horizon. The months that followed would test my ability to persevere and achieve my dreams.

CHAPTER 3:

Foreclosing of a Dream

CASSELBERRY, FL

October 1995–May 1996

Hope provides a delicate bridge between dreams and reality that can easily fall out of balance and break toward despair. For my family, the balance began to tip in the fall of 1995.

In September, my parents separated and began the process of divorce. Stuck in the middle of the situation were my two younger sisters, myself, and my hopes for a successful senior year. When Rick moved into his own apartment, Patty invited a neighbor who was undergoing her own divorce to move into one of our rooms. The tense arrangement lasted a month or two, though it brought me and Mom closer in the beginning.

She also sought to help rectify the dearth of information regarding a hole in my life.

"Ryan, you are never going to believe what I found out about your father," Mom said gleefully as I walked in one afternoon after cross-country practice.

I braced for the news.

"Your father's wife lives in Oviedo. And guess what! You have a brother and sister! I was able to find her by the child support checks."

It turned out that my biological father's estranged wife, Kathy, was sending the child support checks. Through her research, Mom contacted Kathy directly over the phone.

I felt as if I'd had the wind knocked out of me. Having the mystery solved did not dampen my hurt. If anything, it opened a wound I didn't know I had. Here I was, at seventeen, having grown up imagining Bill Carder leading a parallel life in some alternate universe, and my siblings were minutes from my doorstep. Bill could have visited, but he never did.

I eventually talked to Kathy Carder and later Bill on the phone. In the background of one call, I heard my younger siblings making noise. My recollections of the conversations have faded over time, but neither Kathy nor Bill wished to disrupt their children's lives by telling them they had a brother. I was not confident enough to assert that I should be allowed to know them and them to know me. It was not my place, but I felt rejected. From time to time after school, I drove around the Oviedo neighborhoods, looking at homes with children. It became a useful distraction as the situation at home continued to deteriorate.

By December 1995, our temporary roommates were gone and with them the extra money for rent. Mom was already financially strapped when she lost her job two weeks before Christmas. She couldn't afford a babysitter, and her employer decided that her family problems were not reason enough to cut her slack for missing work. As our home life spiraled out of control, her grip on reality began to slip. It was not obvious until the holidays.

Mom cherished Christmas more than any other time of year. She would spend the year planning and saving, ensuring that Santa delivered presents that often exceeded our modest means. In previous years, she put gifts on layaway with the local department store and paid them over time. I took it for granted that it would magically happen.

On Christmas Eve 1995, it did not seem like we were going to have a pleasant holiday. There were no presents under the tree. As my sisters played in their room, I approached Mom in the kitchen and asked, "Mom, were you able to get any presents for the girls?"

Mom paused with a sigh that answered my question but then looked at me with a glimmer in her eye. "Ryan, help me get your sisters in the car."

I helped get my sisters in the back and sat next to Mom as she drove to various stores. We had a positive spirit as we headed out of the neighborhood and admired the lights, but then came despair. The K-Mart was closed. The grocery store was closed. We drove around for about an hour. Nothing was open.

When we woke up that next morning, Santa had not come. It was just another day to be forgotten. I recall only the car ride of despair the night before.

Christmas is obviously about much more than the presents; and it has nothing to do with Santa Claus. It is about celebrating the spirit of love and selflessness and the birth of Jesus Christ. But the absence of gifts, under such a dark mood, marked a crack in the foundation of our family.

By January 1996, my parents' divorce proceedings were anything but amicable. Mom had to give custody of my sisters to Rick, who had the support of his friends and family. Mom had no one to turn to but me. No friends who could help. Her mother and siblings, struggling with alcoholism, were unreliable, though she wouldn't have accepted their help even if they offered.

Losing custody of her girls caused Mom to turn inward, away from the real world. We drifted apart as I focused on my future and she brooded on the past. At home, we lived off canned goods and cereal. Patty did her shopping at the day-old bread store, where we found deeply discounted food items past their expiration. I also ate fast food at half price at work whenever I had a shift at Checkers. I eventually quit around March to work for Cory Frank's dad in construction, doing demolition and cleanup whenever we didn't have a track meet. I often stayed late at Cory's house and ate dinner with his family before returning home with no utilities. I did not discuss my family issues, but the Franks knew something was wrong.

After the dissolution of her marriage in February 1996, Mom drifted further away from reality. She did not eat or sleep and began to suffer from delusions. The pressure caused her to break out in shingles. I watched helplessly, incapable of helping her through her personal crisis, as the bedrock of my support slowly became a stranger.

Danny tried to intervene, stopping at our house one day.

"Come take a ride with me to the store."

When I got in his old beat-up truck, I realized he reeked of alcohol.

"Ryan, your mom is sick. Why aren't you doing anything about it?" Danny yelled at me as he drove out of my neighborhood. I was scared. His slurred rant continued all the way down the road. I leaned on the truck door and considered jumping out, but we were moving too fast. I thought, *Danny, you're sick too.* But I did not want to escalate the situation. I just wanted to go home.

"Take me home, Danny," I begged, restraining my emotions. I already felt the weight of the situation on me. Now this drunk asshole was telling me I wasn't doing enough. Fortunately, Danny complied and dropped me off. He sped off across town, where he lived with Grandma.

Mom and I were better off without that type of help. I'm certain that adding alcohol to the mix would have killed her.

My routine was well defined during those difficult times. Every morning, I got out the door before the light of day could shine on my problems at the house. I put my focus on other things, like school and sports.

At night, I spent time with a study group at Cory Frank's house, where we hammered out homework for our dual-enrollment college courses and Advanced Placement classes. My friends and I were all overachievers. Returning home at night made it easier to ignore the problems. Patty was usually sleeping. I simply found my way through the darkness of the home and crawled into bed—then dreamed of West Point and a state championship.

The state meet was my more immediate future, and I had more control over the outcome, or at least it felt that way. At some near point in the future, though, the twin dreams would either become reality or disappointments; that was a certainty.

For three years, I dreamed of racing down the runway with poise and launching into a vault that would carry me fourteen feet or higher at the state meet. I figured that height would be enough to win that year since there were not a lot of returning vaulters from the year prior. I developed my skills in every aspect possible. I trained through all four seasons.

The track and field championship series included the conference meet between all schools across the county and the district qualifier, regional qualifier, and state meets. In my junior year, I unexpectedly qualified for both the region and state meets by setting personal records in consecutive meets. After my junior year, I set the high expectation to win the state meet in my senior year.

Coach Cashman trained his athletes as champions on the track not by just teaching technique but also by enforcing a championship attitude. During one practice, I came up short and landed gasping on my back from about thirteen in the air. I got my wind back slowly, but my confidence was pierced.

"Okay, Ryan," Coach said with authority. "That was quite a fall. You look fine. Get back on the track and go again."

Reluctantly, I agreed. The next jump after a fall is always the hardest. Confidence in the event is everything, and you don't want a bad jump to be your last. So, I went down the runway one more time. It wasn't my best effort, but I regained some confidence.

Throughout the track season, I detached from Mom's situation as she experienced more delusions. Some revolved around my future, and she would share them as if she were a prognosticator. For a while, it was mostly positive.

"You are going to go to West Point, Ryan, and will become great. You are destined for great things. I know it," she once told me with shining eyes. "Lord knows that I never wished you would join the military, but I'm so proud of you that you are doing it."

Mom's optimism flattered me. "I feel like Charlie from *Willy Wonka*," I said with a smile, "just hoping for that ticket."

"Your golden ticket," she began to sing. "It is going to be your golden ticket out of this." She returned to the misery of the moment. "That is what I'm living for, all I have left here—in this house."

"Mom, I've got to get in first, but I hope you're right," I replied. I tried not to think about the decision, since I could not affect it.

Mom based her own value on the success of my future and the impact I might make. Over time, though, I saw this optimism fade completely away.

Mom looked to everyone but herself as the reason for her troubles. Everyone from her publicly appointed lawyer to Rick to her own family were responsible for the misery of her existence. The shingles exacerbated her mood and compounded her stress.

The downward spiral was clear-cut. The stress of her dissolving marriage left her ill equipped to handle three children and a job. The loss of a job left her unable to provide for her children. The loss of her children left her without a purpose. Divorce then became more about exacting revenge than about what was right for the children, on both sides of the courtroom. Her anger came out in those proceedings and isolated her from anyone who could have provided support. Everyone became her enemy. And so she escaped into a fantasy world, her way of coping and ultimately surviving.

She needed to be confronted directly about her mental issues, or she would die. I did not think I was strong enough to do such a thing—but I would try.

I was content to skip senior prom. Cory Frank decided to skip, and the girl I dreamed of asking ended up going with another guy. She would never know of my crush.

The week before prom night was stressful. I had come off a bad meet, suffering a "no-height," which occurs when a jumper fails to achieve an opening height in three attempts. I put too much pressure on myself and collapsed after I missed my first attempt, missing my second and third tries. My aspirations were in peril. If I no-heighted at the district meet, there would be no regional or state championship.

School pressures also remained high as I realized that a West Point appointment might not come to fruition. Others were in the process of receiving military academy appointment letters. With each passing day, I assumed fewer spots were available. All the golden tickets were being found, and I was losing my dream.

By March 1996, Mom already seemed intent on withering away. Yet part of her desperately wanted me to have my senior-year experience. When I got home the day prom ticket sales ended, I found out that Mom had made a trip to the office to buy me a ticket. It was a noble gesture, but also a sad one. She wanted me to have my senior rite of passage in that house even as it went into foreclosure. Notices had come in the mail, and the die had been cast. The house was gone. It was only a matter of time before we were physically removed from the premises.

But I went ahead and made my prom preparations with Ben Brown and Chris Kempink. I had a tuxedo fitted. My plan was to change at Ben's home and head with him to the event.

When the date of the prom finally arrived, the situation at home was even worse. I had become the only outlet for Mom's frustrations, and it began to wear me down. In the morning before school, we got into a rare argument about the conditions of the home, and she became defensive. I blamed her for my previous week's no-height.

I would later recognize many signs indicative of a cycle of codependency in our relationship. Patty needed me around to validate her purpose in life, even though she had become incapable of serving that purpose. I was dependent on her for emotional support as a parent, but her problems were dragging me down with her, making me more likely to fail. Who would rescue me from failure? Mom would, of course. Except I think, deep down, she recognized that I needed to break away.

The argument kept me at the house a little longer than normal. The sun was shining bright that morning when I finally left with an unfamiliar sense of clarity. I faced the prospect that staying there might undermine my performance, destroying all hope of achieving my goals.

Feeling detached throughout the day, at practice I contemplated what would happen when I returned home. I squarely faced reality: I might not get into West Point and might be stuck in that house—or worse, homeless—with no college prospects.

Danny and Billy always used my grandmother as an excuse for why they moved back home. Their failures in life were masked by a cycle of dependency. They lived in miserable conditions and drank alcohol to forget their problems. The alcohol led to more failures, but at least they had each other. Misery loves company. I saw the patterns repeating with me. Maybe I could help Mom through her ordeal by remaining with her, but I risked losing my own future. I needed to address her condition.

When I walked into the living room that night, I saw that Patty had vandalized our walls with angry messages to Rick. She lay on the couch with candles lit around the room. It was a spooky sight, so I avoided her, but she engaged me in one of her delusions as I was about to leave for prom.

"Ryan, the FBI will be at the prom," she told me as if people were listening to her. "They're on to Grandma and Danny. They also know of your importance, Ryan. You are Paul Atreides Muad'Dib. You are destined for greatness!"

Normally, Mom kept her prophecies about me to herself and would only share bits and pieces. On this occasion, she was intent on involving me in her delusion.

It tore me apart. I admit that part of me wanted to believe her in order to deny the sickness that had taken over her mind. She wasn't intentionally ruining my night. After all, she was the reason I was going to prom.

"Mom, you're sick. I don't know what to do, but the things you're saying . . . I just think you need help," I said, fighting off my emotions.

"I'm sick, huh? Fuck you, Ryan! Get out of my house and don't come back," Mom said with anger I had never witnessed in her before. This was a different person I was dealing with. But I needed her to see her state of mind clearly.

"Mom, it's not normal to write on walls. We have no electricity, no water. I mean, things aren't just going to get better," I said. I realized I'd hit a nerve and tried to reassure her, "Mom, I love you."

"Well, I don't love you, Ryan," she yelled at me. "It's time to get over that and get the fuck out of my house, now!"

"Mom, I love you. Don't do this," I pleaded from the door.

She threatened violence and hammered the final nail into the coffin: "I don't want to see you. Don't come home tonight. I don't love you anymore."

She slammed the door.

Mom forced me out that night in a way that meant there was no going back. Prom was the only place to go. I sat at my table the entire night, feeling empty. I know it was not the sort of moment Patty had envisioned. As my classmates celebrated, I sat in limbo, trying to make it through the night. I told a couple of friends from the track team, but no one else. No one wants to be depressed on prom night.

"You can stay with me and my family," Ben told me after the dance. I roomed with him that night, and a day later, Cory Frank's parents offered me my own room at their home; their oldest son had left for college.

Mom was soon admitted to a mental hospital against her will under a Florida law that allows family members to have loved ones committed. Rick and my grandmother signed the papers. Mom saw it as a betrayal and possibly rightfully so. Our family finally decided to do something for Mom—after there was nothing left to salvage.

Family took on a new meaning for me on prom night, as one life disappeared and a new one emerged.

Terri and Allen Frank were high school sweethearts and got married at a relatively young age. They had two boys, Brandon and Cory, and a daughter, Haley. Brandon was a couple of years older and was attending Florida State University. Haley was three years younger and a freshman in the same high school. Together, the Franks were an all-American family—Catholics that went to church every week, and first to leave after taking Communion to make it home in time for the NFL games at noon.

Allen was the quiet but steady leader of the family. He deferred to Terri on many issues but kept things together anytime drama entered the equation. There was rarely any drama with Allen. He never yelled, and he was patient. Like Rick, Allen worked in construction but was also part owner in a successful local construction business. Terri was a nurse who wore her heart on her sleeve and kept the children in line. She was always concerned with enriching the family in meaningful ways, such as planning family vacations. She was driven in this way and was extremely welcoming in bringing me into the family. They rescued me from the downward spiral.

A few days later, I returned to the home that was now under foreclosure to retrieve items I had left behind. Mom was no longer there. I didn't know what to do with our personal possessions. I couldn't possibly bring it all, and I didn't know if Mom would be able to get her stuff.

Overgrown grass had already crept onto the driveway. An unpainted panel on the front of the house added to the sense of abandonment. Mom had painted the front door gold, and a lock now hung there. To get inside, I lifted the garage door and went through the interior door. The house was a mess, but I sensed that the crisis was over.

Cory was taken aback at the sight and kept quiet as we ventured inside. I rambled on about what had happened, showing him how Patty had painted on the walls. Most of the house was dark, but we could see by the light from the window in my room. I grabbed family photos, some clothes, and my baseball card collection. Uncollected dust filled the air. The bare concrete in the kitchen was now dampened by the humidity.

"Anything I can help you with, Ryan?" Cory asked at one point.

"No, man. That's okay." I didn't really hear him; I was stuck in my memories of life in that house. "On second thought, can you grab that?" I pointed to a component of my stereo system, which had taken over three years to put together. First I got a radio receiver for Christmas—no speakers, just the receiver. For about six months, I had to listen to music on my headphones. Then I used summer lawn-mowing money to buy speakers. The next Christmas, I got a CD player for the system. Finally, I added a tape deck with the money Rick gave me for helping reroof our home.

After I rounded up the stereo system components and wires, I turned to Cory. "How much stuff can I bring over?"

"However much you need—you want," Cory corrected. "We have space."

We grabbed a few other items but left a great deal for whoever would come to clean up the mess. I didn't want to impose.

That was the last time I thought of that place as home. It was anticlimactic in a way. When we got back to Cory's house, I neatly stacked my belongings in the closet and readied my temporary room.

Later that same night, I took a shower and finally allowed my emotions to release. I cried as the hot water sprayed down on my head. For days, I had felt empty. The good memories in my childhood home were now tainted, and there was no going back.

Weakened by the emotional release, I hunched over on the shower floor, staring down at the drain. I remembered making breakfast for Mom on Mother's Day and a Christmas when I got everything I wanted. I remembered playing with my dog, Hawk, in the backyard. I remembered my sisters, my family, and the life we had—all those great memories washed down the drain.

"Why am I living?" I wondered aloud as my tears ran short. It was not a suicidal thought but rather a desire to disappear or give up.

I could have chosen to remain in solitude and prevent hurt by never being close with anyone else again. But I didn't want that; I would rather feel the pain of intense loss than isolate myself. So, I faced the pain head-on and allowed more tears to flow.

The pendulum of emotion began to swing back toward center. *I cannot feel sorry for myself*, I decided. The past was gone, but I still had dreams to carry me into the future. I turned the water nozzle off and prepared for bed and the day ahead. With my last conscious thought that night, I imagined vaulting in the state championship.

Both pole-vaulting and West Point occupied my mind as I sought a diversion from the past, the former allowing me to focus on the moment and the latter providing me hope for the future. In the Frank family's home, I slowly recovered from the traumatic events at my own home. The new environment helped. The Franks offered me a picture of what a family could be—loving, compassionate, and a source of mutual support.

With Patty's situation stabilized, I felt more at ease than I had in a year. Still, I anxiously awaited word from West Point. My focus on admission peaked after I got settled into my new living situation. By April, it was getting late in the process to expect notification, so I reached out to my congressional liaison at John Mica's office. I had previously been told there was no decision yet, but with championship season in track looming, I hoped to relieve some pressure by putting this issue to bed.

"Hello, this is Ryan McDermott again. I was just curious if anything has come down yet?" I asked the assistant who ran appointments to the academy, bracing for potential disappointment.

She responded with some reservation: "Ryan, I am not supposed to release that information yet, but I'd advise you to buy a winter coat."

"What's that?" I asked. "I got in?" I was in disbelief; I was going to West Point.

"Read into it what you want, but you'll need a winter coat."

Two days later, I received an offer packet with an embossed certificate: my golden ticket to a bright future. It was such a relief. I literally danced for joy around the house as it all sank in and shared the news with my friends. It was bittersweet, though, as Mom was not there to celebrate with me.

With the stress of the academy admission finally out of the way, I jumped in the conference championship on the school's senior award night. The rest of the scholars in my class participated in the awards ceremony. An Army officer attended to present my appointment in front of the crowd, but I was absent, and that same night, I added a conference championship to my senior-year achievements.

On the road to my ultimate goal, I won the district and regional championships in the pole vault. As co-captains of the track team, Cory and I also led our team to district and regional team titles. Cory qualified for the state meet in the 800-meter dash while I was ranked second in the state pole vault going into the final. It all came down to one meet.

In May 1996, the state meet was held at the University of Florida track in Gainesville. I felt good going into warm-ups and put up some big practice jumps. On my opening height of the meet, I cleared the bar by over two feet. It might have been the highest jump of the entire competition. However, the height does not count unless there is a bar measuring the result. As I walked back to the waiting area after missing a jump at the next height, I realized that the bottom of the pole had broken off. This was unexpected. I could no longer jump on the pole weighted for me at 160 pounds. I had to move to a pole weighted for 165 pounds. Apprehensively, I grabbed a stiffer pole with less flex. I had jumped on the same pole a couple of weeks prior but had lost additional weight to ensure I could also jump on my primary pole.

"Okay, here we go," I said as I held the pole over my shoulder for my next jump. *Stay in the moment*, I thought as I prepared for my pre-run routine. As I stood some 100 feet from the pit, I lifted the pole high above my head with both hands and imagined the jump one last time before I started down the runway. The dream was becoming reality, but I now had to perform in the moment. I took one step back before launching into my approach run.

"Six, five, four . . ." I counted my approach steps down as I neared the pit. I accelerated the count. "Three, two, one." With both hands, I pressed the pole skyward for the plant and counted out my last two steps in the jump. "Plant, and takeoff." As I leaped toward the sky, I could feel that I had hesitated ever so slightly; an observer probably would not have noticed. I came up short on the jump and stalled over the crossbar.

Unfortunately, my attempt to use that other pole was fruitless, and I went out at that next height. On the next jump, I stalled out over the crossbar yet again. I finished fourth in a meet that I could have won. I felt no anger and little frustration, only total disbelief, as I walked away from the pole-vault pit.

Coach Cashman pulled me aside after the meet. "Ryan, you could have won," he said sympathetically. I could tell he wanted me to win almost as much as I did. "You were good enough to win, but it didn't happen."

My emotions released with my tears as I felt a dream slip away with utter finality. There's no second chance at your senior year. "I wanted this so bad. I wanted it for you as well," I told him with passion. "I let the pole get to me. I shoulda—"

"Shoulda, coulda, woulda. Stop it. It's over, Ryan. Now you need to be a good sportsman and head to the podium. You should be proud. I am."

I struggled to find words, and tears continued.

"Look, you've dealt with more this past year than most people deal with in a lifetime. The ability to persevere in the face of adversity defines a person's character. You won the conference, district, and regional meets. You are a success. You persevered." Coach paused. "You're going to West Point, for God's sake," he concluded with a smile, as he realized that it was time to finally focus his athlete on the next height.

It was disappointing to lose that meet. But the goal gave me something to pursue when everything else was falling apart. The reality is that I would never have made it to that meet or gained admission to West Point without such great friends and a compassionate mentor. My world crashed down around me, and yet there I stood on the podium, all because of the people who supported me in my hour of need. If I did not prove something to others, I certainly proved something to myself. In my heart, I felt like a champion.

CHAPTER 4

Becoming a Poet

WEST POINT, NY

June 1996–May 2000

West Point focused on military discipline, academic rigor, and physical development. The structure of cadet life, with its intense pressures and high standards, left little room for emotional expression. I endured the challenges, gradually became a leader, and completed my academic studies. Yet amid these demands, I found myself turning inward, searching for meaning beyond the mission of the academy: to paraphrase, "educating and training leaders of character for our Army."

Writing afforded a private space to make sense of the hardships I was confronting, both externally and internally—and to explore my identity, spirituality, and my dreams of the love I desired. Poetry became my voice to express what I had to suppress, the part that longed for connection and struggled with loneliness. As I navigated the four years of development at West Point, I was not just becoming a soldier and leader; I was becoming a poet.

Journal Excerpts

September 30, 1996 (Cadet Basic Training Reflections)

My journey to West Point began on an overcast day in late June. I felt like a zombie, stunned that the day had finally arrived. After landing in Newark, I made my way to the airport hotel, where hundreds of other new cadets were staying. Everyone seemed to be top of their class, exuding confidence. Despite trying to get a good night's sleep, the excitement kept me awake.

I awoke at 4 a.m. on Reception Day, otherwise known as R-Day, the biggest day of my life. By 5:20 a.m., I was on the bus, headed to West Point under dreary skies that mirrored my apprehensions. When we arrived, a line of new cadets stretched for a quarter mile outside the Holleder Center. I stood quietly, absorbing the mix of emotions around me—fear, excitement, confidence. Parents beamed with pride, knowing they wouldn't see their children for months. I had already said my goodbyes.

The cadet cadre, essentially our drill sergeants for the summer, began yelling as soon as I stepped into the gymnasium, out of public view. We were lined up, ordered not to look around, and shouted at for the slightest mistake. My first blunder was failing to properly secure a tag to my bag. What followed was a blur of instructions, hurried actions, and relentless pressure.

One memorable tradition was reporting to the cadet in the red sash. I made sure not to step over his line, but my bag tipped over and fell on his foot. I was yelled at but quickly moved on, following the red line to my company area. Exhausted and disoriented, I struggled through the rest of the day.

My chain of command consisted of Cadet Alff, the harshest in the company, who hazed everyone mercilessly. Cadet basic training, called "Beast," was relentless, with nonstop knowledge recitations and drills. My two roommates, Joe Odorizzi and Jeff McFarland, were initially sources of friction due to the stress we were under, but by the end of

Beast, we had become good friends.

Beast was a test of endurance, physically and mentally. We rappelled down cliffs, endured pepper spray, fired M16s, and carried heavy packs during road marches. At the midpoint of Beast, our cadre changed, and I went from the hardest squad leader to the easiest, Cadet Gross. He helped me see the absurdities of military life with humor, though I felt he was too lenient.

Beast ended with the assignment of what would be our companies for the academic year. I was assigned to C-2, known as the Flying Circus, and had to move all my belongings in preparation for the final march to Lake Frederick. That march, though tough, had a purpose, and I felt accomplished upon reaching the destination.

At Lake Frederick, our squad excelled in Squad Stakes, earning the best score in our company. The nights were cold and miserable, especially when it rained, but the march back was satisfying. Each step brought me closer to becoming a cadet, and with each passing day, I felt closer to achieving personal perfection as well. The goal was clear: to become the best version of myself.

October 1

Waking up on Monday at 5:10 a.m., knowing that I have nineteen hours ahead of me until I can sleep again, is one of the hardest parts of West Point. It's a relentless cycle, especially when I have five days in a row like this. Sometimes I swear I won't get out of bed, but the sense of duty and the drive to learn push me forward. Prioritizing has become essential here; learning to do homework for classes where it will be checked has saved me from unnecessary consequences, though I've learned some lessons the hard way. The only solace for a first-year cadet is sleep.

"Sleep"

Sitting, waiting, nothing to do. Grab my pillow and rack for a few.

Lie in bed and fall asleep. Resting my eyes, counting sheep.

Slowly my mind drifts away. Bringing the passing of a new day.

Floating through the cloudless sky. Wondering when I learned to fly.

All the time looking around. Wondering why there is no sound.

It is the world of my own creation. One of absolute elation.

October 10

This week has been a mixed bag. I did well in boxing, winning both of my matches, one by a technical knockout (TKO), but I'm disappointed with my performance on the history exam, where I got a D. Despite the setbacks, I'm determined to keep pushing forward. The fall season is becoming more noticeable, adding a sense of change in the air.

February 9, 1997

Everything has moved so quickly. I was cut from vaulting in December and have returned to intramural boxing. I'm feeling more energetic now, but I sense it might be grating on my new roommate, Steve Dunaway. He has this obsession with listening to the same Tim McGraw song every morning, and it makes me long for home. Despite the homesickness, life feels good. I'm more relaxed and productive than I was last October, focusing on refining my skills rather than just getting things done. Plebe Parent Weekend is close, and I'm looking forward to it, but there's a subtle shift in how I see myself. I'm evolving, and it's noticeable.

February 23

This past week has been productive. I successfully handled my duties as plebe in charge for minutes without major issues, and I'm gearing up for the Army Physical Fitness Test now that boxing is over. My grades are still just below where I want them, but I'm striving harder this semester. I've come to realize that as people, we are forever changing, never the same individual we were the day before. This journal helps me evaluate my progress, and I've noticed how my faith becomes stronger during trials. It's a cycle I'm trying to understand.

March 22

I have felt depressed the past couple days. I realize my ultimate goal in life is to have a happy family. I just feel bad right now because I have no relationship going on. I have never had a strong relationship with a girl, and now I feel sort of hopeless, being here at West Point. I'm not shy like I was before; I think I'm afraid or something. It is frustrating to me. The only thing I need in life is this love, but it seems as though I am on no track to find it here. Maybe my expectations are too high. Plebe Parent Weekend has been a drag in a way. I am actually looking forward to the academic routine.

"Frustration"

Impatience writhing inside, anticipation at the root.

Two worlds, one I soon just leave behind.

Memories grouped together, separated by my environment.

Pushing forward in one world, I look to the other.

Existing as a faded semblance of my former self.

Trying to reanimate myself from my ghostly existence.

Forging a path from one world to the next. Delicate is the manner in which

I must engage on the path, in order to make my soul complete.

I'm trying to reconcile the person I was with the cadet I am becoming. West Point offers a shelter from the outside world, a place to grow, but I'm constantly aware of the challenges that await beyond these walls.

April 15

"Storm Clouds"

I continue to drive on. Through the cloudless day I walk.

Many pleasant thoughts ring through my ears.

Storms are coming, though. I've seen the forecast.

Winds are picking up, and I prepare for the hurricane.

The lightning flashes with the thunder close behind.

Life seems unbearable. Just as I think things can't get worse,

The winds pick up and destroy my home.

My life. What is the source of this destruction?

The pursuit of happiness? Perfection of the day?

Why do we pursue something intangible and elusive

When, if we set our goals to just live, we could be happy?

Reflecting on last year, I see how my family's separation shaped my outlook. These thoughts offer an abstract picture of the emotions I remember feeling during that time. I've come to appreciate the importance of having a well-regimented training program—keeping both my body and mind in shape is essential to maintaining my well-being.

May 2

"The Spring Air"

Spring is finally clear in the air, leaves turning from brown to green.

Everything smells so fair. I look at the mountains, a perfect scene.

Winter is finally over. More and more each day, a little more life

Seems to be present all around. I hear the birds playing their fife.

Oh, such a sweet sound. The summer is upon us.

I'll soon be back home at the beach,

With the sun and sand, and a cocktail in one hand, in the other a peach.

There's so much life in the land. Spring is finally here.

The changing seasons mirror the changes within me. With spring in the air, I'm reminded that I'm over the hump of the semester and heading home soon. I'm focused on finishing strong, knowing that each day brings me closer to the goals I've set for myself.

May 22

Term-end exams (TEE) are over, and it's a huge relief. I studied hard and feel like I did well. By striving for perfection, I've managed to exceed my own expectations. Life is about overcoming obstacles and working toward self-fulfillment. I've come to believe that the spirit we cultivate here on earth is what lives on after we're gone. Whether heaven exists or not, the impact we have on others—the spirit we leave behind—endures.

December 7

I think I would be a good infantry officer, but I would still have a rough transition into that type of life, as I do with any transition. I love training, I am intense, and I am not as afraid to die as some others. I figure that I could get killed just as easily walking across the street or in some stupid accident. I would rather not die at all, but if I had to, I would rather die in combat. I have also developed a desire to become better trained in different soldier skills.

There is something almost romantic about war. War is the one activity that man has participated in throughout the history of his existence. Our lives are bounded by time, and death comes to all. My philosophy is that just living and leaving a small mark in time is enough to satisfy me at this current time—that if heaven exists, which I believe it does in some form, it is a bonus to living. However, I think that our souls experience existence differently after death. While in our physical form, we experience many emotions and adversity and happiness. After death, I think that we come to cherish those emotions because they let us feel our existence and feel alive. Yet after death I think our souls are less tied down by emotions.

I have experienced much mental agony in my life, so much that I think it has permanently scarred me. I haven't cried in more than a year and a half, since my family problems occurred. I feel like I have been drained of emotion. I hardly experience joy anymore. Even when I am home.

January 24, 1998

"The Weeping Willow"

At the edge of the river stands a weeping willow among other trees.

Her long branches drape down like hands, covering her face as she weeps.

All alone stands the willow, without a companion to keep her content.

She cries as wind begins to blow. A plea for help is what she's sent.

She is the black sheep of the forest. Unlike the others, she is all alone.

Saddened by her loneliness, unlike the rest, she calls out in distress with a moan.

This poem represents an image of my mother among her family. My mom has had to deal with more problems with her brother and mother. Her brother Danny assaulted her, and he went to jail. In the process, she ended up in a women's shelter since she could no longer stay with her mother. It would be best if she separated from them and started a new life.

Maybe it's because I'm a thousand miles away, but I did not feel as affected by her ordeal as I think I should. I need to maintain my focus and stay level-headed. People don't realize what it is like to be completely on your own, though I can't say that exactly; I mean having no one in your "real" family. However, real family has new meaning to me. My real family consists of anyone who accepts me as part of their family. The Franks are real family to me. My mom is the only blood relative who I actually relate to as real family and is the most important member. I have considered what I would do if my mom were to die. I would have no one to relate myself to, except my sisters. Maybe I'm the weeping willow.

February 20

I need to revive myself somehow, maybe by going to church. I'm feeling somewhat depressed, but I am still functioning. Philosophy class really has me thinking about life. It also makes me question my future in the Army. I don't think I could ever take another person's life for any cause but to save my country and family. Even then, whose purpose for fighting is right? As Americans, we always seem to be fighting elsewhere. And who is to say that we are fighting for the right reasons? We are always going to think we are right, but there is another side to the issue.

"Will to Fight"

Hurry up and wait! This is the Army way.

What is it that you hate? You have no choice but to stay.

For nine years my life's on hold. Living my life in a slum.

When I get out, I'll be old. All for what? Our country's freedom?

Is that true, or is it all a lie? That I wear Army blue, just so that I may die.

As long as there be reason for and a cause deserving attention,

I am prepared to die in war. Live, serve, and fight with great men.

April 9

My mom is still at the women's center and will be there for at least a few more months. Last semester, I kept a daily routine of focusing on academics. I must admit, it was exhausting. I don't want to burn out, so I take it easy now. But I still study for the big tests and ensure that I understand all the material. One thing making time pass quicker this semester is that I have been sleeping a lot more. I think it is because I've been sick, but it could also be that I'm just depressed. I have started to really miss my family. I have two projects to work on today, a physics lab report and a math project. Both are major graded assignments. I also have to prepare for an in-class philosophy paper tomorrow, which is worth like 10% of my grade in the course. The monotony of this place wears on me often. The academic load is intended to instill strict discipline of the mind and conformity. I must maintain my artistic outlet to keep my sanity.

"Artist's Rhyme"

Sitting, waiting, what's happening—nothing. Listening to someone else sing.

Thoughts, expression, start to pour that have taken a while to lure.

Suddenly, everything is vivid and clear. I'm thinking well from ear to ear.

From my mind to my hand to my pencil and paper.

I feel, I write, and I iterate until my poem becomes sculpture.

This poem captures the essence of the artistic process I've developed. Initiated by a need to create something, to feel productive outside of the monotony of West Point's strict curriculum, I draw upon feelings and emotions to craft ideas into unique prose. Sometimes it works. Most of the time it doesn't. But I find great satisfaction when words and emotion converge to convey something of artistic value.

May 1

I love writing the word "May." My birthday, graduation—just two of many reasons to be glad. My grades are still doing alright. Last semester I thought I had maxed out my academic potential. But it turns out that I need to set my standards higher. I've been able to achieve any standards I set for myself academically. Plebe year, I didn't really have any. Maybe in one class I did, but not across the board like I do now. I should probably expect all A's from now on or at least strive for it. I feel so focused right now. I know that going home is just going to piss me off. Mom has always got problems, which she can't control but probably talks about too much. I always thought my self-confidence was low, but Mom's is probably worse. I feel really confident in my abilities now.

I feel like I have to help develop my own mother, which is frustrating because it should be the other way around. I must give her moral support through her challenges. Her poor self-confidence comes from her support base, her family. It's gone now, and she's searching for a new one. Her brothers constantly get themselves into trouble. It's depression feeding more depression and family members bringing each other down to their lowest level. You take away my mom, and I pretty much have no connections to my family. They are spiteful due to the condition they live in. Regarding how they treat me, it's like an oxymoron; they are proud of me, but they resent me because I've done something with my life.

May 11

How can our soul possibly survive eternity? How is it defined? Are our past experiences and memories a part of it? What defines the essence of a person? One could argue that our genetics and upbringing determine our personality and thus define our soul. However, is personality that closely related to soul?

A big problem with religion is that it focuses on the individuality of humanity. As far as we know from what we see, people are born, they live, and they die. In the middle of all that, many experiences and emotions shape the way the person views the world. Some of this must be genetic, since it deals with the organic framework of the mind. Just as someone's face might develop similarly to their parents', their thought processes and brain structure do also. As a living being with consciousness, we formulate a false sense of importance as an individual. It is important to satisfy the individual needs in order to live a happy and healthy life; however, as far as the afterlife is concerned, I would be happy to know that my spirit will live on.

This is where defining the spirit of a person comes into play. In heaven, I do not think our experiences matter. We may or may not be conscious of our earthly self. In fact, this might be how multiple lives can be explained. A person who has the same spirit might live multiple times. Now, a spirit is that which defines the personality of a person in the most elementary form. The spirit could be defined as energy and the person's experiences the matter. Just as energy and matter are interchangeable, albeit through a complex process, so are human beings and their spirits.

One thing is certain: We overestimate our importance within the universe. Why? Because of our natural instincts to survive. We survive by having some sense of self-centeredness. Why do we seek to survive? Because we are unsure of the afterlife, whether there is one—and if there is, what do we have to do to make it there? We seek to prolong life in order to reach our goals based on our assessment of this question. Those who have faith in the afterlife might search for the qualifications for this afterlife. Must I seek forgiveness? If I do, will I be saved? Must I be earnest with others? Or does it matter at all what I do? We all seek answers to these questions.

"The Gift of Life and Love"

Every day, someone asks what heaven will be like.

But these answers are given in dreams and everyday living,

Through goodness, mercy, devotion and selfless giving.

For if you can dream, you can learn to believe and then live it,

And to live the dream, to experience Heaven, God will always provide it. Every day . . .

Someday . . . The judgment and answers shall come forth,

And the Lord's plan will be revealed.

However, do not think this plan is something so concealed.

God's gift is love and so is the plan.

For Heaven shall be offered to every woman and man. Someday . . .

Today . . . We must try to live out the plan and do God's work.

To truly accept God's gift, we must accept him fully.

Accept his love, embrace his presence, and just believe.

Heaven is God's greatest gift to you.

We can experience his gift of love

Today . . . as long as our faith is true.

May 13

My mom still looks to me to find support. I don't mind lending support, but I hate hearing about all the problems. Summer leave is looking more and more boring, but I don't mind. I might just mess around and do nothing for the two weeks. Mom is getting on me about Thanksgiving leave tickets, and I really don't want to go home. I love her, but there is so much negativity surrounding her. It's a test to overcome, but it still weighs down on me. I have dreams still of the conflicts within my family. I just realized today the impact it has had in my life. It has caused an inner conflict that affects my personality and mood.

May 22

Well, TEEs are over, and what a relief. I studied my ass off like I wanted to, and I think I did well. By striving for perfection, I was able to far exceed my goals. I'm still recovering. I need about a week of sleep, but I'm pumped. I talked to Mom today, and it was refreshing to hear her in a better mood.

Life is about overcoming obstacles and working toward self-fulfillment. It is important to be satisfied with the person you are because when you go to heaven, you are the person that you have developed into. If people perceive heaven as something where they are happier and overall a different person for eternity, then your spirit really isn't there. It is important to be happy and have a strong spirit in order to have any chance for satisfaction after death. For even if no heaven exists, the spirit you exhibit here on earth will be remembered, and others will exhibit the same. These people may have never even known you, but they hold a piece of you within them, a common denominator.

Memories may differ. In fact, those might disappear after death, as does the body. But the spirit you have binds you to whoever shares the same characteristics. The one thing I would hold on to if Mom were to die would be that her spirit resides within me. I don't need her memories or anything of that nature. Our bond is eternal. I must add that I believe in heaven because of a dream I had.

"Heavenly Dream"

I lay there dreaming all through the night.

Suddenly, a warmth so pleasant held me tight.

I was looking at the sky, a wavy bright crystal-blue sea.

I felt its pure beauty and realized my soul's been set free.

It was just a moment, a feeling so good and pure.

This was my heaven; I knew this for sure.

I wanted to swim amongst the waves as almost to give it a big hug.

Similar to bundling next to a loved one by a fire on a nice fur rug.

Breath taken, enlivened, but I felt so much more.

Blessed, humbled, both of these too I felt for sure.

Warmth, security, everything plainly pure.

All this, and so much more, resides within the boundary of Heaven's shore.

The dream of Heaven becomes reality if you choose it to be,

For if you can dream, you may one day believe,

As you know the warmth of the sun. And as long as you believe,

You will one day wet your feet in Heaven's sea,

For the shores of Heaven lie just beyond the horizon.

August 28

I started the process of becoming a Catholic. I will get out of religion what I put in. Understanding and reading in between the lines is vital for spiritual growth. Internalizing the message is the next step. This will come with time and experience. I have already felt a release by reading a little of the Bible last night and today. It's like I have seen the words before. The reason behind this is that the truth is within each one of us. We just have to search for it. Words may not come out the same, but the meaning is the same. I was especially intrigued by the analogy that our bodies are merely a seed, so that when we die our spirit emerges like vegetation in heaven.

In the back of my mind, I planned this year to be the year that I investigate my spirituality. First year, just survive; second year, begin to excel; third year, expand my capacities. I will wait to see what my senior year will bring. Lately, all I can think about is my life after graduation. It's almost two years away, but I want to be ready. I can't stop thinking about starting a family of my own.

As the summer of 1999 drew to a close, I found myself increasingly introspective and feeling the lack of a family structure. The weight of unresolved emotions from my past surfaced, particularly those related to my father. What follows are the poems that came from the school year that followed, and my explanation of what each poem refers to.

August 1999

"To My Father"

There's a man who has no shame, two who love him who do not know,

While another falls victim in the game. But now his face will finally show.

All the boy's life he lived in a shadow, the shadow of another's shame.

The boy is an illegitimate son, forever to carry his bastard name.

It hurts . . . It hurts to be this boy, a boy in the man's body.

Father, why can't you just see how it hurts to be me?

Writing this poem was a way to confront the lingering pain and confusion from my youth: the lack of a relationship with my father. It was an attempt to bring clarity to emotions that had long been buried while lamenting that my siblings were oblivious to my existence. Amid these reflections, I began to think about the nature of strength and resilience. I considered how we often build up walls around ourselves, a false facade, only to realize that our perceived strength can be fragile.

"Sandstone"

Isolated, I am my own rock. No bone in me is weak or feeble.

I look to no one for help or stock. I am a man of stone, impenetrable.

What's this? A rock has no feeling. Can you live without love, all on your own?

Or do you covet this precious thing? Now you appear no stronger than sandstone.

This poem reflects the realization that isolation, while seemingly the purview of the strong-minded, can lead to a hollow existence. It is a reminder that true strength often requires vulnerability and opening up to others. As I grappled with these thoughts, I lost myself in deeper, more existential reflections. The feeling of being adrift, searching for meaning and direction, was pervasive.

"Lost"

In a cave, I stood all alone. With an unsettled voice I call out,

Amidst this tunnel made of stone. Trying to find a route.

A route out of this cave of loneliness, to a place less unbecoming of me.

Never again to experience the darkness. From this place, I wish to flee.

I listen for a possible echo. Somehow it might show me the way.

Or find someone who might know. Where I might find the light of day.

What's this? I think I see a light. Could this be the opportunity I seek?

I journey ahead, full of fright. For a future possibly less bleak.

The imagery in this poem captured my ongoing search for purpose, for a way out of the metaphorical cave in which I often found myself. Hope kept me moving forward, even though the path was unclear.

September 1999

As September arrived, my thoughts turned to the concept of quests and personal journeys we all undertake. I reflected on my own journey, visualizing myself as a knight on a mission, searching for something just out of reach.

"My Quest"

I am a knight on a noble quest, searching for something dear to my heart.

Undergoing many trials and tests, I struggle to find that missing part.

Loneliness has caused my soul to feel incomplete.

In my heart, there is a hole that brings me pain with each beat.

On my quest I've formed a sickness. Only one thing can serve a cure.

It is what gives us purpose, and that is love, wholesome and pure.

On this road I look to each bend, wondering, Will my quest ever end?

This poem encapsulates my yearning for connection and love—something that seemed elusive despite my efforts. Throughout this time, I dwelled on not being in a position to have a relationship. And I found a muse who inspired more affectionate poetry.

"On the Shelf"

She was a princess, I but a pauper. She had great beauty, and I adored her.

Admiration to a point of being excessive. Becoming annoying to her majestic self.

For she already knew she was impressive. I exist only as another item on the shelf.

To be stored away for that rainy day in autumn when things have gone awry.

If she asks for more, I give her some. If she asks me to jump, I ask, "How high?"

All I hope for in return is something for which I eternally yearn.

Whatever she decides to give, I am satisfied and continue to live.

I could only relieve my longing by writing down my thoughts. It was a selfish act. I couldn't have the girl, but I could at least have the poem.

I continued to dwell on a future I could not foretell. The anticipation of what might come stirred within me a mix of excitement and anxiety.

"Future Unknown"

Insomnia! What has brought this about? Anticipation and uncertainty of the future.

Hopefully everything will work out. But of this, you cannot be sure.

Impatiently, my stomach starts turning. The moment has finally come

For me to satisfy my inner yearning and, with it, gain more freedom.

It is best to go with the breeze, enjoy the ride and look around.

It will put your mind at ease, eventually, coming softly to the ground.

This poem reflects my attempts to come to terms with the unknown—to embrace it rather than fear it, and to trust that the journey ahead would unfold as it should. It was inspired by my experience at Airborne School the summer before, where I gained the confidence to take a physical leap. The act of confessing feelings was another leap I felt I needed to take, where I would lay bare my emotions, hoping for reciprocation—or, if nothing else, understanding.

"Confessing My Feelings"

Tonight, I present my heart to you with all my feelings and affection.

This surprises you? I thought you knew. Love has seized my heart, like an infection.

This infection has the feeling of an inferno. My heart burns for your love tonight.

In my veins, passion flows. Resisting was futile. I fought it as hard as I could fight.

I asked the Lord for his mercy. But he pushed me to seek my destiny.

I took the bold leap and confessed my feelings to my muse, who hugged me in that moment by the beach—as a friend.

October 1999

After that moment of awkwardness, I brooded on whether I'd gone too far. I knew that some things cannot be rushed and that beauty often takes time to reveal itself fully.

"Flower Bud"

Today in the garden I found the bud of a flower, its identity covered by its sepal.

It shut itself during a storm shower. I asked others what it was, but no one could tell.

Curiously, I tried to coax the bud to open. With my fingers I tried to unveil its color.

Any rougher and I'd have damaged its skin. So I paused, sat back, and began to wonder.

Should I wait for another day, so the flower doesn't wither away?

I fear someone else will take this beauty, never giving me a fair opportunity.

I hope someday I'll see a flower's bloom, admire its beauty, and smell its sweet perfume.

This poem symbolizes the delicate nature of growth, whether it's in love, personal aspirations, or even in the relationships I'd been yearning for. I wrote it as a reminder to myself that sometimes the best course is to wait and let things unfold naturally.

November 1999

As the year progressed, though, I began to feel the disappointment that my feelings were not reciprocated, despite my expectations being irrational. These reflections often carried a sense of loss and focused on the harsh realities of unmet desires.

"Dream Denied"

I once had a dream denied. A beautiful woman loved me.

Of this, I do confide. Searching the land sea to sea,

The woman that I had dreamed turned out to be someone I already knew.

She might have loved me, or so it seemed. But I was wrong, and I feel blue.

Love tends to be fickle, weighed heavier to one person's side.

Having one's heart torn out with a sickle closely compares to this dream denied.

Not all dreams come true, and realizing that, particularly in the quest for finding love, can be quite painful. It's a moment of reckoning. Some things are not meant to be, no matter how much we desire them.

The emotional toll of these experiences led me to seek refuge in my faith. I found myself praying for relief from the heartache and confusion that had become all too familiar.

"Seeking Asylum"

Lord, grant me asylum from this love I feel.

Give me back my freedom that it seems to steal.

For I don't have my heart's control. I lost it in her eyes somewhere.

I would do anything to regain my soul, venturing where few even dare.

Grant me asylum, I ask you please. The only power I have to turn to.

Can you set my mind at ease? What must I do for you?

What must I do to earn my soul, heart, and dignity?

Which direction must I turn to earn your blessed pity?

I was searching for peace—a way to claim my sense of self after feeling lost in the depths of unrequited love. This poem is a plea for guidance and comfort. I was also starting to realize that to find love, you must first love yourself, and through loving God and embracing His love, you can be ready to receive it.

February 2000

As I entered the new year, the concept of distance—literal and emotional—became a prominent theme. I imagined commissioning and moving to Georgia for the Infantry Basic Officer Leader Course. Maybe there I might meet the girl of my dreams. My longing for that connection often surfaced above other, more pressing concerns. I imagined that the woman I would grow to love was out there somewhere and it was only a matter of time and circumstance that we would finally meet. But I could not know when or where that would happen.

"In the Distance"

I see a beautiful woman off yonder. Would she ever feel for me?

That is what I begin to ponder. She is too far for me to see.

With distance, her image begins to fade, but I hold her picture close to my heart.

From my undying need for her it was made. It keeps us from ever coming apart.

Waiting for the day we finally meet. The picture becoming clear.

Personality, her beauty more complete. Her voice I can almost hear.

April 2000

With my last spring at West Point, I reflected on the seasons of life and equated them to seasons of love. I thought more about the nature of love and faith, how they endure through life's storms like an evergreen tree, unwavering and constant, and about what soil laid the foundation for such strength.

"The Evergreen"

The autumn rain assails the ground, its wind violently blowing the leaves away.

Its cry is the only sound, but all will be restored with the passing of the day,

The leaves, memories of spring, when love was new and pure,

And birds used to sing. Now you're not as sure.

Those leaves now only serve as a reminder, and have possibly fertilized

A love to last an eternity. I pray this dream is realized.

I see an evergreen in our yard, though. Forever lasting through weather most severe.

No wind can possibly disturb it. There is nothing that should cause it fear.

Lasting through the hottest summer and coldest winter,

None of the obstacles provided by Mother Nature

Can ever cause our evergreen to splinter. For our love is with God, innocent.

People come from miles to see our evergreen. All the while, they remain in awe.

Such a sight no one has ever seen, because within our evergreen, there is no flaw.

This beauty was formed by the Lord above, forever giving our evergreen guidance,

And never failing to recognize our love. To give thanks, we take every chance.

The evergreen's beauty becomes ever more magnificent, with each passing day.

From heaven and God, it was sent. Forever it shall be, in our yard of fruitful dedication.

Since it was new, our love has continued to feed our evergreen tree.

How can we hope for an undying love so able?

Only with God above can we hope to have an evergreen,

For only His love can help it stand stable,

Through storms of conflict and obstacles yet seen.

This poem represents my aspiration. I assumed relationships would grow, wither, and die in a natural course. Yet I held hope that I'd share a love with the enduringness of an evergreen.

As I filled page after page with thoughts and emotions that lay beneath the surface, poetry became more than an outlet. With every line, I colored in pieces of my soul and felt more complete. Poetry also helped me see the future my heart desired: one of military service and starting my own family.

PART II

The Iraq War

CHAPTER 5

Counseling—Session 2

WASHINGTON, DC

April 27, 2011

Following the first session with Paul, I felt more confusion than resolution. Recalling how my relationship with my mother deteriorated from being the closest bond in my life caused me great regret and shame. Recalling the absence of my biological father and the impact on my development left me questioning my identity.

As I walked into my second session with Paul Rubin, I burst out, "I thought this was supposed to make things better. Instead, it's like everything is breaking apart. I can't even sleep anymore. My mind won't stop racing. Is this normal? I feel worse."

Paul leaned forward in his chair, his eyes soft but steady, waiting for me to continue. I felt the walls closing in. My life seemed to be tangled up in knots I couldn't begin to untie.

"Worse?" Paul finally asked, his voice low.

I nodded, pressing my palms onto my thighs, trying to ground myself. What was I supposed to say? How could I explain my feelings without sounding like I was complaining?

"I don't know what I'm supposed to feel. I hoped this would help me get rid of the weight, but it feels much heavier. And I don't even know who I am anymore."

"What do you mean by heavier?" he asked as if guiding me to a new insight.

I shook my head and began to reflect. "I thought counseling would help me get past all of it—the war. But now it's in the front of my mind, and I can't ignore it. I don't know what to do."

Paul nodded, but he still didn't offer answers. Nor would he. I found that frustrating.

"I'm not the guy I used to be—the guy who could just push through it all, who could shut out and keep going. But I don't know who I can be now. All I know is I don't like who I've become."

And there it was. The confusion wrapped around me like fog. I couldn't see where I was going because I didn't know who I was. Every time I thought I had a grip on something, it slipped away, leaving me more lost than before.

Paul nodded with a slight smile, giving me a moment to breathe.

"Ryan," he said gently, "I told you this is hard work. Sometimes it has to get worse before it can get better. You must open old wounds and allow them some air. There are lessons you need to pull out, and you must find them for yourself."

"I guess there are some lessons, and I'm proud of what I was able to do despite adversity in high school," I replied. "I survived."

"Yes, you are a survivor," Paul said with a smile. "You are a resilient man, still a young man. We all have to overcome obstacles in our youth. We adopt strategies to survive, and those become behaviors. When we become adults, those behaviors can prevent us from having the relationships we desire."

"That makes a lot of sense," I said with resignation. "My relationships in my youth, with my mother and stepfather, and even how I dealt with the absence of my biological father, all have a common thread."

"What's that?" Paul asked.

"I've purposely lied to myself about the nature of the relationship." I began to cry. "I love and care even when it is very hard. Love is a duty. I overlooked the fact that my father abandoned me and held him in high regard. I overlook my own flaws and that I was not meeting my part of the bargain in the marriage. My way of showing love was to fight and protect, and to provide."

"Do you want to talk about love, Ryan?" Paul asked.

"I guess," I said reluctantly. I thought about how to explain my story in some logical format. My mind was fragmented and all over the place. "I grew up wanting love—desperately. I wanted to find the love of my life. It was all I could think about during my last two years at West Point. I wanted to find my dream girl, but I didn't know how. It was like I knew her before I met her, but that feeling of knowing actually doomed our relationship over time."

"Go on."

"Well, as soon as I had it all, I was sent to war," I said, staring up at the ceiling. "When I got back, Lucy and I thought we were good, but we didn't have a foundation."

Paul expanded upon my logic. "You went to war. You went to Ranger School. You are a fighter. You don't quit."

"I definitely don't quit," I replied with mixed emotion. I realized that my never-quit attitude could be a detriment if I allowed it to erode my capacity. "I came back from Iraq with such a sense of purpose. We came back feeling like heroes."

"You are. You most certainly are," Paul acknowledged. "Why don't you talk about Lucy and your journey to Iraq? Let's explore that."

CHAPTER 6

Becoming a Leader

I must not fear. Fear is the mind-killer. Fear is the little-death that brings total obliteration. I will face my fear. I will permit it to pass over me and through me. And when it has gone past, I will turn the inner eye to see its path. Where fear has gone there will be nothing. Only I will remain.

—FRANK HERBERT, *DUNE*

WEST POINT, NY

May 26, 2000

The path to becoming an officer is paved with challenges that test your resolve and shape your character. On May 26, 2000, I graduated from the United States Military Academy at West Point after branching into the infantry. As I sat next to my classmates, awaiting my degree, I realized this was more than a graduation; it was the beginning of my journey as a leader.

Vice President Al Gore gave a nonpartisan speech and shook each graduate's hand as we received our diplomas. My entire family attended, including the Franks. Mom, Rick, Jessica, and Laura were all there when I pinned my officer rank on my shoulder.

I split time between the Franks and my family during graduation week. Both groups were cordial with each other but had not interacted much. Mom was rebuilding her life, and my sisters had been following Rick around the country wherever work took him. Mom extended the graduation invite to Rick on my behalf, likely to initiate some reconciliation but also to get help paying for the girls' travel. I still harbored resentment toward Rick, but if Mom could get along with him, I could too.

After the cadet first captain gave his final order—"Class dismissed!"—we tossed our white caps high in the air in euphoria. I hugged my roommate, Bob, and gave my friends high-fives before taking pictures with both of my families to mark the occasion. My classmates and I became commissioned officers in the Army, and all departed West Point for long vacations before beginning our new careers. I was granted sixty days leave before I had to report to Fort Benning, Georgia.

Four years of West Point builds toward one goal: developing leaders of character for our Army. I embarked on a journey in the Army not knowing where I was going. I wanted a family, and the increasing instability of my parents and broader family only accelerated my desire to find someone to love, marry, and begin a family with.

As I read back over my journal entries from plebe year and the rest of my time at West Point, it all seems to fit together—the path I chose and where I ended up. I was a momma's boy and illegitimate son. I embarked on the West Point experience as a rite of passage into manhood. Taking on challenges was a way to prove my worth. That translated into choosing the Infantry Branch, as well as attending Ranger School. Still, I sought to stay close to home. When I made the decision to post at Fort Stewart, Georgia, it was out of a desire to reunite with my family, not a calculated career move. Something in my heart took me to Savannah.

I also hoped to improve my chances of meeting someone by being close to established social circles. Instead, I found myself working on my relationship with Mom as she fought to rebuild her life. Her attendance at my graduation was a mutual triumph. We spent more time together during the holidays and in general. Still, something was different. There was a distance, something beneath the surface, and we both knew what it was. It was simply impossible for either of us to discuss what transpired four years earlier.

I spent the summer of 2000 enjoying time at the Franks' home while preparing for the Infantry Basic Officer Leader Course at Fort Benning, Georgia. With sixty days of vacation, I had time to do whatever I wanted. I felt compelled to address a void in my life that, until then, I had lacked the courage to face. It was finally time to confront my Darth Vader, my biological father who had denied paternity and never sought to be part of my life. I wanted to understand why.

Bill Carder and I corresponded while I was at the academy, but barely. When we did, there was little substance to the conversation. He never made an effort to meet me or invite me to visit him in Virginia. His children still did not know I existed. Until this point, I simply didn't have the self-esteem to be more proactive and deal with potential rejection. But I also didn't have the time. Now I did.

In June 2000, Bill was the Republican vice mayor of Roanoke, Virginia, a position voted by the city council. Bill was an affable politician and described by everyone who knew him as a genuine and innovative thinker. He was the general manager of the Patrick Henry Hotel after years working for the Marriott Corporation. Inside the hotel, Bill ran a five-star restaurant that served the best steaks in the city. Bill was a musician and helped establish an annual blues festival in the city. He and his wife, whom he had only recently married, lived in a nice home.

By all measures, Bill was as impressive of a man as I could have hoped for in a father. But something didn't add up. How could he deny I was his son when I was born? When he saw pictures of me and knew I was at West Point, how could he not want to visit me? These were questions for which I sought answers, but I soon realized I'd never get them directly from Bill.

During my senior year of high school, I had dwelled on the fact that Bill's children lived close to me. Four years had gone by, and I finally had enough of living in the shadows. By May 2000, Lauren and Dane, thirteen and ten respectively, were growing up fast and would never identify me as family, though I already did with them.

AOL Instant Messenger was a popular application for communicating over the internet. The platform possessed similar characteristics to Facebook, which would be developed a few years later. There were searchable databases of people, with location and other fields included, but there was no sense of community. One night I was bored and exploring AOL profiles, looking for people who might know my sister. My curiosity had been piqued when Bill mentioned she was in the band at her high school. The facts I had were limited but all I needed.

I stumbled upon a young woman who knew Lauren and tried to explain the situation. Needless to say, that caused a stir on the other end of the keyboard. It must have seemed threatening for a total stranger to be prying about a teenage girl.

A day later, Lauren Carder reached out to me: "Who are you!? Why are you asking about me!?"

I provided her my story and offered to send a picture to prove my genetic relationship.

My West Point senior portrait loaded slowly over the computer, with my eyebrows, which resemble Bill's, confirming the truth. My move was impulsive but also deliberate, as I had waited for so long to be introduced. Her mother, Kathy, told her to call Bill. And Bill acknowledged my existence.

Within two days, I was invited over to the house. Lauren and I bonded immediately. I also developed a good relationship with the woman who would have been my stepmother, Kathy Carder. At that time, Dane was still visiting our father in Roanoke. I met him not long after.

The window of opportunity to build relationships with Lauren and Dane was relatively small, as they would soon reach adulthood. I'd be a footnote in their lives if I didn't make a commitment. For this reason, I spent the better part of my year at Fort Benning, from 2000 to 2001, commuting to Orlando on weekends to spend time with them. We went to local theme parks and hung out at the mall. I realized that our father was almost as absent in their lives as he had been in mine.

ROANOKE, VA

December 2000

I began to solve the puzzle of Bill Carder over the course of that year through casual conversations and then met him for the first time at Christmas. Bill invited me up to Roanoke for a few days.

Our first meeting was somewhat anticlimactic, occurring at the bottom of an airport escalator. It was impossible to know what to expect. Part of me wanted him to instantly convey a sense of regret at not being in my life, or to express appreciation for the man I had become. But he didn't know me and could not convey such feelings. It would have been disingenuous. He didn't see a boy. Bill saw the man I had grown into. I might have been his son in another life, but we shared no life experiences.

The moment we finally met in person was an unmemorable blip of basic courtesy. Still, I wasn't disappointed and proceeded without expectations.

With our awkward introduction out of the way, Bill took me to his house and introduced me to his wife, who gave us space to get to know each other. Bill had purchased all the ingredients needed to make a delicious chili that night. With his culinary expertise, he guided me through the preparation and had me cut up various vegetables and meats. As we both took on accompanying tasks, we connected, albeit slowly.

Our conversation started more superficial but eventually shifted to family history. He described some of the trauma of his childhood. It gave me insight into his soul. We are all the heroes in our own narratives. Bill was a good man who was so troubled by his childhood that he could not be close to anyone. He also seemed unable to empathize with those he might have hurt as a result.

We continued to converse like new friends do as he prepared a gourmet meal. But it was odd that he didn't express a sense of being my father. Instead, he talked of his parents' shortcomings, which seemed ironic given my relationship to him.

"When I was ten years old, my mother up and left our family," Bill confided as he visibly restrained his emotions. His father and mother got married young and raised a large family while Bill Sr. was in the Navy. With so many children, I imagine that his mother hit her breaking point. The void created by her abandonment left him ruminating on his childhood for his entire life, and that left him ill equipped to be present in his other children's lives, much less my own.

"I heard some stuff from my mother," I confessed to Bill and held back further inquiry. I wanted to say in a disconnected way, "Yeah, my father never took time to investigate who I was. Oh, that's you." Instead I shuttered my emotions and tried to understand him.

"My father was a military man, like you. I'll introduce you to him someday."

"That would be great," I said.

This highlighted the challenge with Bill. He wanted control of the relationships, or perhaps he was apathetic about connecting me into his family. While I was at West Point, he had suggested introducing me to his children but never took action. In hindsight, I think it was because he didn't have much involvement with them. Bill was a man present in the immediate surroundings but disconnected from those not in proximity.

"Yeah, my father was a career naval officer and had to manage all the kids on his own," Bill said with pride. "He's a great guy; you'll like him. Here's a picture of us when we had a father-son day of golf."

"I'd love to meet him," I told Bill. *Where was my father-son day of golf? Where were you, Bill?* I asked silently. There were to be no direct answers.

I realized that I could never completely solve the mystery of Bill Carder, but our interaction allowed me to move on. Meeting him allowed me to let go of the insecurities of my youth. I was becoming a more accomplished man, and the fact that I had the courage to reach out to him marked a culmination.

I had gained sufficient insight. It was this simple: Bill could not find a way to balance his need for creating and finding fulfillment at work with spending time with his children. He focused so intently on his own emotions that he neglected those whose emotions contradicted the illusion of his world. When he was approached with my paternity, Bill likely dismissed it as a statistical anomaly, accepted he had to pay child support, and moved on. It was a choice not to be involved, and to be frank, Mom didn't press him about it. In effect, Mom provided me all the love and support he could have provided and an illusion of what Bill might have been. She gave me an ideal to aspire for.

Meeting Bill Carder in person was a positive experience, but I realized I didn't need a relationship with him to become the man I hoped to be. More important were the relationships I had with my sister and brother, who had also missed out on having a father. They played no part in my prior estrangement, and I loved them both instantly.

My relationship with Lauren and Dane Carder formed quickly during that year, yet I knew I would one day focus on my own family, once I had one. Lauren offered to help me find a date, and I agreed to meet anyone she recommended.

CHAPTER 7

Chance Meeting

FORT BENNING, GA

July 2000–April 2001

Fate has a way of bringing people together at just the right moment, often when we aren't even looking. As my vacation came to an end, chance meetings awaited me, one of them setting the stage for an unexpected turn in my journey.

The Infantry Basic Officer Leader Course was the next step in what I believed to be a predictable path. After sixty days of vacation, I departed Orlando and arrived at Fort Benning in early August 2000. The training program, comprising a series of courses, was tailored for new infantry lieutenants based on whether they were assigned to mechanized units, which had armored vehicles, or light units, which used wheeled vehicles. Infantry officers in mechanized units went through additional schooling for maintenance on the Bradley Fighting Vehicle. Officers who were assigned to light units went straight to their units after Ranger School.

The program I was slated for put me in the basic course, which all infantry officers attended, for approximately eighteen weeks. After that, I would have to wait another month before the next Bradley Leader Course began. Finally, I was scheduled to begin Ranger School in May 2001. In total, I was scheduled to spend nearly a year training at Fort Benning.

Much of the basic course entailed tedious classroom curriculum. Most of us had covered the material as cadets at West Point. Every other week, we went to the field to train small-unit tactics. Typically, we were assigned a standard type of mission, such as a hasty ambush, and practiced it several times over the course of the week before conducting a live-fire exercise near the end, using real bullets. These excursions allowed the students to get to know one another and build bonds of friendship. Some of us commissioned from West Point, others from the ROTC, while others came straight from college and a few came from the enlisted ranks.

In general, the prior enlisted noncommissioned officers (NCOs) knew more about tactics than officers because in almost all cases, they had more experience. Officers have the book-smart answers for everything, but NCOs have common sense. Most importantly, NCOs understand soldiers better than their officers because they have lived the life of an enlisted soldier. NCOs are the bridge in a unit, communicating orders from the officer and simplifying complications.

It was during one of the field training exercises that I met Travis Patriquin. He had been enlisted before becoming an officer, and his pragmatism immediately contrasted with my idealism. He stood behind me in every formation, and we talked about the Army, about life, about the future.

Travis intrigued me with his down-to-earth style and knowledge of history. Being at West Point, I always felt out of place among the elite crowd and intellectuals. Patriquin was a soldier's soldier. He deeply valued the arms profession and what it meant to be part of the warrior class. I liked him immediately, as I suspect most people did. His eyes had this sparkle, and his smile carried a warmth that drew others to him.

Travis always looked you in the eyes when he spoke with you. He never tried to one-up anyone. He had humility and confidence. Travis only spoke well of people and admired in others those qualities where he felt short. For example, he widely praised one of our fellow lieutenants for his Jedi-like abilities.

His positive attitude carried me through many boring formations and training events. Travis saw so clearly what I only recognized later: that our job as platoon leaders is to care for soldiers, not just lead them. It was a role that he relished because he genuinely loved soldiers, especially those who chose to serve on the front lines.

The eighteen-week basic course culminated with a weeklong field problem in December 2000. Patriquin and I were paired up during the first leg of the exercise. On the first night, we flew Black Hawks into a simulated battle scenario. In preparation for this movement, most of our gear was pushed forward due to the lack of space on the helicopters, including our cold-weather gear. When we landed, it was already freezing cold in the Georgia swamp. The operation was delayed, and we would not reach our gear before the fight at the first objective, a small mock-up town. We expected to hit the town in the middle of the night and fight opposition forces until morning.

Part of me would have preferred to be snug in my bed on this cold night. But as we flew off in the Black Hawks, I saw Patriquin's enthusiasm build.

"This is good shit, isn't it, McDermott?" he yelled. The helicopter increased the severity of the cold.

"I guess," I responded with muted enthusiasm and a smile. I didn't want to rain on Travis's parade, but the conditions sucked. He loved it.

As we disembarked, the cold began to settle into the lowlands, which was where we were headed to sleep. The approach was meant to be as tactical as possible. We cut through brush, and thorn bushes pierced my skin through my uniform. I didn't like pushing through the woods and questioned whether I had made the right choice in choosing the infantry. The damp chill seeped through my uniform and forced me to keep moving for warmth. Patriquin and I talked quietly as we followed our platoon through the woods.

"McDermott, you got any pogey bait?" Patriquin whispered. Pogey bait was slang for snacks in the field. Patriquin had left all his food in his duffle.

"Yeah, I got a little beef jerky here. Want some?" I offered. I had mastered the art of making myself as comfortable in the field as possible.

Patriquin grabbed some and threw it in his mouth, and we pushed on through the wet brush. We were getting tired, constantly forced to wait as the leaders of the patrol struggled to get us to our objective. At one point we stopped for what seemed like hours, and I started shivering.

"Shit, man, this is fuckin' cold."

"This even has me feeling 'the suck' a little more than I'd like," Patriquin admitted, though you wouldn't know it by looking at him.

"What do you think is up with the patrol leader?"

Travis thought for a minute. "I don't know, McDermott, but if I was leading, I'd probably want support from everyone."

When put in the role of soldier, be the soldier. When put in charge as the leader, then be the leader. That was Travis's lesson.

Time continued to drag on as we staggered through the lowlands. I felt close to hypothermia. Eventually, we stopped so everyone could sleep before proceeding to the objective at dawn. All the guys in the unit paired up with their battle buddies and tried to get comfortable.

"Dude, I'm fucking shivering my ass off here," I said. "I can't stop chattering my teeth."

"McDermott, don't take this the wrong way, but let's huddle up."

I put my back right up against his chest and pulled his arms around me like a blanket. I was a homophobic individual at this point in my life, but the choice was to cuddle close or freeze to death. I went into full spooning mode.

In the morning, we got up to continue the mission.

"I may give up my cold-weather blanket for you," Patriquin teased me as we got ready. "McDermott, you're a spooning motherfucker."

"Hey, man, I was probably close to having hypothermia."

"You're just a cold wuss," Patriquin said with a laugh and grin.

"That's okay; we all have our weaknesses to different 'sucks.'"

"What do you mean?" I asked.

"You know, lack of sleep, lack of food, being wet, being too cold, being too hot. It all sucks." He spoke with simplicity, but there was something profound about what he was saying. I had endured tough conditions but didn't fully appreciate the quality of being resilient through it all. 'Embracing the suck,' as they say, seems to take you to a higher level of consciousness.

"I guess I do better in too-hot situations and maybe with lack of sleep, and food," I said as I considered what sucks I was least susceptible to.

"Maybe I'll suck with lack of food in Ranger School," Patriquin proposed. "All I know is that it is going to suck, but I'm going to love every minute of it."

The next morning, we hit the mock town and completed the field exercise. And I made it through the rest of that field problem with ease and continued to grow stronger as time went on. Warriors care for each other regardless of the circumstances. That was Travis Patriquin all the way—unselfish, strong, and determined. He carried me through that field problem, a challenge I believe prepared me for Ranger School.

Patriquin and I did not keep in touch after my time at Fort Benning. After the basic course, the newly minted officers ended up scattered between other schools—Ranger, Airborne, and the Bradley Leader Course. I went to the Bradley course and was fortunate to not go through Ranger School until May, when it would be much warmer. As the year progressed, I shifted focus to moving to Fort Stewart and getting on with my life in the normal Army, assuming leadership of a platoon, and settling into a new rhythm.

The year of training at Fort Benning was demoralizing at times, the endless training preventing a serious relationship. Spending time with Lauren and Dane helped fill a void, but I wanted purpose beyond that of a warrior. I wanted to find love and start a family. Opportunity in love seemed to avoid my path when I sought it but materialized unexpectedly when I wasn't.

In high school, I was too shy to date and became preoccupied with getting into college. West Point did not offer me time to realistically pursue a relationship. I dated occasionally. There was one girl in Orlando I confessed my affections to, but they were not reciprocated. It was a defining moment in my life because I finally opened my heart and survived.

In April 2001, Lauren came through with her promise to introduce me to a local girl in Orlando. At first, she simply gave me her name, Shannon McGinnis, and an Instant Messenger ID. There were no pictures or other details. I initiated contact online one night at the officer library.

At first, I was skeptical of my sister's judgment and who she would try to connect me with. Shannon and I continued to chat on AOL, and we realized that we had attended the same high school, albeit separated by a couple of years. At this point, I became more skeptical because the name did not ring a bell. Then Shannon said, "Do you know my sister, Lucy?"

That's when I realized who she was. I had known the sisters by a different surname: Devaney. McGinnis was their stepfather's name. The sisters had been the most beautiful girls in school. Lucy was stunning but also a bit eccentric, which I liked. Shannon was too young for me to remember, but she lived in Oviedo, while Lucy lived in North Carolina.

Just before I entered Ranger School, I took Shannon out to lunch. We had a cordial date—if you could call it one, because it felt more like a meeting of friends. Shannon talked more about Lucy than she did herself, as if she sensed I had more connections with her older sister, who was serving in the Army. Shannon aspired to an acting career in New York or Los Angeles, while I was heading off to Ranger School.

After we parted ways, I pushed thoughts of dating to the back of my mind. Becoming a warrior became my focus.

CHAPTER 8

Becoming a Warrior

FORT BENNING, GA

May–August 2001

Ranger School is known for breaking even the most determined soldiers, but it also forges warriors of unmatched resilience. As I prepared to enter Ranger training in May 2001, I braced myself for an experience that would dredge the reserves of my mental and emotional strength. My mission was to complete all the training and earn the coveted Ranger Tab.

Ranger School is designed to be a crucible, with three grueling phases, each approximately three weeks long. The first phase, held at Fort Benning, tests physical fitness and mental endurance. Candidates must negotiate obstacle courses and pass fitness challenges to earn the right to lead a patrol. Failure means either purging from the course or starting all over again.

A patrol is a military maneuver exercise where a team of soldiers is given a geographic objective and tasked with attacking the location by a set "hit time." If all goes well, the leader will pass and get a "go." If not, then the leader must hope for another chance or face failing the course. Normally, each candidate is given two patrols during each phase.

The second phase takes place in the mountains of Dahlonega, Georgia, and the third takes place in the oppressive heat and swamps of Eglin Air Force Base in Florida.

The physical toll—of sleep deprivation, hunger, and the relentless demand for perfection—is immediate. By the end of the first phase, I had navigated the obstacle courses and earned my "Go" to move forward. Yet I already felt the beginnings of something more insidious than physical exhaustion. My body was capable of pushing through, but my mind started to fracture from the strain.

The mountains of Dahlonega, normally breathtaking in their beauty, offered no solace. The picturesque landscape did not soften the rigor of training. The second phase began with a week of knot-tying and mountain-climbing techniques, culminating in a difficult hike up Mount Yonah, where candidates had to successfully climb lanes along the mountain. The second and third weeks were devoted to patrols around the mountainous terrain. Again, candidates rotated into and out of leadership positions, where they were graded on a pass-fail basis.

I failed to get a Go during my first attempt through the three-week test and had to recycle. I also learned that Hawk, the family Lab, had been put down. The loss reminded me that life continued on the outside, and I set aside my grief to focus on my goal. Until then, for fear of failure, I had been hiding amid the formation, hoping to pass quietly to the next phase. But I learned a lesson when I was forced to recycle: I could not hold anything back if I was to pass the course.

In the time before the next class arrived, I fully committed to earning the Ranger Tab. There was a three-week break. The other candidate recycles and I ran to the top of a local mountain every morning and repaired our physical maladies along the way. Most of the Ranger instructors were on leave during the recycle phase, so the environment felt far different. Ranger School became like a home, although we were still clearly second-class citizens in the camp.

During the recycle break, I devoted myself to becoming proficient at preparing operations orders and mission planning. I felt a need to differentiate my skill set from those of the other candidates to demonstrate my worthiness of the tab. There are smart Rangers, and there are strong Rangers; you can either get through the school with your wits or you have to be strong enough to endure the physical strains. Learning to write the operations order would make me a resource when the next class arrived.

Our respite as recycle candidates came to an end when the new class of trainees arrived. As soon as the trainees exited the bus and the RIs began yelling and screaming, it was chaos and confusion. First the new batch of Ranger trainees had to go to the trucks to secure all their bags. The Ranger instructors were all over them.

"Get off the fuckin' bus, Rangers!" one yelled at the top of his lungs. Another Ranger instructor called up to the recycle Rangers, "Get the fuck down, now!" We immediately had to join the new class in a punishment, and I regretted purchasing an excess of supplies. Now I had to run all my stuff in laps around a parking lot until the RIs could inspect the gear and get us moved back into the barracks where we were already settled.

The punishment didn't stop for hours. I had three full duffle bags and a rucksack to carry. It doesn't look possible, but I intended to die before quitting.

"Faster," one RI demanded. Round and round about eighty students went around this parking lot, with all our bags and supplies. And then, finally, the RIs told all of us except for two students to stop. Two students were told to keep going. After a few additional laps, the RIs told them that they only had one more lap to do, and they would be done. The rest of the students, including myself, cheered these guys on and encouraged them to finish. Both made the lap with all their gear just fine. And then I sensed the doom in the air. As soon as they reached the finish line, both dropped their bags, only to be told, "Take another lap. I didn't tell you to drop your bags."

One Ranger candidate, a recycle, leaned over in exhaustion, and his eyes showed he had quit before his lips moved. He could have just not said anything. Instead, he came out in a quiet but defiant way, telling the RI, "I quit."

It was disappointing to watch someone put in so much effort only to quit. No matter the pain, I would never have uttered those two words.

Unfortunately, that day was one of the easier days during my second rotation through Mountains.

During the rope-training week, we learned how to set up a rope bridge. The RIs sat us in some bleachers as they demonstrated the steps to constructing the rope apparatus. At one point, an RI provided a briefing in a monotone seemingly designed to entice us to sleep. The other RIs warned us several times not to. Then one RI called someone out who had dozed off.

"Out of the bleachers, Rangers. We're going to wake you up," he said gleefully.

Instead of having us do push-ups, the RIs had us lift the bleachers above our heads. At first, the aluminum structure was light enough to hold with everyone putting in equal effort. Slowly, though, our arms became exhausted, and the bleachers were resting on our Kevlar helmets. My neck strained from the compression. When the lesson was over, we put the bleachers down, but our hazing did not end.

At Mount Yonah, the supposed "gentlemen's portion" of the course where students learn mountaineering and climbing techniques, the RIs were equally unforgiving. Unscheduled physical fitness sessions were routine. On one occasion, an RI challenged a student who was about seventy feet up a steep embankment to look down at the Ranger he was partnered with.

The Ranger student hesitated.

"Ranger, what the fuck are you doing? Are you scared?"

"I can't look down," the student said with the fear of a child.

With an evil eye, the RI said, "I believe you can fly. Do you believe you can fly?" This RI had been known to throw Rangers around while properly fastened to rope lines. "Because if you don't look down that fucking mountain, I'm going to throw you down." The RI then motioned the student to stand up, to which the student finally submitted. The RI proceeded to adjust the rope fastening the student so that he could now stand up and look down the mountain.

"I want to hear you sing it," laughed the RI. "'I believe I can fly. I believe I can touch the sky.'"

The student looked out at the blue sky and landscape below him and complied with a nervous stutter: "I believe I can fly . . ."

"Now flap your wings, Ranger." The student flapped his wings and sang as he gazed out into the wide-open sky. As this was going on, the rest of the Ranger candidates continued rope climbing. Then one of the other students laughed.

"Oh, you think this is funny, do you, Ranger? Let's let you enjoy the fun."

Oh shit! I thought. *Here it comes.*

"Get on your backs, Rangers, and face the open sky," ordered the RI.

With little room to navigate on the side of the mountain, we prepared to execute flutter kicks.

"Let's begin. One, two, three, one, two, three." As the RI called out the cadence, the Ranger at the top of the hill continued singing his song. "I believe I can fly; I believe I can touch the sky . . ."

During these sessions, I went to my happy place. I looked at the cloudless sky and tried to separate my soul from my body. If I could somehow detach from my pain, then I might be able to appreciate the beauty I was looking at.

The count continued. We echoed with the number of full counts completed. "Ninety-nine, one hundred . . . a hundred and one . . ."

"Shit," I said out loud to myself. "We're going over a hundred." *Time to go back to my happy place.*

Stars dotted my vision, and I was reminded of my heavenly dream of swimming in a clear blue ocean. I achieved a physical high as I endured the flutter kicks and surrendered to the moment. God was helping me get through—or maybe it was an adrenaline rush. Either way, I made it.

"Alright, Rangers, let's get back to climbing," the RI said as he finally ceased the count. "No more fucking around!"

Mountain phase taught me a critical lesson about success and failure. Success breeds success, just as failure breeds failure. After wrapping up our climbing tests at Mount Yonah, we prepared for the patrol phase.

Our first field problem got off to a bad start because of a self-centered field-grade officer who sacrificed time to sleep for more robust planning. I'd observed during the first rotation that rest was essential for the first mission, but the major demanded more elaborate tables and drawings for the planning phase than necessary, which took excessive time. Admittedly, he gave an excellent briefing the next day, but of no more substance than if you wrote it on the back of a cardboard box. For that, no one in the platoon got more than three hours of sleep.

It was a disaster. We missed our hit time on the objective, got disoriented on enemy contact, and the RIs used artillery simulators to send a clear message: The patrol phase was a No Go for all students in leadership positions. Yet the major got his Go for the planning segment.

It was during the endless strain of Mountains that I learned how close to the edge I could be pushed. The emotional disconnect started subtly—a growing sense that I was alone, even in a group. We were a team, but each man fought his own battles, with the one exception being my Ranger buddy, who pulled me through.

Each Ranger candidate is paired with another specifically to care for one another. My Ranger buddy was another recycle, Mike Moynahan, a lieutenant like me who had completed other officer training at Fort Benning before attending Ranger training. We had mutual respect for one another, but the environment did not afford many opportunities for a normal friendship. What bound us was our common commitment to succeeding.

When we returned from the field after four days of patrolling, we were told that few people had Gos. My patrol had been very quick with my task to link up with the rest of the platoon after assaulting an objective. Moynahan did well on his patrol, but it was unclear whether I did. For our next series of patrols, we held out hope for more success.

However, the RIs didn't relent and kept the pressure on us during refit, and we went into the next five-day field problem equally exhausted. Failure breeds more failure.

The RIs made it clear they wanted to punish the platoon. On one occasion, we walked toward a mountain that seemed to slant straight up.

"This is going to be fun, Rangers. And I'm going to make it easy for you," cackled one RI as he pulled out an artillery simulator.

"Fucking shit," I said under my breath as our group started scrambling up the mountain, taking cover just as the simulator exploded. The RIs then assessed casualties.

"You are dead, you are wounded, and you're wounded," the RI told several fellow students. Those who were able had to pick them up and continue the climb up the steep slope. I had the radio, so I was left to struggle with the heaviest rucksack. My Ranger buddy slowly crawled up with another student on his back.

"Get up the fucking mountain, Rangers, or I'm going to pull another arty on you! We can all just die here. We'll leave one guy alive to carry you all up."

We all screamed at each other to comply with the order. I grabbed onto small branches to help me climb. It took an hour to get up the hill.

When we finally finished scaling the slope, we were close to missing our hit time for the mission. I was on radio watch over the gear and rucksacks, and as we set up in the objective release point, I felt like I could relax. The rest of the platoon would go forward to the objective area. "No sleeping," ordered an RI as they marched off to the objective area some 400 meters away.

Moynahan sat with the platoon's gear. I had the radio microphone propped in my Kevlar and secured on my chin strap. As the last Rangers were leaving the release point, darkness set in.

"WHAT THE FUCK ARE YOU DOING, RANGER?!"

An RI grabbed my weapon from my clutches and began firing toward the sky right in front of my face, the hot brass casings peppering my body. "Get the fuck up! Get to the objective area! We're going to have some additional training!"

"Oh shit!"

I had drifted off to sleep. That's what no sleep for three days will do to you.

Moynahan and I joined our student peers at the objective area, where we all were cussed out on a poor performance. The RIs decided to have us repeat actions on the objective—a task that required a great deal of running. After the exhausting sprints, one particularly sadistic RI, Sergeant Mac, sat down with us in the open field.

"Listen, Rangers, I know you all think this is a game, but this is fucking reality. Your job as Rangers is to kill motherfuckers. This pussyfooting around the objective is not going to cut it. You get to the objective with a purpose and assault like your family's life depends on it."

Sergeant Mac continued, "Look, in combat, either you go home in a body bag and the enemy goes home, or it's you that buries them in their holes, and you can go home to fuck whoever you want. That's why women love Rangers. We kill so they can be protected and live their happy little lives."

Sergeant Mac wasn't dealing with a full deck, but his attitude highlighted simple realities of human nature. War is a contest of will and strength. And as General Patton famously said, "No bastard ever won a war by dying for his country. He won it by making the other poor dumb bastard die for his country." Ranger School seemed to house some of the most sexist and politically incorrect soldiers I ever knew. Several years later, there was a crackdown on the school to focus it more on practical tasks in war.

It was another night with no sleep and another No-Go patrol for the Rangers who were in leadership positions.

"There are going to be a lot of Rangers going to the house," one RI admitted to the group. That was another way of saying a lot of people would be dropped from the course. We had about a 45 percent pass rate during that rotation. Fortunately, Moynahan and I were some of the lucky ones. Those of us who passed did an airborne jump into the Florida phase.

The swamp phase was the capstone exercise for the entire course, a nine-day field problem that would test our bodies and our mental toughness.

Our platoon learned lessons in Mountains. When we finally began planning our first mission in Swamp, we got a good night's sleep. The first night would be a long one, an airborne insertion and ambush. Then we would roll straight into the next mission-planning segment with no sleep. We knew what to expect. The key to success was to get the second mission executed on time.

That night we geared up and prepared for the jump with a full combat load. Fear had been purged in the mountains of Dahlonega. I took time on the brief flight to relax ahead of the jump. I was in the present moment. The past and future were nonexistent.

We were given the orders: "Stand up. Hook up."

I stared ahead at the red light and waited for the color to change and the jumpmaster to give the order to go. The light turned green, and the order was given. Students in full gear and tight file shuffled to the door, holding our static line. As I approached the door, the jumpmaster looked me in the eye, and I thrust my static line to him as I took a firm step into the darkness.

Under the moonlight, I saw the outlines of other students and their parachutes and focused on the timing to lower my combat gear. I hit the ground without incident.

The mission did not execute well afterward because of how long it took the students to regroup after the landing. That made it a long night, and we did not get any sleep before making it to the patrol base.

As I prepared to eat that morning, I got the call: "Ranger Five-Eleven."

I quickly threw myself into the act of planning and pretended like I knew what was going on. Coming off the line, you fake it until you make it.

In the minutes that followed, I was given a verbal order from the RI, copied copious notes, and quickly got to work. I ordered the assigned platoon sergeant to secure the perimeter while I cracked out a written order by the book. It reminded me of cramming at West Point with the deadline rapidly approaching. As soon as I got it close to complete, I called the squad leaders to the center to issue the order. It didn't need to be perfect; we needed to get going, or we wouldn't complete the mission.

Line by line, I went through the order and explained our task. We made our time of departure, but no one got sleep. I charged my lead squad leader with getting us to the objective. Unfortunately, he took us slightly off course. Nature also slowed us down. At one point, we were halted due to a storm, and I wondered if I would be gigged for the patrol, despite a solid plan. As soon as the storm ended, we came under attack by the OPFOR (opposing forces).

There was confusion. None of the squad leaders reacted immediately. I tried to get them situated for an attack, but I failed to have them move their squads. The RIs pounced on us and began throwing artillery simulators everywhere, which then forced us to run all over the place. The good news was that we got to the objective and eventually to our patrol base, and we even got three hours of sleep that night—more than we had gotten since the first phase during a field problem.

The next day, we did a river crossing with a rope line and swam across with all our gear. The water drenched our socks, and subsequent walking took a big toll on my feet. By the third morning, when the medic checked, the bottom of my foot looked like a porous sponge. I had trench foot. The medic told me he had never seen someone's foot look so bad so early in the phase. It was painful.

My body was in a race against time. My feet had to make it six more days through endless patrolling, or I would have to do it all over again. Fortunately, our unit continued to execute missions well, and we got to patrol bases with time to sleep. Once in patrol base, I immediately took my boots off to let them dry off while we were digging our foxholes for the night. In the mornings, I put my boots back on with fresh socks and fill up the foxhole. That was the routine. Walk all day, hit a mission, walk for a few hours, dig a hole, take off socks, and get a little sleep.

The last day of the field problem was anticlimactic. We were supposed to march ten miles back to camp but ended up being trucked into base camp due to a tropical storm. The next day, we all found out who made the cut to earn the coveted tab. When I went in for my counseling, I was told I got a Go on my planning patrol. I was equally happy to find out that every other member of the platoon had also earned the Ranger Tab.

The Ranger class flew back to Fort Benning following the notification of our passing status. It gave us time to pack calories into our bodies and put some weight back on. A few days later, we attended the graduation ceremony, where we would finally receive the tab. It was not certain until the day before graduation whether my family would attend my graduation. Mom hated driving, and her car was in bad shape. Still, she found a way to get to the field that day in August and even accepted the honor of pinning the tab on my shoulder.

"Ryan, I'm so proud of you," she began. "It is difficult knowing you're in the Army. I worry constantly. But I'm so proud that you've been able to accomplish your goals."

"Thanks, Mom," I said with a smile. I had a friend at the ready with a camera, and we captured this major moment of triumph in my career. It remains one of my proudest accomplishments.

Mom was emotional and proud, but I sensed she was holding back. She sensed the reality of my future in the Army. No longer was I wearing the pristine cadet parade uniform. I wore the same fatigues that men and women wore into combat.

U.S. ARMY

CHAPTER 9

Unexpected Turn

OVIEDO, FL & SAVANNAH, GA

August–September 2001

The river of life is rarely straight. As I faced the next leg of my journey, a fork appeared that I hadn't planned for.

Coming out of Ranger School, my personal life was not a priority. Everyone went their separate ways after graduation. I packed up my car with my clothes and headed east to Savannah. My Beast roommate, Jeff McFarland, and I agreed to be roommates once again. Jeff picked out a townhome in the historic downtown district but needed to share it to afford rent. I would buy furniture to fill my room but had to pick up my other personal items from my mom's house now that I was going to be a real adult.

Coincidently, Shannon McGinnis invited me to her birthday party the same weekend I was scheduled to arrive in town.

Every great romance has a unique prologue. In some cases, people cross paths multiple times before embarking on that journey. In others, couples describe falling in love at first sight. With Lucy, it was a little bit of both.

As the middle child among her siblings, Lucy experienced a childhood out of the spotlight and was innately shy. She loved to play the piano and read books for leisure. And she was in a league of her own in high school.

She had the beauty of a prom queen, but Lucy wasn't about all that. She was quirky, didn't pursue popularity, and was kind to everyone. I saw her in the halls but didn't know much about her beyond that.

Picture the woman Axl Rose describes in the song "Sweet Child of Mine," and that's Lucy. Her eyes were of the bluest skies, or as if the Hope diamond, a heavenly blue sky, and the ocean deeps had melded to create an element of pure beauty. Her blond hair was thick and lush, like a warm, safe place. And her smile was simply sweet. Lucy broke hearts throughout her teenage years since no one was good enough for her.

I had a chance now, though. She was descended from a long line of Army officers dating back to the Civil War, and her family had a West Point lineage of its own, two of her ancestors having graduated from there. Unbeknownst to me, Shannon helped set me up with Lucy long before we met. She sent Lucy my West Point senior picture and told her all about me.

Shannon still lived with her parents in the same Oviedo neighborhood as the Frank family. When I arrived at the house, I saw a few people in the front parlor through the front window as I knocked on the door.

"Hi, Ryan! Thanks for coming," Shannon greeted me. "I want to introduce you to my sister, Lucy."

When our eyes met, I couldn't look away. I did not plan to spend the entire night talking to Lucy, but she captivated me. Her eyes, which I had admired in high school from afar, were hypnotic as they gazed into mine. They held me hostage in flattering conversation about my recent experience in Ranger training. Her Eastern European face had perfect symmetry, with her bone structure highlighting the softness of her peach-colored skin.

Lucy's beauty was intimidating, but as she smiled at me, I felt calm.

Shannon had about fifteen or so guests at the party, but I scarcely remember any other conversations. Lucy and I spoke the same language. No one else in that room understood Army life as we both did. And that was what held me back.

Before the night ended, the party moved to a bar in downtown Orlando, where we ordered drinks. I got to interact with one of Lucy's closest high school friends, Jennifer, and hid my desire for Lucy's attention by sharing mine with the rest of the table. When I ordered my drink, I saw a hint of hope.

"I'd like a mudslide martini," I told the waiter. Lucy seemed hopelessly engaged with Jennifer across the table.

Then, when the waiter moved to Lucy, she said with the slightest smile, "I'll have the same thing."

My heart secretly delighted that she was in tune with me and paying attention. At that moment, I knew we liked each other. But the moment was constrained by time and the friends surrounding us. I also didn't want to send mixed signals. After all, I had technically gone on a date with her sister.

At the end of the night, I said good night to everyone in the group and goodbye to Lucy individually. I held back asking for her phone number because there were a lot of people around and I didn't know how Shannon would react.

"It was very nice to meet you," I told her. As I drove to my new home in Savannah, I wondered whether we'd connect again, but I chose to leave it to fate. My mind shifted back to my new life and the unit I would report to shortly.

In the first week of September, I moved into the townhome. After we completed the basic in-processing with the unit, Jeff and I planned to take a week off to settle into our apartment. It is typical for the Army to allow such leave. Jeff was assigned to 3-7 Infantry, while I was assigned to 2-7 Infantry. Permissive leave was granted, and so we returned the following Tuesday, September 11, 2001, to sign out.

It was cool outside and a beautiful, clear morning. Both Jeff and I wanted to sign out early so we could have enough time to enjoy the day in Savannah. We embarked from our apartment around 8 a.m. to Fort Stewart. The last segment, the "green tunnel" through the forest, is a boring thirty-minute drive. Every turn looks the same as the last; so we listened to the radio and chatted.

"I think I'll go to a museum today," Jeff started. "Do you want to go?"

"That would be cool. With the weather, though, I think we should eat outside. There are some great places on the river."

"Okay, let's clean up a little when we get back and try to head out by eleven." Jeff was always more methodical in his approach to planning, wanting to get the house ordered first.

When we reached the gate, we simply drove onto post and headed toward our unit areas. Just as we prepared to exit the car, we heard a strange radio report: "A fire has been reported at the World Trade Center towers."

I thought it bizarre, but I went inside and signed out without a second thought before heading back out with Jeff. And then what seemed merely an odd occurrence transformed into a national nightmare.

Jeff and I listened to the horrific description of what had happened to the North Tower of the World Trade Center in New York. At first we imagined that a small prop plane had crashed into the building but soon realized that something much more devastating had occurred.

"What the hell!" I exclaimed to Jeff as he drove us back. "What does this— This is not happening, is it?" There was no precedent for something like this happening in the United States. Not on this scale.

Jeff sat stoically for a time. "I don't know, Ryan, but let's get home. There's nothing we can do about it."

We arrived back at the townhouse, where we were still settling into our lives, and tried to ready the place as the news continued to come in. We watched the South Tower disappear in a cloud of dust.

"Did it just collapse?" I asked in astonishment.

Jeff was still calm. "I don't know. It looked like it might have."

"This was a terrorist attack. It has to be. Two planes—I mean, four planes? This is fucking crazy."

The next day, I got a call from the battalion executive officer, Major Lumpkins.

"Lieutenant McDermott, your permissive leave is over. We need you to come in and take charge of your platoon."

The day after the call from Lumpkins, I stood in front of the thirty-two soldiers who comprised the "Black Sheep" platoon.

Before addressing my men, I had met my company commander outside the headquarters area. As Captain Todd "TK" Kelly and I shook hands, he teased me, "Nice haircut, Lieutenant McDermott." My hair had yet to grow out from Ranger School. "This"—he pointed to his lush head of hair—"is the standard. Grow it out a little, or continue to be the butt of my jokes." Captain Kelly laughed again and then said lightheartedly, "I like to joke a lot, so get used to that. I'll make you famous!"

I appreciated his allusion to *Young Guns*. Perhaps Captain Kelly saw himself as the gregarious Billy the Kid, played by Emilio Estevez, and saw me as a new cowboy joining the crew. I immediately knew he was the cheerful type and would be good to work for. It seemed that September 11 had little effect on his attitude; he was ready for war whenever it came.

A few weeks into my new job, I took my guys out for my first field training as their platoon leader. The exercise involved gunnery qualification for Bradley Fighting Vehicles and a dismounted infantry squad. I played a coordinating and evaluator role, critiquing my squads and taking notes. My first infantry squad leader, Staff Sergeant Foreman, ran his squad through flawlessly. He maintained communications with the tracks as his squad moved forward, and the Bradleys supported with covering fire. We wrapped up feeling that the training exercise had been a success.

As I returned from the live-fire range and closed in on the control tower, I received a call from the company executive officer, Mike Pecina, to head over to see the brigade commander, call sign Raider Six, Colonel Vincent Brooks. He wanted to talk with me.

The brigade commander was in charge of roughly 4,000 soldiers. Below his command, he had several battalion commanders whose units numbered close to a thousand. And below the battalion level were numerous companies of 100 to 150 soldiers each. Needless to say, Raider Six was an important person in my chain of command.

At first, I thought, *Wow, he must have seen me run my first squad through the lane with some good training. Maybe he wants to give me some words of encouragement.*

As I ascended the stairs to the control tower, a shadow stretched down from above, and there he was, standing over me, between the first and second floor.

"Sir, I'm Lieutenant McDermott. I was told—"

"Get to the position of attention when talking to me," Brooks barked. His eyes pierced my confidence. I had no clue what I was being corrected for but figured it was my fault for not knowing.

Colonel Brooks's baritone voice was firm and articulate, much like Darth Vader's, as he ranted, "I'll fire you and replace you with one of your privates if you can't control your platoon . . ."

At some point, all you can do is rattle off the simple responses: "Yes sir," "No sir," and "No excuse, sir." Keeping control of my platoon was a professional point of pride for me, and I didn't know what part I'd lost control of.

It turned out that my gunner and other dismount squad leader had been joking lewdly over the radio. The brigade commander overheard the entire conversation and at one point was rebuffed by my gunner when he tried to intervene over the radio.

I learned that there is always someone watching and listening.

Communications must be limited to the mission. I corrected the men's behavior the only way I could—by telling them I took a heat round for them and that I felt let down. We were now a country at war. Training was serious business. Plus, we had real-world missions at home.

In October, my platoon was tasked with serving as a quick reaction force for the post, as the Army was on heightened alert. There was a scare with anthrax mail around the same time. We were to be ready in case of an attack, however improbable.

This left us with a significant amount of downtime. My platoon was stuck in a building, so I offered classes to pass the hours. I decided to do a class on personal finance because I had grown up in a lower income home and did not learn much about personal finance until I reached West Point.

My cell phone rang while I was teaching my soldiers. I ignored it the first time, but then it rang again and again. The phone number was associated with Kathy McGinnis, Shannon's mom. All thirty soldiers regarded me with interest. I didn't want to disrupt my presentation, but I wondered why she might be calling.

Kathy had appreciated that I was a West Point graduate. Her great-grandfather, Henry Jervey, was the top graduate in 1888 and retired as a major general, having served as an officer in the Army Corps of Engineers and distinguished himself as a founding member of the War Department during World War I. His son also graduated from West Point and served as a signal officer before retiring as a colonel.

I answered the phone as my soldiers watched.

"Hi, Kathy," I said quietly. "How can I help you?"

"Hey, Ryan," Kathy said. "Paul and I are planning to visit Savannah next weekend. Is that offer to be a tour guide still good?"

"Of course," I agreed without elaboration. "I'm teaching a class right now, so just call me closer to next weekend, and we can coordinate."

Kathy agreed and then told me she'd have company. "Lucy is going to meet us in Savannah, so she will be there if that's alright."

My heart jumped unexpectedly.

"Of course," I acknowledged with tempered excitement. I did not want to show such a personal side in front of my soldiers or reveal my reaction to Kathy, but my feelings for Lucy clearly went deeper than I knew. And Lucy would be making quite an effort in driving from North Carolina to Georgia simply to see her parents. Was she interested in me?

As the date of Kathy and Paul's trip to Savannah neared in late October, my anticipation increasingly occupied my mind. I took care to prepare my room and planned for Lucy's arrival. When the day came, she called to let me know she was close to town. We communicated politely, perhaps both of us holding back.

"I'm just pulling off of I-95 and plan to stop at the first exit to get gas," she informed me.

"Okay," I acknowledged. "I know the exit and will come meet you there so you can follow me into town."

The plan was simple. Lucy would come to my apartment, and we'd link up with her parents later that evening for dinner.

At Shannon's party, our interaction had been totally spontaneous and without expectations. By the time of this visit, nearly two months later, we'd had time to process our chemistry. Tension filled the air between us at my apartment, but I was still able to open up. Her parents' arrival helped to ease the pressure. We all got in one car for a tour downtown, and I listened carefully as Lucy chatted with her parents, trying to pick up clues about her dating life.

"How is Seymour treating you these days?" Paul asked.

"Seymour is great," Lucy said as my heart palpitated. This was the first I had heard of Seymour.

I leaned over to Kathy and asked as casually as I could feign, "Who is Seymour?"

"Oh, that's Seymour Johnson. You know, Seymour Johnson Air Force Base."

"Oh, yeah, the base. That makes sense," I said with relief, my jealousy at the prospect that Lucy might be talking to a guy named Seymour having confirmed my feelings: I genuinely liked her. But I still did not know whether she was dating anyone.

Kathy shared their plans as we tooled around the downtown area. "Paul and I are going to check into the hotel and shop the antiques, and you two can meet up with us at the restaurant at seven."

Lucy and I had been paired off rather fortuitously, or perhaps that was precisely Kathy's plan. Either way, I was elated to be in her company. I decided to take her on a tour of River Street, where candy shops, restaurants, and bars line a cobblestone road. The formality in our interactions gradually subsided as we took in the sights and smells of the historic district.

"Check this out, Lucy," I suggested, leading her into River Street Sweets. "This place has amazing taffy. You have to try it."

"Okay, let's try it," Lucy answered with a smile.

She joined me at the counter to try a sample fresh from the machine.

"That's so good."

Lucy and I were left alone for several hours to take in the fall weather and chat about where we were in our early careers. She enjoyed my Ranger School stories.

"Looks like we have about fifteen minutes until we meet up with your parents," I mused as we neared the restaurant. "Why don't we sit over by the river?"

"Okay, sounds good to me," Lucy said. "We've been on our feet for quite a while." We both took a seat on the bench. The sun was about a half hour from setting.

After a few quiet moments, I shared some Savannah trivia. "You know, a couple recent movies were filmed here—*Midnight in the*

Garden of Good and Evil, Forrest Gump."

"I know Forrest Gump but haven't seen the other movie," Lucy said.

I impulsively turned my body forward and put my hands in my lap to go into character. "Hi, my name is Forrest Gump. Momma told me life is like a box of chocolates."

Lucy laughed. "That's perfect! You are Forrest Gump!"

I smiled, then did my best impression of Lieutenant Dan: "The day you are a shrimp boat captain, I'll be your first mate." Skipping to another scene, I hollered, "I was supposed to die in the field!"

"You are really good at that," Lucy said. "I have all the lines from the movie *French Kiss* memorized. In basic training, I entertained my squad mates by reciting the entire movie." She performed a couple of lines as if she could hear the dialogue in her head. I was impressed. With my guard down, Lucy changed the subject.

"You know, Ryan, I think you should be patient with Shannon to let her get to know you. Don't give up."

I had not fully appreciated the dynamic between myself, Lucy, and Shannon. To be honest, Shannon and I did not seem to have chemistry beyond friendship. Plus, I figured she had been planting seeds by talking so much about Lucy. I took a moment to consider Lucy's advice. Was this a test? It makes no sense to wait for someone to come around; it is either a natural fit or not.

After a pause, I simply told her, "Well, I would like to get to know you better."

Lucy smiled.

At that moment, a local vendor pushed a flower on me. "Flower for the pretty lady?"

"Sure," I agreed. "How much?"

"Five dollars," the vendor said and quickly handed the flower to Lucy.

That night during dinner, neither Lucy nor I ate much. I had a chicken Caesar salad and could not find the appetite to finish my meal. We both knew there was chemistry, and the tension built over the course of the night. At the end of the dinner with her parents, sleeping arrangements were discussed. Her parents did not want her staying in the hotel with them, and I offered her my bed. I would sleep on the couch.

Before heading back to the townhouse, Lucy and I strolled down River Street, stopping at more shops along the way. We talked about the Army, life, and occasionally recited more lines from our favorite movies. And we enjoyed the silence as we shared each other's company. When we arrived at my townhouse, we watched TV, and then I prepared my room.

"Okay, the room is all set," I told Lucy as she entered, and I began my descent downstairs.

Lucy looked at me sympathetically and said, "You don't have to sleep on that uncomfortable couch. I trust you; you can stay here."

We got into our pajamas and simply slept next to one another. A hug good night became an embrace that lasted all night long. We did not do anything beyond cuddling—not even a kiss—and yet, it was clear. We were falling in love.

Our friendship quickly blossomed into love over the next days, weeks, and months. Lucy and I spent every weekend we could together and talked every night. After months of dating, we knew we wanted to be with each other and eventually start a family. It might be irrational to hurry into a relationship. However, it would have been irrational not to pursue it, knowing I had found the woman I wanted to marry.

We faced obstacles, though. My unit was scheduled to deploy to Kuwait, and eventually I'd be gone for at least six months. With the war ongoing and another war on the horizon, we threw caution to the wind as training and preparations intensified.

CHAPTER 10

Training for War

FORT IRWIN, CA, NATIONAL TRAINING CENTER

April 2002

War isn't fought on the battlefield alone. It's also waged in the rigorous days of training, where every moment is a rehearsal for survival. It is waged through preparations at home, with families who provide love and support for our soldiers.

Charlie Company received orders to deploy to the National Training Center (NTC) for a March-to-April rotation as the opposition force. The NTC sits in the desert about midway between Los Angeles and Las Vegas. The open desert provides ample space for mechanized units to maneuver their tanks and large formations. Often, the NTC supplements its own training force with units from other posts, such as those in the 3rd Infantry Division.

The OPFOR rotation served Charlie well for two reasons. First, it built company cohesiveness. We bonded as a team—and a family. Second, it brought unconventional warfare to the foreground of our minds, tactically. By playing as OPFOR, Charlie Company learned to think like the enemy and how to target mechanized forces with anti-tank systems.

One mission in particular demonstrated the steady determination of our company. The afternoon before our mission, we set up on the northeasternmost side of the central corridor near a terrain feature referred to as Salt and Pepper. Our mission was to conduct a night infiltration and dismount and destroy the infantry strongpoint suspected to be securing a mine-wire obstacle in the central corridor. The night was cold, but we only expected a few hours to dismount and a 3 a.m. hit time.

We rolled out with my truck probably fourth in order of movement. We stayed in the wadis to avoid detection in the main corridor. However, the system of wadis was perpendicular to our movement, which made our movement challenging.

It took all night to navigate the wadis in what I remember as one of the most frustrating experiences of my Army career. Even Captain Kelly, who was always calm, called several times over the net, "This mission will not happen if you do not get up here." And I heard him curse for the first time. Right when I was about to lose hope of meeting our hit time, we stopped, dismounted, and charged the high ground.

Lieutenant Gleason's platoon took contact first and sought to fix the enemy on the first hill. As he was fighting, my platoon and the hodgepodge of soldiers left over conducted a penetration around the left flank of the hill. We got behind the enemy's front line and attempted to get our anti-tank system into the fight.

One squad was sent back to envelop the remaining forces fighting on the hill that Gleason's platoon had taken. Most of the platoon was wiped out at this point. I ended up getting notionally killed in the battle, while some of my dismounts made it to the top.

Our mission was a success for the most part. Tactically, we executed some basic dismount maneuvers. We also got a flavor of motorized fighting. Most importantly, we learned how to persevere through adversity as a unit. We were a stronger team. Our unit cohesion was beginning to peak in a tactical and interpersonal sense. But this was just the start of many lessons to be learned and bonds to be formed.

LAS VEGAS, NV

April 2002

What happens in Vegas stays in Vegas, or so the saying goes. If one of the many strengths Captain Kelly possessed could be viewed as a distinguishing feature, it was his ability to build a team. He did so by creating a social environment that nevertheless retained the hierarchical bounds of a military organization.

Some things go unsaid in the infantry world. Partying is one of them. Captain Kelly organized a company trip to Las Vegas as a reward to the soldiers. It was a risky venture considering the trouble our guys normally got into. The officers planned to go out together. My hope was to go gambling.

Lieutenant Gleason and I were trying our hand at the slot machines when the first sergeant appeared in the lobby with Lieutenant Morseth. First Sergeant looked excited.

"Sirs. How are you young LTs doing tonight?"

"Great, First Sergeant. You look ready for a night on the town," Gleason said.

"When you're my age, you'll take every opportunity to live it up when you get a hall pass. It has been too long," First Sergeant said with a grin.

"I've only been married a year, and I can appreciate that," said Morseth.

"I guess I'm not there yet," I responded with reservation.

"Lieutenant McDermott, just wait. Eventually you'll be looking forward to deployments," First Sergeant predicted.

"I don't think so," I said firmly.

"You'll tire of each other." But First Sergeant backed off when he sensed I was getting a little sensitive about the matter. "Okay, maybe not."

Captain Kelly finally joined the group. He looked energized. "First Sergeant, ready to roll? How are my young LTs doing? Giving you a hard time?"

"We're just discussing professional development. But I wanted to say you guys did a good job out there this week. I'm sure I speak for all the NCOs. That means something, because if you weren't ready, you'd be out of a job," the first sergeant finished with a quick reality check. He had the power to remove any of the platoon leaders if he didn't feel we were capable leaders. It was his responsibility to ensure the soldiers in the unit were cared for, which included competent leadership.

"Don't butter them up too much, First Sergeant," Kelly quipped. "There's always room for improvement." He smiled with pride, knowing we had performed well and that there was great promise in the company.

Gleason refocused the conversation. "Sir, we were debating whether to play craps or blackjack. Any preference?"

Kelly thought for a second and scanned the group to gauge our expressions. "First Sergeant, since you're the oldest one here, I defer to you."

"Fuck you, sir," the first sergeant said, laughing. "But since I am the oldest motherfucker here and probably won't get another hall pass anytime soon, my vote is for getting fuckin' drunk and seeing some big-ass titties."

"Gentlemen?" Kelly looked around the group again for approval. "She's got a couple of major-league yabbos." Another movie quote, I figured, but I didn't know this one.

Justin said, "Beverly!" The rest of the group laughed; I remained in the dark.

"Ryan, you know *Animal House*, right?" Captain Kelly asked with disbelief. I shrugged in shame. "Ryan! Come on! *Animal House*!" He was genuinely shocked. "You haven't seen one of the greatest comedies of all time." Everyone laughed.

"I may have seen it a long time ago," I defended myself.

"Ryan, what good are my movie allusions if you haven't seen any of them? Much to learn, young Jedi." He moved in to pat my back, taking the sting out of it. "Let's go to the Luxor. First Sergeant can hit the club on his own."

We gambled as a group for a while, and I stayed up all night playing craps. At the end of the night, I was up $300.

During the trip, I learned that Lucy was pregnant. We had suspected prior to my deployment, but she confirmed the news. On that night out, I reflected on the impact her pregnancy would have on my life. Part of me wanted to enjoy the moment, but the other half wished to hold her in my arms.

SAVANNAH, GA

May–September 2002

Lucy and I were eager to build our own family and left it to fate when she got pregnant. Perhaps it was 9/11 or what seemed an inevitable war in Iraq, but we didn't want to wait.

Circumstances were not ideal. We were not yet married and had a baby on the way. Still, Lucy and I both knew we would be married eventually. We did weekend trips to Myrtle Beach and several other towns in South Carolina during the summer of 2002. Not long after I returned from NTC, I purchased a diamond ring and planned a marriage proposal.

Lucy might have suspected I planned to propose to her one weekend when we were staying at Myrtle Beach. We had a great time despite the rain, spending most of our time huddled up inside our new tent. I wanted something special for that moment and didn't think a tent was the ideal place.

Lucy came down to Savannah the weekend after the beach trip to drive to the Disney World resort together. I planned to pop the question in Savannah before the drive.

Lucy called me about thirty minutes out from Savannah, and I toyed with her a little to keep her focus off the prospect of the proposal. I put the ring in an empty film casing and placed it in my pocket.

When she arrived at the townhome, I suggested we go out to dinner, which was meant to feel spontaneous but was all part of my plan.

"Lucy, let's take a walk over to the Six Pence pub for dinner."

We were thrilled to see each other as always, but I was nervous. I tried to hide my nerves by discussing plans for the weekend. As we walked toward Forsythe Park, I casually suggested we take a detour to the famous fountain walkway. Lucy did not realize what was going to happen until I stopped her midway down the path and gazed into her eyes.

"Lucy, you are my soulmate. I love you so much, and this is the perfect place." I paused, trying to compose myself. "I have something for you."

I reached into my pocket for the diamond ring and got down on one knee and made my proposal. It was the most nervous I've ever been, but not because I was afraid of her answer. Rather, I was caught up in the moment we were going to commit our lives to one another. In Lucy, I valued her genuineness. She forced me to live in the present even as she inspired me to pull my head out of the clouds to focus on the future. Most importantly, we viewed love and life in the same way.

Lucy lit up and stuck her hand out forcefully for me to place the ring on her finger. After she accepted my proposal, we walked over to the pub, where we dined and talked about wedding plans. The schedule would be tough, since I was training for a deployment and ultimately war. For that night, though, we aimed for the moon as I anticipated becoming a father and building the family I had always dreamed of—one that would bring stability, love, and a sense of belonging and fill the voids of the past.

CHAPTER 11

Becoming a Father

As Lucy and I moved forward, I realized that creating our family would be more challenging than I first imagined. Financial and time constraints prohibited a big wedding. We eventually settled on a small ceremony at her parents' home. I also had to go to the NTC again, and our baby was due to be born within a few weeks of my return. We settled on a November 23 wedding date.

Within a matter of three months, I would deploy to California, marry Lucy in Oviedo, welcome a baby in Jacksonville, and prepare to deploy again from Savannah, but this time the destination would be Kuwait. It was a lot to do, but together Lucy and I had the strength to get it done. Lucy would spend the latter part of her third trimester in Orlando, and I would stay in hotels during the week and drive to Orlando on the weekends.

FORT IRWIN, CA, NATIONAL TRAINING CENTER

October 2002

When we deployed to the NTC, we had no doubt who we were preparing to fight and that we would be called to Iraq sooner than our planned April deployment. Our packing was coordinated to potentially deploy to Kuwait from California. We sent everything to the NTC.

As the movement officer for the company, it was my responsibility to make sure all our unit equipment was packed and accounted for. I also had to supervise the rail loading of our company vehicles.

The focus of the NTC rotation was entirely on fighting the Iraqi Army. Preparations were made to facilitate that training. Our first mission was a movement to contact. We executed an armored vehicle-launched bridge crossing to simulate breaching the berm. We crossed with our plows, something of an experiment at the time. The process worked well if the tanks went slow.

Our attack took us to terrain known as the Whale Gap as we approached from the southwest. The OPFOR took positions in the north. We ended up racing through the desert to the Whale Gap, making contact on our left flank. The battle was more of a stalemate, administratively ended before casualties mounted. However, it gave me a taste of the unpredictability of battle. Not every battle has a clear objective, and the enemy is a mobile force that won't necessarily behave the way you expect.

Our next mission at the NTC was another movement to contact. It was a night mission. We attacked from the Whale Gap to Red Lake Pass. My platoon secured the far side of an observation hill just before the pass and established our support-by-fire line. We observed vehicular movement on the western high ground of the pass. Our company engaged with direct and indirect fire. Unfortunately, the vehicles we observed were friendly. I never found out the reason why that happened, but lessons were learned about clearing fires.

Once we began the assault, I took my Bradley section up to the high ground. My intent was to limit their exposure and conserve their energy. I also wanted to experiment with the capability of the Bradley, which is highly mobile. I positioned my vehicle in a location high up a ridge that looked otherwise off-limits. However, I lost the ability to maneuver and became bottlenecked. This taught another important lesson I would eventually apply in combat: Stay back a little to keep your maneuver options open; when the decisive maneuver point is identified, race to it decisively.

The next two days focused on the same mission. We called it the causeway mission. The scenario seemed too specific not to be a simulation for a planned objective in Iraq. The concept was simple: to stay on the road or else get mired in the mud. The end of the road, we were told, opened up into desert, and we expected additional defensive positions behind that. That was where the notional enemy would likely establish a trench system. Road barriers would block our path to slow our movement.

The first iteration of the mission was a disaster from a training perspective. We never got off the causeway before the entire company was taken out of the fight. The second day went a little better, but much of Charlie Company was taken out of the fight by simulated artillery and anti-tank systems. We still felt our plan was correct because the OPFOR has the tendency to exaggerate enemy abilities. I believe at some level we validated our approach to the mission, but it would not be discussed again until we made it to Kuwait.

Following our causeway experiment, we went into another deliberate attack against a defending enemy in the north. Our company took the eastern boundary of the reservation up to the point of breach, with wire spread across the desert from east to west. Our objective was to secure the eastern foothold. We learned about the limitations of tanks when moving through wadis. They are slow. Bradley Vehicles are more maneuverable.

The mission itself was uneventful from my perspective. I came away with a little more insight on how to integrate tanks, Bradley Vehicles, and infantry dismounts in a fight. Task organization should be terrain dependent. With this sort of mission, the tanks should stay in the west where the ground is flatter and leave the rough terrain to the infantry. Tanks kill the enemy out deep, while infantry are the jack-of-all-trades when it comes to terrain. By matching capabilities with the battlefield, efficiency is gained.

Our live-fire exercises integrated all the firepower we would see in use in Iraq. I got my first look at white phosphorus artillery at about three kilometers distance. It explodes in the air and sprays downward. By the end of the NTC rotation, I felt well prepared for combat should we be called to go to war. But I was not ready to leave my family.

ORLANDO, FL

November–December 2002

I was allowed to return early from the NTC to spend more time with Lucy, in expectation of the delivery of our son. We were married right around Thanksgiving. I will never forget Lucy in her dress, fully pregnant and as beautiful as ever. Cory Frank was my best man. Lucy and I exchanged vows and enjoyed the ceremony with our families.

By late November, the baby was due any day. As December began, my mind was completely focused on the baby. When I got the call on the night of December 3, I notified my company commander.

"Captain Kelly, I just got the call."

"Good luck, Ryan. Take all the time you need," Captain Kelly said. He rarely called me by my first name. He and his wife had welcomed a baby girl a couple of days before.

I drove down to Jacksonville and made it to the hospital in time to be with Lucy long before the delivery. She delivered an eight-pound, nine-ounce boy in under an hour of pushing. I looked into my son's eyes as he was placed on a scale and the nurses applied cream. They were a beautiful blue, like Lucy's, and his face had such a serene countenance, even as a baby.

"Shores of Heaven"

I once dreamed that I walked the shores of heaven.

The crystal-blue water vibrantly gleaming.

I felt heaven for a moment as I wetted my feet in the sea.

But I knew I was just dreaming.

For I was not worthy to gain entrance into a place so magnificent.

And so quickly, my dream came to an end.

When I saw you, I realized you were heaven sent.

In your eyes, I see the shores of heaven.

Deep blue sapphires—like your mother's—shine through and humble me.

They make me realize that I'm not worthy.

As I am not worthy to swim along the shores of heaven.

Like the dream, your eyes remind me that I need to be a better person.

They make me regret my mistakes, seek penance and forgiveness.

In your eyes, I walk the shores of heaven.

Which is why I am making some changes.

I want to be able to swim in that great blue sea

As I want to look into your eyes and feel that I'm worthy.

I may sometimes fall short in what I can provide

But I will become a worthy father, you will see.

And with God's guidance, I will one day swim in that crystal-blue tide.

Seeing my son born shifted my perspective. Brandon represented the love Lucy and I shared, formed into a new life. As I mentally prepared for combat, I saw my new purpose clearly: coming home alive.

CHAPTER 12

Saying Goodbye

Every goodbye carries with it the weight of memories and the uncertainty of what lies ahead. As I prepared for the next chapter of my life, saying goodbye meant letting go of more than a place; it meant leaving behind a part of myself.

By mid-December, I had married the woman of my dreams and had a beautiful baby boy. We celebrated Christmas in Orlando at Lucy's parents' house. Financially, we were a little more strapped as a family of three, but we didn't need gifts. Brandon was our gift. While we enjoyed spending time with our little guy, it was an emotional time because I would soon be pulled away.

Before winter break, soldiers in my unit were told to expect a call ordering our early deployment, but we did not know precisely when the call would come. My call came the day after Christmas. My unit would deploy in thirty days for an undisclosed amount of time. The rest of our Christmas break fell under the pall of pending deployment as the politicians in Washington resumed beating the drums of war.

"Saying Goodbye"

Hey, honey, do you hear the drums? Their beat grows louder now.

They call for me. Hey, honey, we knew this would be when we had our wedding cake.

Something we prepared for but were never sure—now they're talking about yellowcake.

A nightmare we hoped we would never live. So much we would have to give.

Time is getting close now. They've called for me. Have to go now.

Do you hear the beat of the drum? The time has finally come.

The beat of your heart is beginning to fade, now that I hear the beat of the drums.

As I leave, I make a promise to you, something I'll do to make it right.

When the beat of the drums finally subside, this I confide, our days will be bright.

And you will see how much we can be. But right now, I have a war to fight.

I promise when we come home that I'll hold you tight. We'll make it right.

And we will have a good life, with children who know the love of a beating heart.

We'll forget the sound of the fife and beating drums, and our life can finally start.

Everything you've ever hoped for will be reality, when I get back from the war.

FORT STEWART, GA

January 2003

After my vacation time was up, I drove my new family back to Savannah. Lucy, Brandon, and I stayed at a local Best Western just off-post, a rather cozy accommodation with nice amenities. The hotel offered free breakfast every morning and a comfortable room for Lucy and Brandon to continue bonding. Unfortunately, those two and a half weeks flew by. I had a lot of work to do to coordinate the movement of our unit equipment. The next thing we knew, Lucy and I were preparing to say goodbye.

Two nights before I was to deploy to Kuwait, Lucy and I stayed at on-post lodging. The amenities were not as comfortable, but the location offered proximity to my departure point. It brought my family closer to the experience I was about to embark upon. There was little else to do but wait. Lucy and I took pictures in the room with our baby, and I privately wondered if these would be our last memories together. Lucy and I had decided we didn't want something as personal as our goodbyes to be in public, and I needed to know she had gotten back safely to her parents' home in Oviedo before I flew to Kuwait.

I held on to every precious moment leading to that inevitable goodbye. After putting Lucy's luggage back in her Volkswagen Jetta, I tucked Brandon safely in his car seat. There wasn't much left to say. Brandon, now sleeping, was too young to comprehend what was happening. I felt at peace knowing he was with Lucy, who loved him so much.

"Lucy," I said, looking into her blue eyes one last time. "I love you so much and will think of you every day. Be strong for us, and take good care of Brandon."

Lucy gazed back as tears filled her eyes. "I want you to focus on what you have to do over there." After a brief pause, she continued, "We will be fine. You are a wonderful father—and husband. I love you."

Kissing my son's sleeping face and sharing one last embrace with Lucy served as my goodbye. Lucy pulled out of the car lot, and we waved to each other.

I headed off to my unit's company area, where other soldiers were already gathering and preparing to board their buses to the airport.

Saying goodbye that day was the hardest thing I have ever faced in my life. It is burned into my mind and serves as a reminder of the sacrifice Lucy, Brandon, and I made. Words cannot capture the emotion. It lingered for weeks.

Letting go of your family is impossible yet necessary for a soldier. Only those who have served know what that type of sacrifice means. I cried later that night as I accepted that I might have seen my child for the last time.

Thankfully, the next morning was busy with activity. I was satisfied to have my goodbye out of the way. Other soldiers were still saying theirs. Sharing the obligation and burdens of service carries soldiers through tough times.

We flew out of Hunter Army Airfield on a chilly day near the end of January. Along the way, we stopped in Germany. It was cold in the terminal, and we ran into some 82nd Airborne Division personnel en route to Kuwait on another flight. As I looked through the window, I saw evergreen trees and mountains in the distance. The layover was not long. Soon, we got back on the plane, and the next thing I knew, we were in Kuwait. We secured our bags, got on buses, and headed out to Camp Arifjan to begin vehicle draw. We left crews there to sign for vehicles. Everyone else boarded a bus destined for Camp Pennsylvania.

The ride to the camp was memorable. The chartered bus was made for children, so the seats were tiny. It was nearly impossible to get comfortable or sleep. Most of us were so tired, though, that we managed to grab a little shuteye. The drive was extremely boring. All we saw for miles was open-desert nothingness. Then, after hours of this, an indistinguishable berm appeared out of nowhere, and behind that, a gate materialized. Inside the perimeter was a sprawling camp of vehicles, tents, and structures resembling a small city.

NORTHWEST KUWAITI DESERT, CAMP PENNSYLVANIA

January–February 2003

For the first couple of weeks at Camp Pennsylvania, I fell under a depression at the separation from my new family. The feeling was compounded by a mystery ailment. I slept a lot. Then I tried to put my focus on the task at hand: preparing for war.

Under my leadership, I had two M1A2 Abrams tanks, two Bradley Fighting Vehicles, and one dismount squad. My job as a platoon leader was to maneuver this force in combat by taking orders sent from Captain Kelly, then interpreting and filling in the necessary details for my platoon to accomplish the mission.

When we began our platoon training, I ironed out the leadership team and prepared for the missions we were assigned, focusing on how we would maneuver our hunter-killer team of tanks and infantry. I studied the Battalion Tactical Standard Operating Procedures, or TACSOP, and battle plans. I drew diagrams to hammer in the need to be flexible in formation. In the end, it was an evolution: Infantry get you to the fight and find the enemy; tanks lead the way when contact is imminent.

We took the liberty of personalizing our newly issued vehicles to fit our unit's character. Many vehicle commanders named their tracks, though I never named mine. We took apart Air Force pallet systems to create a netting device that allowed us to carry more supplies on the sides. Units that had been in Kuwait longer had fashioned mounted steel racks to their vehicles, but we did not have the luxury of time.

We officers were a tight group, though we weren't without our feuds. Still, we always came together as a team and genuinely got along. Captain Kelly informally had us eat every meal together. Although Gleason was assigned to the scout platoon, he often joined us for meals.

"Dermo, how's Lucy and Brandon?" Captain Kelly asked me one night. He knew I had called home earlier in the day. I typically avoided discussion about my family because I was not dealing with the situation well. It made me emotional thinking about them.

"They're good, sir. How are your wife and Olivia doing?"

"Great, Ryan," he said with enthusiasm. He seemed to be dealing with the separation well.

"Looks like a steak dinner tonight," Morseth piped up from the front as we moved through the cafeteria line. "Captain Kelly, you mind giving me one of yours? I know you've been watching your weight lately. I need the protein for building muscle. I've been lifting. Even McDermott has been going. Why don't you?"

"Ha ha, Justin. Or should I say, Meathead. You are such a meathead," Captain Kelly came back with a laugh and smile. "Truth be told, I have been working out."

"Really? Oh," Morseth said with sarcastic surprise. "Sir, now that I'm looking . . ."

"I go at night," the captain admitted. "I actually work during the day, unlike you platoon leaders."

Gleason chimed in at that point: "Sir, you're going to have to bulk up to beat back the boys from your daughter." This playful conversation was a rare opportunity for the platoon leaders to land a few punches on their commander.

Morseth said, "Sir, it is such sweet justice that you of all people had a girl. You get what you deserve."

"In that case, Justin," I said, "I'm sure you're going to have a whole litter of girls." Everyone laughed in agreement. Justin prided himself on his fraternity days at Denison College.

"No way. Males dominate my family. I'm going to have a strong Nordic son." He paused to consider the reality. "I might name him Lief."

"Steve, you and Meg plan to have kids?" I asked on the side.

"Yeah," Gleason replied. "We started trying right before we deployed, but no success yet."

We proceeded to grab our food and sit down to eat. I grabbed a chocolate bar for dessert to satisfy my sweet tooth.

"You sure like those chocolate bars," Captain Kelly said. "One day, you won't be able to get away with eating those so often." He patted his belly.

"I just like them for the pirate. Arrr, shiver me timbers."

We ate our meals and headed outside, where the Kuwaiti desert and winds reminded us how far away from home and family we were.

We moved out of the comfort of Camp Pennsylvania around the middle of February. The 101st Airborne Division needed to occupy the area to secure ammunition and conduct last-minute combat rehearsals. We waited in the desert, parked in widely distributed and interlocking perimeters. Our new environment did not offer much recreation beyond playing cards and eating competitions. Each day, we listened to news updates on the radio—a chaotic contrast to the tranquility of the open desert. I also wrote letters home to Lucy and on occasion directly to Brandon. The process helped me feel better about the separation.

In my letters to Lucy, I conveyed my love and attempted to maintain a sense of normalcy in our relationship. In my letters to my Brandon, I wrote about life far beyond what his mind could comprehend. He was too young to understand where I was or why I was gone. But I wanted him to know me, to know the kind of man I hoped to be, and to understand why I had chosen this path. I didn't want him to think I left because I didn't care. I wanted him to know I thought of him every day.

CHAPTER 13

Letter Home March 10, 2003

KUWAITI DESERT

March 2003

The Kuwaiti desert stretched out around us, an endless expanse of sand that blurred the boundary between earth and sky. We had prepared for months in the United States, and now the time was nearing for a mission we could not be sure would materialize. Would Saddam Hussein concede to the demands set by the United States? Would President Bush order us to cross the border and execute the war plan?

As much as we tried to focus on our mission, the quiet moments, those times when there was nothing to do but wait, became harder to bear—longing for Lucy's embrace, Brandon's sweet smile.

As I sat in my track in the middle of the open desert, I felt a heaviness in my chest that I hadn't felt before. There was something about this moment, this quiet before the storm, that made the distance from my family unbearable. What I wrote might truly be the last words I ever sent to my son. And so I chose my words carefully, hoping that if nothing else, he would know how much I loved him.

Hey Brandon,

How are you doing? I hope you are healthy and getting stronger each day. I'm sure Mom is ensuring that. Are you having fun with her? Mom is wonderful, isn't she? Anyway, I figure you won't understand much of this letter or others for a while. I want you to know that I think of you every day. I wonder what sort of man you will be. What virtues will you seek to embody? I can't wait to see you grow, though. It is unfortunate and out of my control that I am on the other side of the world. I wish I could be over there with you and mom. Believe me.

One day, you may ask me why I joined the Army and why the Infantry. I'm still not sure. However, I've always thrived [on] challenge. I initially decided that West Point was the best college for me. I knew that [. . .] West Point would set me up for success throughout my life. Attending and graduating from West Point requires Army commitment. I chose Infantry because it is the heart of the Army. Plus, it left me with more options should I choose to stay in.

One lesson you can apply throughout your life is to leave your options open. You also have to [. . .] choose [a path] for yourself. That is internal. This should spring from your passion and desire. I just hope virtue is the basis for your pursuits, not just ambition. Ambition can lead to selfishness, which can lead to a lonely life. However, there is a healthy level of ambition. [. . .] Brandon, you are the world to me. I look forward to playing with you when I get home. I'll be changing your diapers as well. I may get out of practice, but I'll pick it up quickly.

Brandon, I hope you remember me when I finally get home. You probably won't, but that is okay. I was just remembering the day you were born. You were very alert once you were delivered. We got to look at each other, and I knew you looked like your mom. The doctor thought you [would be] smaller than what you were. You weighed 8 lbs. 9 oz. That is pretty big. Your mom took great care of you while you were inside of her. She ate well and stayed in great shape.

Son, when I get home, we're going to have some father-son time. I look forward to it. But I have a job to do here. One day it may be in the history books. I'm here because it is my job, not for any glory. I would be there with you if I could. I love you very much. Keep Mom in good company and good spirits.

Love, Dad

I folded the letter carefully, placing it in an envelope as if it contained all the hopes and dreams I had for Brandon. It was a strange thing, writing to a child who couldn't comprehend language. But I knew that one day, he would understand. One day, if he asked why I had gone, why I had left him and his mother to fight in a war a world away, I hoped this letter would give him the answers he needed.

CHAPTER 14

Crossing the Border

Every border we cross marks a transition. As I neared the border to Iraq, the burden of distance from my family grew heavier. Now there were no computers to connect us to home. There were no phones to call our loved ones. Our letters took even longer to process both ways. Mail from Lucy was delayed by one to two weeks. It was impossible to connect to how she was feeling in the moment, but at least I understood how she felt two weeks ago.

Our lives also grew further apart. Lucy wrote more about her daily life with Brandon and her family. In some instances, she referred to a letter I had written several weeks before. By March 17, 2003, I had finally written all I could possibly say to Brandon and Lucy. I let go of my ruminations on the possibility of dying and focused on the mission. I also focused on the fact that others were sharing in this separation.

Moving to the desert marked a distinct step toward war, but the news we received regarding the ongoing political discussions and national decision-making was distant from us. We received mission updates down the chain of command but otherwise were left to imagine what might happen. We simply had to be prepared for combat. I spent my downtime playing cards.

For weeks, we were repeatedly briefed and updated, constantly breaking our missions down in fine detail. The next step toward war would be the order to move into an assault position at the Kuwait–Iraq border. We expected to stay in that location for as long as two weeks—but as soon as we got to the border, the time frame accelerated.

KUWAIT–IRAQ BORDER, ASSAULT POSITION

March 19, 2003

Just as we reached our assault position near the border, my platoon was tasked with a security mission in the north along the Marine sector, with the expectation of crossing the border the following day. Not all the information was filtering to my level, and we had heard little about the ultimatum President Bush gave Saddam Hussein. My dismounted soldiers dug hasty foxhole positions in case we were there for several days.

We were caught off guard when Captain Kelly ordered my platoon back to the staging area. "When you get back, get into your MOPP gear," he said with uncharacteristic urgency. This was not an exercise. This was real. We were crossing the border. We were going to war.

I immediately gave the order to my guys to move out, and we rendezvoused with our company in a column formation. We put on our chemical suits and waited for further orders. There was a flurry of activity as vehicles maneuvered around one another to get into the proper formation.

Within an hour, we observed the first munitions fired in the war—rockets and missiles launched from behind our position and over our heads. Until this point, doubts had lingered as to whether we would cross the border that night, if at all. That doubt vanished with the rockets.

Operation Iraqi Freedom officially began on March 20, 2003. Charlie Company's first task was to secure the seven-mile stretch of road into Iraq for the task force by destroying three objectives. My platoon's objective, code-named Objective Garfield, was positioned just beyond the berm slightly to the north. It could be seen from the border in daylight but was obscured by the night. Our thermal sights would have to illuminate our advance.

We conducted last-minute radio rehearsals and other weapon test fires. As soon as the artillery finished their barrage, we began our assault across the border. My goal was to execute our mission as quickly as possible, to limit confusion from follow-on units. The biggest threat at that point was that an adjacent unit might mistake us for the enemy.

As soon as we observed Garfield at two kilometers, I gave the order to begin firing on the position with our 25 mm Bradley cannons. My platoon sergeant identified what appeared to be a tank hull from the First Gulf War and fired his sabot rounds into it just to confirm.

We had test-fired our weapons, but not with war-stock ammunition. The lethality of our systems was reassuring. It was overkill, however. Upon reaching the objective, as the plow tanks moved to the far side of the objective to secure the area, dismounts quickly moved out to search. In the darkness, I yelled at my dismount squad leader, Staff Sergeant Faver, "Give me an up once the area is cleared!"

Faver yelled back, confused at my order: "Sir, there's nothing to clear. The area is rubble."

When all was said and done, Objective Garfield was cleared. After passing through our platoon objective area, we moved to our initial holding area within Iraq. One platoon secured the site on foot while the rest of us established our next holding area. Then we got whatever sleep we could.

The night was cold, and my adrenaline prevented me from sleeping. My soldiers slept outside the back of the Bradley while I maintained communications on the company network.

The platoon securing the Iraqi command post was the first to see enemy casualties. And we would soon get our first daylight glimpse of Iraq.

Charlie Company's next movement order arrived at dawn. The sky was clear, and it was a beautiful day.

The route, code-named Aspen, took us through a defensive corridor of sorts, with slightly higher ground on our left flank and rough terrain on our right. Our tanks and Bradley Vehicles coasted through the terrain. Military vehicle positions existed all around, but our only company consisted of nomadic Iraqis, sheep, goats, and dogs. The dogs enjoyed running after us; imagine the pride a dog feels chasing off an M1A2 Abrams tank.

Jalibah Airfield, Objective Charlie, was also a strategic objective during Operation Desert Storm. In fact, 3-69 Armor had been a part of the battle, one in which fratricide took place. I hoped history didn't repeat itself. But our unit's confidence couldn't have been higher, and more extensive measures to limit fratricide had been put in place. The FBCB2 system on every commander and executive officer's track allowed adjacent units to track unit movements on a digital map. Combat Identification Panels made vehicles more distinguishable.

Intelligence reported that we could expect enemy scouts. When we finally reached our point of expected enemy contact, our Bradleys deployed in attack formation and raced across the desert toward our objective. We halted at the forward edge of Jalibah, which had unexploded ordnance from end to end, and waited for the Iraqis. But Iraqis were nowhere to be found.

After firing at a bunker position, we determined the airfield was vacant. Within hours the area was cleared and helicopters were staged for deep operations into Iraq. Other units crossed in front of our positions, north toward Nasiriyah. Later that night, rockets launched continuously into the sky. But most of us were too exhausted to watch and rested in anticipation of a long drive the next morning.

After fueling our vehicles and sleeping at the airfield, my company set off in a convoy along a highway to An Najaf. With such little resistance thus far, I wondered if we would get all the way to Baghdad without firing a single shot. I would have been perfectly fine with that.

We drove all day and night without sleeping. Along the way, I learned that another unit had advanced ahead of us to secure areas around An Najaf. It was not clear to me what our mission would entail.

Around midday, we ran into the remains of a small battlefield, which turned out to be Objective Rams, the 2nd Brigade objective. It was a swampy rural area southwest of Najaf, where it appeared that elements of the Iraqi Army had tried to wage battle using pickup trucks mounted with machine guns. This was a bad idea against M1s and Bradleys. The 2nd Brigade had secured the area and were repairing their vehicles while addressing other maintenance issues. After a brief pause within the friendly perimeter, Captain Kelly informed us over the radio that we would be taking the high ground, referred to as the escarpment. This was the causeway mission!

The escarpment ran from east to west, with only a few trafficable roads to support movement to the north. On either side of the single-lane road was swampland with sparse vegetation. This meant there would be little cover to our approach for a couple of miles. It looked exactly like the mission we'd practiced at NTC—where we'd all died, albeit notionally.

It was the third full day of the war, and we were already worn out from lack of sleep. Reality started to settle in. On the side of the road, I spotted a destroyed Iraqi truck, still smoldering. Amid the charred remains were human ribs. Combat felt nearer and more real.

"Did you see that guy? Extra crispy," Sergeant Creeley commented over the platoon radio.

I swallowed my fear. Seeing a dead person for the first time up close, and so gruesomely, was a wake-up call. The stakes of war are as simple as life and death.

I wasn't sure whether we would be moving forward or holding a position south of the escarpment before taking the high ground. I did not have to wait long for an answer. As we neared the objective area, Captain Kelly came on the net: "Guidons, this is Rock Six. Report in sequence. Over."

All the platoon leaders acknowledged, including myself.

Captain Kelly continued, "Be advised, we are conducting a hasty assault on the escarpment. Order of march is Steel, Red, Blue. Red, you will assault the high ground. Steel and Blue, I need your suppressive fires on the ridge as soon as we are within range. Break. Steel and Blue, be prepared to assault north to phase line Foxtrot and be prepared to provide dismount support. How copy? Over."

All the platoon leaders again acknowledged receipt of the orders. Our point man then radioed with a checkpoint update. "Rock Six, this is Steel Four. Reached checkpoint Bravo-One-Five-Niner. Negative contact, continue mission. Over."

Mud stretched before us, parted by one road heading toward the escarpment on the horizon. We could see the escarpment from at least seven kilometers away. Which meant that the enemy could see us.

Captain Kelly reinforced the necessity to "move quickly" through the swamp area and up through the passage. Over the company radio network, our fire support officer announced that the Air Force would be dropping bombs on a target over the escarpment. A few seconds later, a huge explosion reverberated in the distance, to the east, near Najaf. We were too close to the escarpment for them to risk hitting our crossing point, and commanders did not want to damage the road.

We moved closer, with the company point man again reporting our position. "Rock Six, this is Steel Four. Reached checkpoint Bravo-One-Six-Zero. Negative contact, continue mission. Over."

As Charlie Company continued movement up the escarpment, the defending Iraqis on the high ground apparently became impatient. They attempted to engage our vehicles with rocket propelled grenades (RPGs) and AK-47s while we were still well out of range of their weapons. Fortunately for us, the Iraqis were within range of ours. The issue became how quickly we could get up the escarpment and find and neutralize any indirect assets they might employ against us.

As the situation intensified, our point man identified the checkpoint. "Rock Six, uhh . . . we got enemy. Engaging, uhh . . . Reached checkpoint Bravo One-Six-One. Negative contact, continue mission. Over."

Our company point man was feeling the pressure of the fight. I decided to lighten the mood on the platoon net with Creeley. "Blue One, Blue Four. Do you think ole Steel Four has lost it? He just said negative contact. Break. Looks to me someone needs to tell him. Break. That there's a whole bunch of Iraqis that want to kill him. Over."

Creeley responded with quick wit as always: "Roger. I'm just glad he's in front of me shooting, and not behind me. Over."

Two company vehicles took the initiative to move off the side of the road to get a shot lined up. However, what had appeared to be trafficable terrain turned out to be sludge. "Bones" reported over the net, "Rock Six, Steel One. I'm stuck in the mud. It didn't look that bad. Over."

Captain Kelly responded, "Roger. Get your men up that fuckin' hill, with or without you. Break. I'll get the eighty-eight. Break. Rock Five, Rock Six. Have the eighty-eight ready. Over."

One of the lead vehicles, commanded by Staff Sergeant Sorenson, identified and destroyed an Iraqi truck mounted with an anti-armor weapon system sitting in the open at the crest of the cliff. The explosion devastated the Iraqis' morale. The direct fire ceased quickly after that. My platoon continued to distribute fires along the cliff as we took up the rear of the company convoy. Arrayed in a column, we were able to engage off our flanks and suppress the cliff on either side of the pass. For a moment, I felt a sense of sheer power and desire to kill that I had never felt before in training. It was primal.

Captain Kelly finally called my platoon off. "Blue One, Rock Six. Cease fire. Red Platoon is about to assault. Over."

I acknowledged and complied, relaying it to my own platoon

network. Upon reaching the summit of the escarpment, a couple of infantry squads dismounted to seize the high ground surrounding the passage. They assaulted positions with direct fire, including grenades. One bobbled throw caused two soldiers to take shrapnel, one to the chin and the other on the arm. Within minutes, the Iraqis gave up their arms and surrendered.

Mortar rounds began to impact sporadically, the majority in the rear of our column. As this was happening, Captain Kelly ordered my platoon through the pass to set up a security perimeter north. Behind us, the Iraqis finally reached the escarpment with their mortars. On the radio, a soldier was in panic, trying to find his squad leader, as a mortar round had landed within twenty feet of his position. The resistance soon subsided, and we gathered up prisoners.

Captain Kelly again radioed. "Blue and Steel Platoons, I need you to assault north to phase line Foxtrot. Blue, take the right side; Steel, go left. Break. We're expecting enemy movement in the vicinity of the compound. Break. That is not our objective. Break. Be prepared as enemy are flushed out. Over."

I echoed the command to my platoon and executed the order. As we faced the north, my gunner spotted dismounts in the distance. We sprayed the area with coax 7.62 mm rounds. Later, another platoon maneuvered into position as mine pulled overwatch, taking prisoners. Setting up in our screen line just south of Objective Raiders, we processed our enemy prisoners and reassessed our own readiness status. By the end of the afternoon, the area was cleared, with a company total of fifty or so enemy prisoners. Approximately fifteen had been located by our screen line position, while the majority had taken positions along the escarpment. During initial interrogations, we realized that the Iraqis in our possession had been forced to surrender so that others could escape.

The trip into Iraq so far had yielded few maintenance problems for my platoon. Now, though, one of my tanks broke a torsion bar, which would need to be fixed before moving too far. I had to stay with my tank while the rest of the company moved north. Fortunately, Charlie Company did not take any serious casualties that day.

Later that night, there was a great deal of bombing in the nearby city of An Najaf. I took up a position just outside the city in the desert, where several vehicle crews had remained to do maintenance. The rest of Charlie Company continued north to Objective Raiders and formed a perimeter with the rest of the brigade.

In the dark of the moonlit desert, visibility was less than ten meters, though ambient light came from the towns along the Euphrates River. The maintenance issue stifled the tank crew. Mechanics worked diligently for hours to fix the torsion bar, but we had pushed ourselves to exhaustion and could not function anymore. I was so tired that I would have accepted death as a form of sleep. At some point, I gave in, and my gunner covered for me on the radio and in the turret.

During my deep slumber, I had an intense nightmare, the horror of which words cannot adequately convey. I dreamed of a disembodied eye resembling the Eye of Sauron, seething and trying to draw me closer to its power. The pulsing bright-red eye stood silent, but I sensed it wanted me to embrace the power to kill and thereby give over my soul. And I knew there could be no worse fate than my soul becoming nothingness.

Boom!

Never have I slept so hard to be awoken so suddenly and violently. I thought I was dead. At that moment, another bomb hit the town nearby, amplified by the metal hull of the Bradley. I thought for certain that our vehicle had just been directly hit. It took a moment to remember I was in a war zone.

Outside the Bradley, the sound was not so deafening. Using the flash-to-bang method, though, I decided we were too close for comfort.

Apprehensive about none of our vehicles being registered in the FBCB2 system, I sought to expedite our maintenance efforts. The mechanics were zombies. I pulled over a section leader who had been catching up on sleep.

"Guys, we need to get the fuck out of here. Where's the maintenance chief?"

"He's over there." The soldier pointed to a vehicle about twenty meters away. I roused the maintenance chief and we got to work. The problem was fixed with relative ease following our few hours' rest.

Within a half hour, we were on our way and swiftly linked up with our unit. By dawn, we had reestablished contact with the company and were set up in a tactical assembly area northwest of Najaf. We spent the next week waiting out red dust storms before advancing further north toward Baghdad.

CHAPTER 15

The Karbala Gap

DESERT NORTHWEST OF NAJAF, SOUTH OF KARBALA

March 2003

From March 24 to 31, my unit stayed in a perimeter in the desert around Najaf, occasionally supporting missions probing potential crossing points along the Euphrates River. A massive once-in-a-century dust storm prevented us from advancing further through the desert. Fortunately, the storm also allowed our supply chains time to catch up and a respite to recover from the initial thrust into Iraq. Without food, fuel, and, most importantly, water, we could go nowhere. By the time we got the order to advance through the Karbala Gap on March 31, we were fully recovered and eager to attack.

On April 1, we moved into an assault position in preparation for an attack north through the Karbala Gap with the intent of continuing north to the river-crossing site at Objective Peach. My unit then waited until the early morning to begin a thrust that would keep us moving nonstop all the way to Baghdad.

Before our assault, Coalition forces "softened up" Iraqi defenses with an incredible artillery barrage on objectives around Karbala. I couldn't sleep and don't think any other soldiers could either. In battle, you can never plan for when the call comes to attack nor choose the flow of battle once it starts. Why sleep when you might be dead soon?

The artillery barrage engaged more firepower than I had ever witnessed before. Counting the number of rounds in the sky all at once, I once reached twenty-five. There could have been more. At night, the rounds flew with a red glow and seemed to stop at their apex, then accelerate back down to the earth, converging on their targets. Flashes appeared in the distance. Moments later, the sound of the explosions rolled through like thunder. That was when you realized the impact of what was happening.

As the barrages continued into the next night, the finale came with targets directly north of our position. Shortly after the barrage, Captain Kelly came over the company network and gave the order to move out. Our task force moved through the outskirts of Karbala as the sun emerged along the horizon, meeting pockets of resistance along the way north and eliminating a majority of the threats for the follow-on units.

Our battalion task force would make two crossings over the canal that marked the northern boundary of the Karbala Gap. While my platoon was in trail through the gap, I was ordered to clear a trench of Iraqis attempting to surrender. Quickly my dismount squad took action. They secured ten prisoners—and killed one who posed an armed threat.

When Sergeant Grizzle emerged from the trench, I saw concern on his face.

"What is it, Grizzle? Get them tied up, leave them, and you get your guys back in the Bradley."

"Sir, I just shot one of them in the chest. He was hiding in a hole. I saw a weapon. I think he's dead."

Detached from the situation and focused on the mission, I responded, "Okay, good. Clear the area, get them tied up, and get back on the track."

Time was of the essence. My soldiers bound the Iraqis with zip ties and left them on the side of the road with the expectation that follow-on units would take them into custody. While my platoon was occupied with this task, the rest of Charlie Company pressed forward to cross the canal. However, there was some confusion over which crossing point was ours. By the time my platoon was moving again, we easily caught up with our company as it circled back to find an alternate route to the canal crossing point.

The crossing point, when we found it, was nothing like I visualized. Maps never capture the three-dimensional reality. Vegetation and foliage along with rough terrain provided many hiding places for dismounted soldiers. We saw Iraqis on the far side of the land bridge. The lead platoons simply bypassed most threats, shooting only that which time allowed. Sergeant Verdun was able to destroy an apparent ammo cache near one of their bunker positions as Sergeants Hall and Creeley took out two trucks. Secondary explosions indicated the presence of incendiaries and small-arms ammunition.

A trench lined the side of the road to our right. Sergeant Hall suppressed the area with his machine guns and reported that he took some of them out. Without clearing the trench, we pushed north and eventually bypassed it to find ourselves in familiar terrain: more open desert. This was where the Iraqis trained their military. With such open terrain, I saw us reaching the Euphrates that same day.

No firm timeline had been put together—at least, not that was sent down to my level. It seemed event-driven: We went after each follow-on objective, one right after the other, until we could go no further.

Our route toward the Euphrates took one simple but major turn toward the north. To ensure that no unit missed the turn, Captain Kelly ordered my platoon to establish a security line along the flank and direct follow-on units. My dismounts pulled rear and flank security for our vehicles, focusing on lines of sight in which vehicle sights were not as useful.

While we were at that blocking position, an Iraqi truck suddenly barreled toward one of my tanks, threatening the intersection. The truck breached our established 400-meter threshold, and we fired warning shots. A few seconds later, Sergeant Hall destroyed the vehicle with a main tank round. The truck became a fireball and flipped over backward.

I had my tanks blow out their V-PAC air filters while we were stopped. If they became clogged, the vehicles would break down.

My dismounted infantry also took advantage of the time and rotated through weapons maintenance and chow. It was a successful refit operation. My platoon was then relieved from the screen-line mission and ordered to link up with the rest of our company closer to the Euphrates River objective.

By the time we reached the assembly area, we had thirty minutes to prepare for our assault on the bridge. The big fight was about to unfold. That was when I realized my vehicle's night sights were inoperable. But I did not think twice about the vehicle malfunction; my track would just use the auxiliary sight in battle. The damage didn't matter for a day fight nearly as much but made my track useless at night.

Sergeant Verdun and I did some weapons checks and reloaded ammunition, and I drank a nutrition shake. Twenty-four hours had passed since being told to move into the assault position south of Karbala. Twenty-four hours since we had slept.

As we waited for the order to move forward, I felt delirious but alert. I had conserved my energy throughout the day and sucked on dehydrated coffee. I would have been more tired if not for the constant flow of adrenaline.

Weeks of anticipation all came down to the hours ahead, and actions measured in minutes and seconds would determine success or failure. A carnival-like crowd of news media and units converged on Objective Peach. The road leading to the bridge was lined with US military vehicles in what resembled a traffic jam. My company eventually got the call to move to the front.

As we progressed through the column of traffic, the desert gradually turned into a tropical paradise. It was a beautiful area with palm trees. The landscape near the river was lush, the dry sand becoming mud and the endless horizons obscured by tree lines. There was cover for our advance.

However, the landscape also provided cover for the Iraqis. Apache helicopters found it difficult to assault forward of our position because of small-arms fire from concealed areas. As other companies cleared their assigned sectors, we waited at the rear of the task force for the order to move into our final assault position. We were eager to cross the bridge and finish the war.

CHAPTER 16

Crossing the River

AL-KAED BRIDGE, "OBJECTIVE PEACH," EIGHTEEN MILES SW OF BAGHDAD, IRAQ

April 2, 2003

Rivers carve through landscapes, leaving marks that last for generations. As we approached the river southwest of Baghdad, we knew this crossing would leave its own indelible mark on us. The battle we had awaited for weeks finally arrived on the afternoon of April 2. I was at the base of the bridge, looking across into the unknown. The bridge was the last major obstacle for the 3rd Infantry Division before its inevitable attack on Baghdad. After we secured the crossing site, the next stop for my unit would be Saddam International Airport. From there, we naively believed we would fly home within a few weeks. Getting across the bridge would be one giant step toward holding our loved ones.

If we failed to secure the bridge, we would have to look for a bridge further downriver, in an area less advantageous for our attack on Baghdad.

The plan to attack a key bridge south of Baghdad was first briefed to my unit in February 2003, when we were still in Kuwait. Of the many objectives briefed before the war, this mission was on my mind constantly. The strategic importance was obvious; it represented a choke point and last major obstacle before reaching Baghdad. My platoon was designated to be the first mechanized unit to cross the bridge.

For less than a minute of the war, my platoon would be the main effort of the Coalition fight. Leaders in the Pentagon, Coalition headquarters, division headquarters, brigade headquarters—they would all have their attention fixed on the bridge and the outcome of the battle. The stakes were high. Secure the bridge, and the Coalition forces could go to Baghdad. Lose the bridge, and the whole war plan would go out of the window, and popular support at home would undoubtedly be tested.

We were provided rudimentary intelligence to inform our attack compared to what is available today. A satellite photo showed the bridge from high altitude. Our maps were of a scale that made it impossible to interpret the contours of the terrain, and the picture provided only marginally more detail, showing an outline of the river, banks on each side, and what appeared to be a narrow two-span bridge. We could not discern areas that might conceal enemy threats; the photos lacked depth in that regard. But we had enough information to form our plan.

In those weeks between receiving the plan and arriving at the bridge, I contemplated the fight in my quiet moments. I dreamed of the impending battle and anticipated various tactics from the Iraqis. Blowing up the bridge ahead of us would slow our advance, but we could still maneuver to a new location. I imagined the possibility of crossing the bridge and being stranded after it was blown up. I also imagined they might allow some vehicles to cross the bridge before blowing it, thereby miring our unit and creating chaos.

There were only a handful of bridges over the Euphrates in the vicinity of Baghdad. Army units had crossed bridges further south to draw the enemy's attention away from the capital. The bridge at Objective Peach was always intended to be the crossing point for the main body of the US Army's 3rd Infantry Division. Other bridges would force Coalition forces through miles of urban terrain.

From the bridge at Objective Peach, the 3rd Infantry Division could assault key intersections in Baghdad, cripple the Republican Guard, and end the war quicker. Our hope was that we might show such force that the Hussein regime would surrender, preventing the need for an all-out assault into Baghdad.

In the afternoon on April 2, the crest of the bridge was as far as we could see, but we finally felt Baghdad was in striking distance. The skies were clear and the temperature tolerable. It was a perfect day for the Coalition to attack, but of course it was also a perfect day for the enemy to defend.

I sat in the turret of my Bradley, in the cramped space next to my gunner, Sergeant Verdun, and kept my driver, Specialist Rosa, on his toes. "Move us just a little more forward, Rosa—and that should do it."

Indignant with my constant adjustments and micromanagement, Rosa quipped, "Sir, do you want to get down here and drive? I'll gladly sit in your spot."

I continued to pester Rosa so that he stayed alert, but it was also important to sustain internal communication from the commander's hatch to the driver. Occasionally, we lost connection inside the Bradley and he did not realize it. When it happened, there was no way to get him to check his radio in his separate compartment. Either a guy in the back of the track had to throw a magazine clip at his head or I had to get out of the track and kick on his hatch. I also enjoyed the banter. Rosa could be funny when he was being a smart-ass.

"Fine, I'll stop micromanaging you, Rosa," I finally relented. "Just make sure you're ready to go when I give the order. I don't need you dozing off on me."

"Fat chance of that happening," Rosa retorted. "I can't wait to the far side so I can drop this load. I have had to take a crap for three hours. I want to be the first American to take a shit in Baghdad."

We all laughed.

"We won't be quite to Baghdad once we cross, but we'll be close," I replied.

We had all grown accustomed to gross humor; it alleviated the stress of the moment. I had been shy of peeing in the turret next to my gunner just weeks before. Now, at the base of the bridge, decorum seemed unnecessary. No one wants to be killed in the act of taking a piss.

With the incoming artillery, I closed my hatch and swiveled the turret to keep the exhaust fumes out. Depending on the wind, they could fill the turret, making my eyes burn. There was no escaping the smell, though, and frankly, I came to like the smell of burning JP-8 over time. The smell and the sounds of gunfire and explosions combined to create a unique atmosphere.

While Rosa and I bantered, Sergeant Verdun kept mostly silent, resting his brow on the gunner's sight. He didn't need to sustain an active scan, and I did not want him to when we were behind the front lines because of the focus required to discern enemy targets from friendly forces. I wanted his mind fresh when it was time to cross. It was a matter of life and death when he squeezed the trigger.

When I did provide an order to Verdun, he usually replied with a simple "Roger." By this point, we operated with such synchronicity that we often didn't need to communicate. For weeks, we sat practically on top of each other, so we got to know each other quite well.

After the endless day of assault, we were all uncomfortable. My nerves were tested as the explosions encroached on our position. I kept pulling out my piss bottle to relieve myself. My protective gear made me even more claustrophobic, but I knew my guys in the back had it worse. They wore more gear and had less room to move; plus, they could not see any of the action. They had been able to dismount the vehicle a few times earlier in the day, but now they were stuck until we reached the far side of the bridge.

The waiting game continued as we listened to incoming and outgoing bullets and artillery. The Bradley-amplified explosions made me increasingly anxious to get over the bridge.

With all that was at stake, it was impossible not to think about the purpose of war. Why were we fighting? I did not think this war was worth fighting even if Iraq had chemical weapons, but I had sworn an oath. A soldier must serve faithfully so long as the orders are lawful. My purpose was rooted in the aspect of selfless service I had so appreciated in Travis Patriquin; our soldiers deserve good leadership no matter what. Whether war is necessary is not my decision. Officers have the duty to lead, fight, accomplish the mission, and bring our troops home. I assumed the same was true of the Iraqi officers on the other side.

Minutes felt like hours passing. Then, finally, Captain Kelly came on the net to take accountability. "Guidons, this is Rock Six. Respond in sequence." My fellow platoon leaders and I acknowledged. Kelly continued: "Red One, take your unit to the south side of the bridge and secure the near side. Break. Steel Platoon, extend security to the north of the bridge and link up with Rock Five. Break. Blue One, move into assault position behind my vehicle and remain at REDCON One. How copy? Over." The other platoon leaders and I acknowledged and moved our platoons into our respective positions.

I opened my hatch as I directed my platoon. In front of us, two tanks got mired in the mud as they moved toward the river—one of them the same tank that got stuck south of the escarpment and at the NTC. Previously, having a tank stuck in mud had offered some comic relief, but this time, what was about to happen was too important.

Agitated, Captain Kelly maintained focus on the mission and ordered a smoke platoon into position to provide concealment. "Rock Five, this is Rock Six. Take the smoker platoon into position north of the bridge to get concealment."

"Roger, Rock Six. Moving out. Over," the XO, Captain Mike Pecina, acknowledged. He escorted the team to a spot north of the bridge and west of the riverbank, where the smoke could properly conceal the activity at the bridge. Once Pecina settled into position, he happened to find a position with the best fields of fire and began to suppress the far side of the bridge.

The gruff XO always carried out business in a matter-of-fact manner on the radio. His job was to essentially do all the worrying for our company logistics support so that the commander could concentrate on the job in the fight. Pecina made sure our vehicles got fixed and that we had food and water to eat and drink. Normally, he was in the rear with the gear, so to speak, but he was a fighting XO for this battle.

"Rock Six, this is Rock Five," Pecina called to Captain Kelly, who promptly acknowledged. "Roger, we just destroyed two trucks on the far side—continuing to suppress from this position." Pecina continued to put 25 mm rounds on the objective area. The fighting XO would make my fight much easier, as he was able to minimize the threat on the closest part of the river's far side.

As the situation developed, a traffic jam of activity accumulated, requiring me to tighten up my vehicles behind Kelly's track at the base of the bridge. Everyone wanted to see the big show, but the congestion also made for an enemy target. I continued to monitor the radio in my hatch at the near side of the bridge, waiting for the order to assault.

Time dragged on whenever there was little chatter on the radio. I had access to both my company and platoon radio networks. This allowed me to hear from my company commander on one network and relay orders to my guys on another. My company commander monitored his higher headquarters at the battalion level as well as the company networks. I knew that while the company network was quiet, there was likely an abundance of radio traffic on the battalion network.

It's hard to be patient when people are shooting at you. Small-arms fire came from homes across the river, and an occasional artillery round landed in the vicinity. The explosions rattled the Bradley with varying degrees of intensity. I kept my headset on tight to shield from the sounds and decided to close my hatch again. I felt insulated and vulnerable at the same time. I could not control whether an artillery round landed on my vehicle and killed me and my men, though a direct hit is rare, not unlike being struck by lightning.

I considered spiritual well-being while waiting for the order to move ahead. As a combatant, I could not be assured that my spirit would be saved from damnation. It did not seem clear to me whether our cause was more justified than that of the Iraqis on the east side of the river. These thoughts stewed in my head as I flashed back to holding my son, Brandon. Before I allowed myself to get emotional, I remembered what mattered at that moment: my men.

I said a prayer to God that I might lead my men to safety even though we were not worthy of such salvation. I felt at peace. Prayer offered me relief, allowing me to monitor the situation with a more machine-like focus. If I failed my mission, I wanted to have done everything right and without hesitation.

When I peeked out of my hatch at the bridge, I noticed a couple of civilian cars had been destroyed in the oncoming traffic lane. Soldiers from Red Platoon were tending to the civilian casualties.

Trucks brought forward boats to cross under the bridge as smoke billowed across the river. I knew from previous planning briefings that their mission was to secure the underside of the bridge to ensure safe passage for our tanks and Bradley Vehicles. From my position, I could not see them cross, nor did I know if the bridge was intact on the far side.

As the gunfire intensified, I ordered my two tanks to position up front, with my platoon sergeant and my vehicle in trail behind them. They waited offset behind Captain Kelly's track. We were going to use both spans of the bridge until Kelly broke the silence on the company network.

"Blue One, Rock Six. Be advised that the southernmost bridge span has been blown up, you will use only the left lane to cross. How copy?"

While we were waiting, the sapper engineers crossed the river under fire to clear the underside of the bridge of explosives.

"Guidons, this is Rock Six," Captain Kelly called out over the company net. "Be advised that sappers have identified explosives and will be cutting wires. I say again. Break. Be advised that sappers are going to be cutting wires to explosives. Blue One, get your platoon to REDCON One and ready to go."

Normally, I might have dwelled on the fact that one span had been blown, but I trusted the engineers to accomplish their mission. I distributed the information on my platoon net and offered one last silent prayer in my turret. This was it: our big moment.

Then the order seemed to come with no other preparation. "Blue One, assault the bridge!" Captain Kelly ordered over the radio. "I say again, Blue Platoon assault the bridge!"

I quickly acknowledged the order on one radio frequency and passed the information down to my platoon on the other. My men responded quickly, adjusting our two-lane plan to one lane. The tank commanders were responsive and began to accelerate toward the crest of the bridge.

Finally, I gave Rosa the command. "Punch it, Rosa. Let's go! Gunner, shoot suppressive fires deep into the objective area and angle off to the right of the vehicles in front of us!"

"Roger," Rosa and Verdun responded sequentially, the Bradley accelerating up the bridge with the 25 mm cannon shooting bursts. One moment we were waiting, and in the next we were in battle and facing the unexpected.

As Staff Sergeant Currence's tank picked up speed, he expressed concern about an injured Iraqi on the bridge: "Blue One, what do I do if I have to run over this person?"

It was impossible to judge whether he would hit the person as he drove by them.

With all eyes on my platoon and no seconds to spare, I offered my best advice. "Do what you can to avoid them, but get to the other side and shoot suppressive fire. They know we're coming. Get to the other side now." I suspected Currence wanted my go-ahead to do what he knew had to be done. Leaders make the tough calls that impact whether people live or die. Fortunately, we avoided the injured person.

Out front, the lead tank pushed the vehicles blocking our path out of the way, sending a body flying into the bridge rail. My tankers' gunners manned the main guns to engage suspected Iraqi positions while the tank commanders used their .50-caliber machine guns.

The slope of the bridge did not allow visibility to the far bank until it was crested. This created the ultimate kill zone for an enemy force. Knowing this vulnerability, we continued to lead with direct fire.

It is difficult to take in all the little moments in battle and harder to see everything, but as we crested the bridge, it was clear we had met the enemy. We took and returned fire with all our weapon systems heavily engaged. My lead tank shot at suspected positions directly in front of the column, with the second tank angled off the lead track's right shoulder. I authorized both Bradley Vehicles to shoot high explosive rounds to deep targets because the angle of the barrel would not put our tankers at risk. Verdun shot off bursts.

My mission was to support the passage of Charlie 3-69 Armor forward through the objective area, and my goal was to put as many rounds as possible downrange in our minute at the tip of the spear so that the Iraqis would think the entire brigade had just crossed. I wanted them scared and running. And I wanted them dead if they chose to stay and fight.

Once set into position, I had the lead tanks orient their turrets from ten to twelve o'clock and from twelve to two o'clock, with reference to the road facing east. The Bradleys, which trailed, picked up scans from the nine-to-eleven o'clock and one-to-three o'clock positions. This provided coverage over the entire area that might possibly threaten the bridge. We continued taking sporadic fire as we provided fires toward the north to northeast.

I briefly opened my hatch to confirm my platoon's orientation on the battlefield and with follow-on units. I needed to make sure that units could cross through our position without slowing down. Looking up, I spotted an airburst of smoke artillery. The fragments landed right on the front of my Bradley; I yelled over the radio that we were taking friendly artillery. It turned out to be white phosphorous smoke. No harm was done, and I was probably never in danger, but it demonstrated the speed and chaos of battle and, literally, the fog of war.

My vehicles on the left side of the road were in the best position to engage the Iraqi threats, and they did so with main tank, 50-caliber machine gun, 25 mm, and 7.62 mm rounds. When we stopped firing and the follow-on companies continued the assault, I looked at all the vehicles that had been destroyed by Sergeants Creeley and Currence within 400 meters of our position. A picture of war was painted across the landscape. The air filled with the smell of burning munitions and smoke plumes from the destroyed Iraqi tank hulls lining the roadway. We had been spared casualties in my platoon, though one of my tank commanders pulled the remnant of an RPG round off his track.

The scene was reminiscent of *Apocalypse Now*, with helicopters firing from the sky and infantry shooting on the ground. I paused to take a picture with my disposable camera.

Although it was safe enough for me to capture the moment, my mission on Objective Peach was not over. Our job as a support-by-fire element being obsolete, we found work in clearing within our area of operations. The two Bradleys provided overwatch while my dismount squad cleared a total of eight buildings, primarily residential, all of which appeared to have housed soldiers. We found multiple bunkers, a mortar position, and a cache of weapons that would be destroyed.

Finally, what had been unknown to us as we waited on the other side of the bridge became increasingly clear on this side: the enemy's defensive posture. The Iraqis had used civilian Jeeps to push supplies to this frontline position. They must have used motorcycles as well, as there were approximately twelve in the vicinity of the mortar position. We found a night vision device, which led me to believe that special Republican Guard forces may have been present, possibly as an early alert force.

The battle forged on as we cleaned up our sector. While new plumes rose along the roadway ahead, my soldiers filed in and out of buildings, busting down doors as they went. Within a short period, we had friendly artillery vehicles in close proximity. Normally, the big guns are reserved for the rear, but our commander was aggressive in pulling them forward to touch Baghdad.

It made me feel more at ease, seeing the rockets fire from our position while my guys secured and consolidated enemy munitions into piles. Gunfire grew faint as it moved ever forward. Apache helicopters that had circled above us now passed to deeper targets. Vehicles burned less intensely now but continued to provide a distinct odor of expended diesel and munitions. Bombs came more frequently, exploding in the distance as artillery continued to impact nearby.

One thing remained perfectly quiet, and that was the enemy dead, still in their fighting positions.

I considered the flow of battle as my guys completed their clearing missions. The battle for the bridge had exceeded my expectations in its intensity, but it went as smoothly as I could have hoped for. Though the bridge had been partially blown on one span, the span that remained could handle the weight of the 3rd Infantry Division in the days to come. I stood proudly atop the prize, gazing out at the battle scene and feeling a sense of victory and great relief. When all eyes were on my platoon, we held our own.

I finally felt the situation had stabilized enough to let Rosa out of the hatch. "Rosa, do you still need to go?"

"Fuck yeah, sir!" he exclaimed. I had him park at the base of the bridge on the far side so we didn't block traffic before letting him join the dismounts in a nearby home search to use a bathroom. Verdun used the downtime to reload our ammunition before taking a break himself. I continued to monitor the radio and coordinate with my dismounts on the ground.

The brigade tactical operations center soon followed as the battle pressed on. Captain Kelly ordered my platoon to remain as guard at the foothold of the bridge for the night. It felt like our trophy. Smoke rose hazily on the horizon above flashes in the direction of Baghdad. Fewer Apaches flew over our position as it cleared for artillery and rocket fire. We could still hear far-off machine guns and the thud of the Bradleys' 25 mm guns. On occasion, we heard the thunderous explosion of an Abrams tank's main round, but we were safe in our position when my commander approached me at the bridge.

Captain Kelly pulled me to the side.

"Good job, Ryan," he said in a serious tone. "You and your men deserve a good amount of credit."

I could tell he was tired. We had accomplished the mission with no major incident, and the battle continued to roll forward. I considered his praise and his leadership, both before we crossed the berm and during combat. He had believed in my ability throughout training. I was humbled by his confidence in me and greatly appreciated his words.

"Thanks for trusting us with the mission," I said. "Do you think we'll stay in this position for long?" There had been talk of holding outside of Baghdad in case diplomatic efforts ended major combat operations. However, the road thus far—the friends we had lost along the way over in Bravo Company—made that seem impossible. There would be no pause. We were going to have to fight all the way to Baghdad. The only question was when we would continue forward.

Captain Kelly stared out at the horizon and into the sky. He closed his eyes and took a breath in through his nose. When he exhaled, he looked at me and said simply, "I would not expect to stay here long. Get some sleep while you can."

This was not a time for words. We were both too exhausted.

Lives on our side were changed forever in those moments on the bridge, but many lives on the Iraqi side were lost. Within twenty feet of my position was the dead Iraqi soldier who had been thrown into the rail.

As I approached his body, I saw his face clearly, turned up toward the sky as it was. Where his eyes would have been were empty sockets. It is possible they were shot out. Yet it wasn't clear to me how that could happen because the sockets were completely empty. Perhaps his eyes simply fell out when his face impacted the pavement.

Staring at the soldier's remains, I sensed no life. The blood stains on his clothes were already turning brown. His body remained fixed in an unnatural contorted position.

You don't see dead people all that often, but when you do, it is obvious they are dead. Most people only see the deceased at funerals. It was difficult for me to imagine that the soldier had a life before this battle and that he had died only hours before. I'm sure he had loved ones and possibly children. But I did not think about it that way at that time. His body became an artifact of the battlefield, much like a destroyed vehicle or other inanimate object that would only be moved when it was necessary to do so. My men were warfighters who needed sleep and food. I decided to leave the body there until the next morning, when we moved it to a more suitable location.

"The End of War"

There must be peace in death as the body lies still.

The man has taken his last breath. His remains begin to chill.

No more battles will be fought, yet I have many more.

Though I wish to stop, I cannot, for only the dead know the end of war.

The body on the bridge was not the first dead man I saw, nor would it be the last. Still, my proximity to him left a permanent mark upon me, one of many ghosts I still carry from the war. To this day, I can't cross a bridge without being reminded of those moments. The chaos of the war lingers still.

Twenty-four hours after speaking to Captain Kelly, we would be at the gates of Saddam International Airport.

CHAPTER 17

Saddam International Airport

Some places carry weight far greater than their mere physical presence. Saddam International Airport was one such place, and as dawn broke, 1st Brigade prepared for the attack that would mark a turning point in our mission. This was also the last of the missions we had rehearsed pre-invasion.

Before my unit advanced, 2nd Brigade passed through our area onto Objective Saints, a key highway system controlling access into south Baghdad. My guys on the bridge waved them over the crest of the bridge secured less than twenty-four hours prior.

As the Bradley Vehicles and Abrams tanks rolled through, I saw a familiar face among the many commanders—none other than Jeff McFarland. From our journey through Beast and Camp Buckner and our shared experience on 9/11 in Savannah, Jeff and I seemed to cross paths at critical moments throughout our Army careers. We crossed paths again on the bridge of Objective Peach. I felt proud to see my old roommate moving forward as I prepared to continue with my unit to Baghdad.

The original plan, as I understood it, indicated this was the limit of advance, code-named Phase Line Vermont. Phase Line Vermont represented a line we would not cross until leaders in Washington decided a diplomatic solution was impossible. Would we hold up at Phase Line Vermont? Would we get rest?

It was not to be.

Objective Lions, known to the public as Saddam International

Airport, had long been our prize. Lieutenant Colonel Marcone had already staked our claim on one of the nearby palaces. In my mind, and I'm sure I wasn't alone in this, once we took the airport, the war would be over, and we would be relieved and fly straight home. The hope that we were weeks away from seeing our loved ones motivated this last push.

However, we soon realized that more needed to be done. It was about noon when word came down that we would be leaving the area shortly and would have to fight all the way to the airport. "Guidons, this is Rock Six. Meet at my track in five mikes. We're going to the airport today."

At his track, Captain Kelly began, "The order of march is Steel, Red, Headquarters, and Blue. We will depart in two-zero mikes at thirteen hundred hours. Make sure your ammo is reloaded and topped off." He pulled out a map with the route to the airport. "We will follow this route and enter the airport at this location. Once we get onto the tarmac, we will get online and assault in this direction. Three-Seven Infantry will be to our north, our right flank. Steel Company will be to our left flank.

"We have to wait until Task Force Two-Seven has set up the blocking position at the airport gates before we can assault. While this is going on, Second Brigade will continue to hold their position at Objective Saints," Captain Kelly finished, referring to the intersection just south of Baghdad.

The plan focused on simplicity: Get to a start point for the assault, get online, drive straight forward, and shoot to kill. Our task force took two points of entry onto the airport grounds. Charlie Company would lead the way to the westernmost point and gain a foothold on the airport tarmac.

Little time was allowed for dissemination of information. However, at our level, all we needed to do was follow the leader. The move out from the bridge site was chaotic to say the least. Here you had what seemed to be a hundred vehicles in an area that did not support that type of congestion. Yet, under pressure, things somehow fell into place with minimal setbacks.

Once we started moving in the early afternoon, tension settled quickly. First we rolled through the area where our rounds had impacted the day prior. Little did I know how many dismounted Iraqi troops had lined the trenches and foxholes along the road. Over the next two miles, I must have seen a few hundred dead Iraqi soldiers in their foxholes. Multiple armored vehicles were nothing but charred scrap metal. The soldiers looked like they were sleeping, dust layered on their skin as if they had been frozen in the moment of their death.

Better them than me, I thought. I tried not to look at them at great length. To do so might endanger my soldiers. Key to keeping my head was to focus on active threats, not threats already eliminated.

We drove through a small town just south of Baghdad, Al Yusufiyah. People lined the streets in curiosity. Children offered us applause, and the adults seemed shocked to see us. Some embraced our presence openly, while others scowled. In one suspicious incident, a couple of men feuded in our presence, one seemingly being admonished for openly supporting US occupation. But we didn't have time for local disputes. Young men seemed especially suspicious. I imagined them in a foxhole the day before, leaving their uniforms behind as our front units arrived. They were everywhere. It did not surprise me later to find out that support units had been ambushed in these areas.

Canals lined the narrow roads to Highway 1, which would take us directly to the airport. The roads were not fit for tracked vehicle maneuver, affording little room for a driver's mistake. It would have been easy to land in the canal with a slipup. In fact, on April 4, reporter Michael Kelly and Staff Sergeant Wilbert Davis drowned in a vehicle in our task force after veering into a canal while trying to evade enemy fire.

Our company had remained unscathed so far, though, and we reached the highway before dusk. Then, before it even mattered, we hit enemy contact on both flanks of the highway. One scout was critically wounded after an RPG hit his vehicle. We returned fire with 25 mm high explosive rounds and coax machine-gun rounds.

The situation from my perspective was vague at this point. Positions lined the highway, but at more of a distance than at Objective Peach. Our approach was to bombard the positions with sufficient fire so as to neutralize the threat without having to slow down. In simple terms, we did a drive-by shooting. At one point, we had to drive in between a friendly unit who was engaging the Iraqis on our other flank. We didn't have time to coordinate at our level; we just hoped the friendly cavalry unit saw us.

Once we passed through forward friendly lines, we found our turn to the airport. The Iraqis had set up positions on both sides of the road, and the way the corner was defended made it difficult to assault once our convoy started to make the turn. The lead vehicle was able to engage with no restrictions. However, vehicles that had not made the turn yet could not fire upon the target, as any overshooting would impact the area in which the lead vehicles had turned. Vegetation limits visibility. This highlights the importance of situational awareness and sectors of fire. In a sense, the enemy split our forces without making a move. The only vehicles that could safely engage would have to be at the point, directed on-target.

While we were engaging an enemy dismount with 7.62 mm coax, one of the links in the feed shoot broke off. With my gear on, I made a quick assessment. Sergeant Verdun had misfed the links into the ammo cans. The ammo belts are stored in two separate cans. We had yet to go through one can at any given time in the war. Sergeant Verdun was typically superb in reloading the ammunition after each fight. He even ensured that the ammo was dusted off following the sandstorms, to prevent a misfire. However, on this occasion, the rounds were fed on top of themselves; once the rounds began pulling from the second can, we had a jam.

"What the fuck! You fed this shit backwards," I yelled at Verdun. "We are in the middle of battle and have no way to shoot. Fuckin' idiot! What the fuck!" I was livid.

With enemy dismounts in the area and the inability to shoot 25 mm at close range, I worked fast to reload the gun. I pulled all the rounds out of the second can and added more rounds on the end. At that point, I had a string of rounds all over the turret; it was like a taffy machine as I tried to straighten the links. The process took about five minutes.

When your life is on the line, you find the means to perform. Regrettably, I lost my cool with Sergeant Verdun. I had never chastised him before, and it was unnecessary. The lack of sleep and adrenaline had made me an asshole.

"I'm sorry, man. I shouldn't have snapped at you," I said as I finally calmed.

"It's alright, sir," Verdun said. He was a great gunner and took my bullshit with grace.

As dusk fell, we aligned our company along a narrow dirt trail leading to the airport and waited for the order to move forward. Other units also positioned themselves for the attack. Anti-aircraft fire was visible all around. We passed one Iraqi position right off the road and destroyed it with coax fire.

It seemed strange that the defensive position around the airport lacked depth. We didn't need to conduct a breaching operation. The limiting factor for our own navigation was our ability to read a map and direct ourselves through a system of walls and gates. Perhaps the Iraqis didn't imagine we would slip in the back door. They must have thought the attack was going to be an airborne one. They weren't prepared to defend the ground.

Daylight had so far allowed our swift advance to the airport. But darkness causes confusion like no other element. Here we were at the gate, and as soon as we got the word to move forward, we couldn't find the doorknob to let ourselves in, so to speak. The lead platoon reached an airport wall and attempted to shoot through, to minimal effect.

We failed to recognize the first option when you reach any obstacle: Look for a bypass or another way around. Soldiers in the lead platoon could have looked for a bypass on foot before having the vehicles go down a dead-end. This would have allowed our tracked vehicles freedom of maneuver. Instead, we were bottlenecked. I probably didn't help matters with my aggressiveness over the radio, but my platoon was eager to get into the fight.

"Rock Six, Blue One. Get us up there, and we'll punch through," I asserted. "That's our mission—main effort. Let us do our job."

Kelly rebuffed my offer firmly but professionally. "Hold steady, Blue One."

I think he appreciated my aggressiveness but took it upon himself to conduct a recon on foot and found a bypass that was illuminated by a fire caused by a tank round. His action reinvigorated our momentum.

Kelly got back on his track and gave out more orders. "Guidons, this is Rock Six. I need Red Platoon to circle back and follow my track. Steel, take up the rear. Over."

The lead platoon now became the trail platoon, and Red moved forward through the maze of walls and fences. Shortly thereafter, they too took a wrong turn, which brought my platoon in the back all the way up to the front.

"Rock Six, this is Blue One. We're going to take the lead," I said over the company net. "Blue Four is taking point."

Kelly could better navigate from the rear with the FBCB2 system. His computer system allowed for more precise directions. On our maps, we lacked the exactness to make sound directional moves. Sergeant Creeley simply sent grid locations directly to Captain Kelly, who then translated the position for the computer and finally provided directions to the tarmac. At one point, we reached a fenced gate.

"Rock Six, this is Blue Four," Creeley called over the radio. "I've reached a fence and I'm getting out to check it out." He dismounted his vehicle in the lead and reconnoitered the area, found a bypass, and then remounted his vehicle. With a couple of turns down some trail roads, our platoon finally ended up on the tarmac. We were the first unit to reach the objective.

There was no significant resistance on arrival. We were on the south side of the airport, which served as a great seat for watching the war all around us. We adjusted our line, identifying the boundaries of our assault lane, which was simplified by the natural lanes of the airstrip. Once we had the brigade online and other conditions were set, we would assault en masse.

The company support vehicles lagged behind our column and were misdirected for several hours. The fighting was not with us but all around us. Here we stood, having slipped in unnoticed through the back door. To our east, we heard and later saw battles between other mechanized forces. The darkness was periodically illuminated by Air Force bombs in the distance, revealing the terminal grounds of the airport.

Once our line was established, I dismounted my infantry to pull rear security. We went to 50 percent security. My exhausted soldiers rotated through a sleep plan.

Forty or so tanks and Bradleys worked to destroy enemy positions through the night. Rounds crisscrossed the sky like a laser light show. By the end of our brigade's assault, the sun was shining over the carnage. We felt victorious, but work remained.

Isolated shots still sounded. At one point, we heard the pop of a round near our position. The sound of a bullet is different depending on whether it is incoming or not; if it is coming at you, the sound of the bullet cutting the air precedes the pop of the gunpowder from the firing weapon.

After a day of clearing operations, Charlie Company was finally given time to refit. Reporters came to conduct interviews about the day's events. All the days seem to meld into one. From the time we were in Karbala until now felt like one long day. My vehicle weapon's sight was still inoperable, so we used our recovery time to get to the unit maintenance collection point. Then my crew and I explored a nearby terminal. We came across many pictures of Saddam Hussein and other artifacts from his regime.

Enemy artillery rounds continued impacting around our position as we toured, closing in and increasing in volume. Apparently, the war was continuing without our active involvement. Charlie Company did not remain at the airport for long. Orders came down to clear a nearby palace in the complex northeast of the airport.

As we approached the island palace adjacent to the east border of the airport grounds, it became apparent how lavishly Saddam Hussein lived as dictator. We entered with our dismounted troops and cleared room by room, floor by floor. The palace was empty but for one Iraqi civilian hiding in a refrigerator. Securing the palace served as a symbolic victory, as Fox News reported outside the front door, where Lieutenant Colonel Marcone was interviewed. It felt bizarre that we could watch the war on TV as it happened around us.

Our units took over buildings on the palace grounds in an ad hoc fashion. One of my dismount squads took refuge in an opulent home, while others remained with their vehicles. Our mission was to basically hold our ground. Later, we went through Republican Guard barracks within the compound. We found pictures of family and the human side of our enemy. The mess included gas masks and nuclear, biological, and chemical (NBC) protective suits. A safe yielded a load of Iraqi dinar (currency), which was turned in. An arms room provided us with shotgun shells for the shotguns we'd never received rounds for.

I asked Sergeant Grizzle to clear a bunker in the vicinity of our sleeping area. He took a grenade, threw it in the hole, and called it out: "Grenade!"

The explosion caught Captain Kelly's attention. "Ryan, what the fuck?"

"We were clearing bunkers, and it needed a grenade. Won't happen again," I said. Over the past week, I had become much more prone to action on the battlefield, and that aggressiveness stuck with me as we gradually transitioned to less intense battles.

Charlie Company stayed in villas near Saddam Hussein's great palace for a couple of nights, after which we were asked to move again. Charlie Company was assigned living quarters in a hunting lodge within the palace grounds. Platoons set up in local cottages. There was a little bit of squabbling over which platoons had ownership of each facility, but we weren't static long enough for it to build into anything.

For the mission that became known as the Thunder Run, my platoon provided flank security for an engineer company clearing a massive minefield on Highway 8, near the airport. There was no direct contact, but there was a risk of a mine going off or being ambushed. Once the highway was cleared of mines, there was still a great number of RPGs and other weapons to secure. Soon, though, the highway was trafficable, which opened up the western end of the Thunder Run. My unit stayed stationary at the location, securing the area around the entrance to the airport as vehicles raced through the city center and to the airport grounds.

On the blocking position at the highway entrance, we mostly dealt with press trying to go to and from the airport grounds. However, there were also Iraqi civilians attempting to locate their loved ones, some of whom had died just down the road. For several days, the highway remained littered with the carnage of war. A few dead bodies and destroyed vehicles lay within our half-mile stretch.

With pressure to open the highway, Charlie Company was tasked with cleaning up the enemy dead. We nicknamed some of the dead. Perhaps doing so humanized our former adversaries. One soldier in particular, nicknamed George, was in the advanced stages of decay when a dog began chewing on his body. He and other dead Iraqis were buried in shallow graves along the highway so that family members could come back to claim them later.

One day, we were in all-out war; the next we were on a mission to meet the people.

In preparation for our new mission, Captain Kelly emphasized both caution and the need to make a positive first impression with the Iraqi public. With our sector assigned, we went forth into the community and shook hands with the locals. It was surreal, like being on parade. Later that day, several of us shared tea with locals in the street. The honeymoon was off to a great start.

"What are the issues you need addressed? Food, water, or other services?" Captain Kelly asked a local elder.

"We need security; that is all," the elder responded. "We have food, as you can see. We have water—but no security."

Children brought flowers to the soldiers. Sergeant Faver even ended up on the cover of *USA Today* with a girl offering him flowers. Adults asked the tough questions. "When will we have security?" That was the recurring theme. By the time we were reassigned a sector on the east side of the Tigris, it became evident that many loyalists populated our old sector and challenges would long remain.

CHAPTER 18

Gate Guard

EAST BAGHDAD, IRAQ

April–May 2003

In a place where threats can come from any direction, even the simple mission of standing guard becomes a test of vigilance. A couple weeks after major hostilities ended, my company repositioned on the eastern side of the Tigris River in Baghdad at the Martyr's Memorial, a landmark analogous to the Vietnam Memorial in our nation's capital. It was an odd choice, but the landmark stood in a large unpopulated area perfect for a large unit to consolidate safely. From that location, we patrolled the surrounding suburbs in Baghdad to promote security.

Patrol days went by fast and furiously. The task kept us busy and exhausted. At first, we drove our Bradley Vehicles and M1 tanks down streets, mainly waving at the people since we didn't know what else to do. None of us could speak the local language. Most Iraqis gave us a warm reception, but quite a few didn't. Occasionally, we dismounted our vehicles and walked the city markets to show our presence and deter lawlessness. Our mechanized vehicles weren't exactly made for stability operations inside city limits, though; they tore up the roads and crushed concrete curbs regularly. We soon stopped patrolling in our M1 tanks but continued to use our tanklike Bradleys through June.

Rotating to gate guard every few days was a welcome assignment. The gate we blocked at Martyr's Memorial tied in directly to the wall of a zoo, and a break in the wall allowed the zoo's camel to stick his head through right next to our guard position. The smell was disgusting, and the camel attracted flies and was filthy and malnourished, yet there was something amusing about having it nearby, along with the other animals. On a less amusing occasion, one of our mechanics plowed through the zoo wall while trying to move some of the captured Iraqi vehicles staged near the gate, releasing a baboon that the soldiers could not control. When it posed a direct threat to the soldiers, an NCO was forced to kill the animal with his shotgun.

Gate guard was mostly uneventful, other than dealing with Iraqi civilians looking for answers or support. And to call it a gate is inaccurate, because there was no gate, only barbed wire. It was difficult to keep the public away from our area, and though we wanted to help, we were not equipped to deal with their issues. We could only pass people on to other authorities.

Tragically, a family brought a young boy, probably six to eight years old, who was badly burned all over his body. When I saw him, I predicted his wounds would get infected, leading to death if he did not get adequate care.

"We need help," the boy's mother cried in broken English. "A bomb blew up my boy."

One of my soldiers at the gate took the lead. "Ma'am, let me check to see what we can do." He came to my vehicle and informed me of the situation.

I called the company operations center. "Rock X-Ray, this is Blue One. Do we have the ability to handle a burn case?"

The response: "Negative, Blue One; they need to go to their local hospital. We don't have enough supplies to treat every person who comes up here."

It was easy for the anonymous soldier on the other end of the radio to deny aid since they were not personally connected to the situation.

There was little I could do. We didn't have the facilities to care for the boy, nor a plan for how to deal with such situations.

"Ma'am," I told the mother with firm compassion, "we can't fix your son here. We don't have the medical supplies or tools." I paused as she cried. "You need to take him to an Iraqi hospital. We don't have the ability to help." A local Iraqi interpreted. But as I looked at the mother's tears, I yelled back to Sergeant Verdun, "Get the medic! Get him on the radio and tell him to bring his kit bag over here now. I don't give a fuck if we need to save our supplies."

When the medic arrived at the gate, he used supplies meant for US soldiers to dress the boy's wounds where possible, but the prognosis for his life remained grim. We weren't humanitarians. This horrific memory later changed how I thought about this war—about any war.

Seeing the young boy and mother made me think of Lucy and Brandon. The love that mother had for her son was the same love Lucy and I felt for Brandon. The thought of talking to Lucy again preoccupied my mind. I missed her. I missed Brandon.

"Missing You"

As the sun must miss our sky at night, I miss your radiant smile.

For the sky, it has been a while since it's seen the light.

I've been missing you since we were last together. You are the sun in my skies.

I've been missing you all the while. I've been missing the sight of deep blue eyes.

I've been missing your smile. I've been missing you every night—my starlight.

CHAPTER 19

The Godfather

EAST BAGHDAD, IRAQ

May–June 2003.

Every unit has leaders whose presence commands respect and whose decisions carry the weight of experience. Captain Kelly's reputation for cool behavior under pressure preceded him. As he approached the last weeks of his command in May 2003, I sensed he wanted to finish strong, but he seemed to burn himself out in the process.

Kelly went out with every patrol as the platoons rotated on guard and rest. He also sought ways to improve the living conditions within our hastily established base. On one patrol, Kelly made contact with a local man named Ziad Cattan, an entrepreneurial polyglot who seemed more than willing to help our efforts. Ziad later introduced us to a bunch of supposed retired Iraqi generals. I was suspicious of him.

Ziad had a salesman's charm and could just as easily have been a godfather-like figure—a power player shrewd enough to know it was to his advantage if we thought he was a bit player. I'm not sure if we ever figured out his business, but it must have involved relationships. He might have been an arms dealer. Who else would speak so many languages and have the confidence of Iraqi generals? Ziad seemed out of place in that group. With that said, he did some positive things for us.

We gathered in a local school, with a full company securing the perimeter. The discussion focused on the direction of the community and gaining general intelligence on area threats. The Iraqi generals seemed like honorable men and proud of their profession. A connection formed between us that transcended the politics of the moment, a mutual respect as we shook hands with our former adversaries. The key question: Former?

As the discussion progressed, everyone had a different opinion, but no one was willing to step up. This unwillingness to lead frustrated Captain Kelly. He tried to find a solution.

"Is there someone here of rank who wants to be in charge?"

No one in that room wanted to be seen as opportunistic. Who held power remained ambiguous.

"No one?"

I chimed in. "Sir, I think they should consolidate ideas and come back to us as a group—"

Captains Pecina and Kelly stared back at me with such extreme displeasure that I immediately shut up. In combat, I was used to pushing my platoon to the front when I saw opportunity. That did not serve me well in these circumstances.

Captain Kelly pulled me aside after the meeting.

"Ryan, I'm sorry I had to shut you down like that, but I have to be seen as 'the Man' in there with those guys," he said. "Do you remember in *The Godfather* when Sonny jumps into the negotiation with Sollozzo? Never do that again." Captain Kelly grinned as he grabbed my shoulder.

"I haven't seen *The Godfather*," I admitted.

"Ryan, Ryan, Ryan. Come on. *The Godfather*?!" The captain laughed in disbelief. "You have a lot of homework to do when we get back to the States. I expect a report on *The Godfather* and *Animal House*."

We sensed a growing air of frustration among the Iraqis. They did not like Saddam Hussein, but he got stuff accomplished. The entire social fabric and local economy centered around the Saddam way of running Iraq. Results mattered, and the locals seemed more impatient with each passing day. Comments of an indirect nature implied they would resent an occupation force. In other words, they were not happy we were there.

This was the moment of opportunity for the Coalition forces to transition effectively, but we were missing it already. Though diligent, we lacked a plan of action to execute a viable transition of power. Instead, we implemented an ad hoc campaign designed to hand over authority to the next military unit. We simply did not have enough people on the ground to rise to the moment.

I imagine some of those Iraqi generals were assessing our abilities and intentions then. They probably gave us the benefit of the doubt. However, when the Provisional Authority decided to shut down the Iraqi Army and stopped paying them, the consequences were inevitable. The military of any nation only knows one task: defend their soil. We defeated them and then insulted them.

Shortly after President Bush declared mission accomplished in early May 2003, rumors spread that we might be home as early as the end of the month. Our units began decompression activities at Martyr's Memorial, undergoing redeployment briefings, and timelines for redeployment were issued. We believed that once the 1st Armored Division arrived, we would be relieved and sent home.

That did not happen. Instead, my unit was tasked with more stability operations and presence patrols.

Patrolling the streets was monotonous and revealed the destitute circumstances of the Iraqis—which we could not directly improve. Trash lined the streets, the piles growing until they were eventually set on fire. The scent of burning litter stuck with us as the particles gradually layered over our nasal passages

We did make some progress with our own quality of living, though. Once it became clear that some soldiers were calling home on phones in the local community, with a few traveling to the Palestine Hotel to use phones belonging to embedded media, I moved quickly to get my soldiers that same access. Inequality breeds resentment, which in turn breeds a decrease in performance. That is a recipe for disaster in war. Some leaders rationalize a double standard based on rank and responsibility. But you cannot get a soldier to rationalize why he or she should be treated differently.

My company leadership decided to allow our soldiers to use civilian satellite phones at $1 a minute, a price negotiated with a local Iraqi. We maintained our tactical posture, set up on a side road, pulled security, and rotated all the men through calls home. I waited until every soldier made at least one call before making my own. The one exception was a soldier who was unable to make contact after two tries.

I dialed the number out and got a ring. Lucy answered.

"Hello, who is this?"

Needless to say, my exuberance was palpable. "Honey, it's me, Ryan."

"Oh my God, Ryan! How are you? Where are you?"

I choked up at the relief in her voice. I had no idea what she was up to and did not even know what time it was. It just felt so good to hear her voice after nearly three months.

"Look, honey, I can only talk for ten minutes here. What's the date of my last letter you received?"

To my astonishment, she was about three weeks behind. She had not received any updates since just after we got to Baghdad.

"Well, I'm in Baghdad and out on the streets right now, using an Iraqi phone," I told her with pride. "I miss you so much."

"I miss you too. When are you coming home?" Lucy asked.

We thought we would be coming home soon, which is what I told her. The minutes passed quickly. For that moment, though, we regained the hope that we would soon be together. Before we hung up, Lucy had a special guest.

"Ryan, talk to your son before you go. He's awake with me right now."

Lucy put Brandon close to the phone, and I tried to get him to say something. He spoke some baby babble in response. My heart filled with love, and my spirit soared.

CHAPTER 20

Coming Home

BAGHDAD, IRAQ

July–August 2003

After the chaos of war, the thought of coming home filled me with both hope and apprehension. We were already looking forward to leaving Iraq for good, but the events unfolding around us served as a stark reminder that the conflict was far from over.

On July 22, Saddam Hussein's sons were killed by the 101st Airborne Division in Mosul. That night in Baghdad, celebratory gunfire filled the sky—Uday and Qusay were dead. Gleason and I, intrigued by this dramatic turn of events, journeyed to the rooftop of a Ministry of Interior building to watch. We kept our heads down, even though it was unlikely a stray bullet could make it so far up.

"Do you think this gets us home any sooner?" I asked.

"I hope so." Gleason was a tough soldier, but the deployment was wearing on him as well.

"Maybe when we get Saddam, we'll start to see troops start to come home, but that has to happen first," I concluded.

"I can't wait to get back and have Meg cook me that famous Italian dish of hers. We've got to have you and Lucy over sometime; it's awesome." It was no secret that the key to Gleason's heart was through his stomach and that Meg had won him over with pasta.

"I can't wait to hold my son again. It's crazy how big he's getting," I said.

"I bet. Meg and I really want kids. We're at that point where we need to start now or potentially it won't happen."

I tried to lighten the conversation. "Well, I guess you have your work cut out for you when you get back."

Gleason laughed, and we continued to watch the tracers in the night sky. After a few minutes, we headed back downstairs. With the Hussein regime soundly eliminated, minus Saddam himself, our presence might not be necessary soon. Still, we waited for the word while continuing our missions.

AUGUST 2003

"Coming Home"

Hard rock soldier, you're finally going to hold her.

The one true love who is now just beyond the door.

Hard rock soldier, you've fought your last battle

And won the war. It is time to get off your saddle

And hold the one you adore. You've done your duty

And shed your share of blood. You've fought with honor,

Sleeping most nights in the mud. Hard rock soldier,

You've made your country proud. One final salute for your glory

And the applause grows loud. The hard rock soldier's tour is done.

But it is not the end of your story . . .

In early August, we finally got the order to redeploy. Our unit would do one last convoy down to Kuwait and remain there until flying home.

We departed the forward operating base at around 3 a.m. in a 2½-

ton truck. The ride to the airport was memorable only in how uneventful and serene Baghdad seemed compared to when we first arrived. The streets were completely empty. But there was no complacency. All the soldiers seemed aware of the significance of this last trip; we were more alert, with our rifles at the ready. Only when we finally reached the airport did I begin to feel a weight lift.

When we took off, the aircraft took evasive maneuvers as a standard operating procedure. The flight from Baghdad to Kuwait City was only about an hour. We landed on the tarmac, and buses took us straight to Camp New York, which now had air-conditioned tents. The mess hall had been upgraded; the food was better than at stateside dining facilities. We played cards, loaded our bags in MILVANs, and enjoyed the recreation tent. For two weeks, it was like being on a vacation. I finally allowed myself to look forward to holding my son in my arms and being a father—and being a husband again.

On our last day in Kuwait, we loaded the buses in the early hours and departed Camp New York for the airport. The bus ride seemed longer than previous trips to Kuwait City, the anticipation making the moment drag.

Once we arrived, we had to wait. Sleeping was not easy, so I joined in a game of charades. Then, out of nowhere, a soldier announced we would now board our aircraft.

On the plane, I slept as much as I could but never soundly. We stopped in Germany again. This time the area was slightly cool and the landscape green. Our stop lasted an hour or so, just enough to stretch the legs. The rest of the trip remained uneventful.

The plane touched down with a subtle jolt, and the engine revved to slow the aircraft, drowning out the buzzing in my head. *Home.* The word felt foreign as I stared out the window. Yet, in an instant, it was like no time had passed, and I recalled the flight back in January. Iraq became a distant memory, as if I had awoken from a dream.

The air smelled of earth, rain, and trees, but I felt a strange yearning for the scent of dust, the acrid stench of burning trash, and the glory of the battlefield. And then, as I closed my eyes, the image of the man with no eyes and the boy who was badly burned appeared. I winced and opened my eyes to see our greeters on the tarmac. My family would be waiting for me. I had longed to see them as more than faces in a pouch full of pictures for so long.

We arrived in Savannah the same calendar day we left Kuwait, having crossed many time zones. We gained six hours coming home, which made the journey seem like an eternity; it was in fact the longest of my life. Our rear-detachment soldiers awaited our arrival and took our weapons and sensitive items out of our possession. We were then guided to a holding area, where veterans welcomed us with gift bags filled with snacks and sodas. I called Lucy to let her know we had arrived, and our anticipation peaked.

After boarding buses at Hunter Army Airfield, we journeyed to Fort Stewart, which took about an hour, part of it back through the green tunnel. Banners on the gates of the fort welcomed our arrival. I sensed the presence of my family. Emotions overwhelmed me as exhaustion took its toll. I was proud of going to war but regretted leaving my family for such a long time.

When the bus made its way to the parade field, I spotted the crowd in the stands, a sizable welcoming party. The bus took us to the far side of the field, where we would form up to march in front of the commanding general before reuniting with our loved ones. Married soldiers were allowed to stand up front because we had family in attendance. I eagerly accepted this opportunity.

We had not practiced drill and ceremony in many months, and it seemed an inopportune time to do our biggest review without a rehearsal. But we took pride as we marched in step and paraded on the field of victory. The crowd attending, numbering in the thousands, erupted with cheers. Once we were all in formation, the commander of the 3rd ID, General Blount, said a couple of words, as did the brigade commander, Colonel Grimsley, none of which I can remember. My eyes immediately fixed on Lucy when I stepped onto the field. She found me in formation as I attempted to motion to her without disrupting the formation. And, in her arms, there was Brandon, my son. Pure joy.

When the general finished his remarks, I was the first to run out of the formation. Lucy ran toward me, and we met at the center of the parade field. She was beautiful—perhaps the most beautiful I'd ever seen her. If there was a purpose for having gone to war, it was my family. As far as who I fought for, let there be no doubt that the soldiers of Charlie Company fought for each other. We fought together for survival so that we might share in this moment of reuniting.

Lucy and I embraced as physical strangers. We had only known each other as pen pals for eight months. I was skinnier and tan, and she was fully recovered from having the baby. I told her with delight, "You look so beautiful. Wow—smokin' hot!"

"I'm so glad you're back," Lucy said with great emotion. Our lips met for a passionate public kiss, uncharacteristic for us. But this moment felt as special as our wedding day.

"We're finally together," I rejoiced. "And where's my little guy?"

Lucy handed me my son. Brandon was a new person. The baby I had left in the car so many months ago was now a big toddler with curly blond hair. I had worried that he would shy away from me when I saw him and hoped we still had our bond.

Brandon reached out to touch my face. He must have seen my face in pictures, and now here I was in person. He did not understand the role I would play in his life, but there was a familiarity and an undeniable connection.

I gazed into eyes that resembled his mother's. "I missed you, little guy. Wow, you've gotten big. Mommy's been taking good care of you, hasn't she? Man, you are big—you're ten months now? Wow!" I babbled.

"You're delirious," Lucy said, laughing. We found it somewhat awkward talking in person again.

Our long road to being back together had finally come to an end—or so we thought. Lucy and I set off to celebrate with family in Savannah and then spend the night in a nice hotel room with a bottle of champagne. As we drove off-post, though, my vigilance regarding imagined threats on the roadside foreshadowed a longer journey home. We just didn't realize it.

That night, I lay awake in bed. I was back in civilization. I was home. There was cool air-conditioning, and I had felt the touch of the woman I loved and who loved me—the woman who had cared for our son while I was away at war, not knowing if I was alive or dead.

But I was also still over there, thinking about the mission that wasn't over. Right before I went to sleep, I looked at Brandon in his cradle, thankful I'd gotten home alive.

PART III

The Collapse

CHAPTER 21

Counseling—Session 3

WASHINGTON, DC

May 4, 2011

Paul opened our third session with a question. "Have you found some relief in breathing?"

"I'm a little better this week, and yes, the breathing helps," I said. "I never considered how that freedom to simply breathe in and out can be empowering." So much in life can be taken from you. The one thing I could still control in the spring of 2011 was my ability to breathe.

"That's good to hear," Paul said with an affirming smile. "What do you want to talk about today? Your war stories tell quite a tale of the journey you've been on. I commend you for your service." He seemed to be assessing my mood.

"Thank you. I often feel proud of my military service and don't think many people who haven't served can relate," I told Paul with some resentment. "When we were over there, we did things that we were very proud of and came home to our families who were proud of us." I glanced at some of his pictures, then turned back to him. "I guess I need to let go of the fact that not everyone cares or values that as much."

"Well, Ryan, I for one am grateful for your service," Paul reassured me. "I grew up during the Vietnam era but was too young to have been called to serve myself." He paused. "Imagine those guys, Ryan. How hard they had it when they came back."

"That is so true," I acknowledged. At least we hadn't been tormented by war protestors.

My mind returned to those months after the deployment and recalled how the parade marked the pinnacle of my life in a way.

"When I went to war, I had so much to live for—a beautiful wife and newborn son. A family. My family! I felt my dreams were so close. And then came my nightmares. What could I have done differently?" I asked. But the words felt hollow. I had been asking myself the same question for years, but no answers ever came. The decisions I had made—choosing the military, choosing the Wall Street path—were carved in stone. The question felt like a trap. Did it even matter?

Except maybe something underlying the question was crucial to solving the puzzle, to freeing myself to live a happy life.

"Ryan, let's explore this a bit," Paul probed, likely sensing that I wanted to talk about what came after my return from the war. "How does an essentially homeless teenager get through West Point, go through Ranger School, go to war, and then go to business school?" In some disbelief, he continued, "How did you end up at Lehman Brothers?"

"Well, that is a good question."

"Let's talk about that," Paul said, "but I want you to be thinking about another question: Why? Why did you take the job at Lehman Brothers?"

CHAPTER 22

The Nightmare

Though I may come to the Shire, it will not seem the same; for I shall not be the same.

—J. R. R. TOLKIEN,
THE RETURN OF THE KING

SAVANNAH, GA

September 2003–June 2004

What begins as a dream can quickly turn into a nightmare when harsh realities strike.

The move to a new place was supposed to be a fresh start. Lucy found us a two-bedroom apartment in a popular complex for junior officers just off I-95. For months after the redeployment, I remained at a heightened state of alertness and anxiety as I adjusted from being in a combat zone. Driving down the road, I was frustrated by not having the same control as I did in a Bradley Vehicle. I found myself keeping an eye out for IEDs out of habit.

Following a week of reestablishing our company areas at Fort Stewart, we took two weeks of leave. The leave simply did not last long enough. Life in the garrison environment felt different from before the deployment. We were at war on two fronts, in Afghanistan and Iraq.

It was clear to everyone that the 3rd Infantry Division would soon deploy back to Iraq. There simply weren't enough deployable troops in the Army to rotate in and out while allowing for adequate training and dwell time. The celebrations ended after we came off break, and many soldiers transferred to other units across the Army; some of them would deploy before the 3rd Infantry Division returned.

With Lucy at home with Brandon, I weighed my career options. I could either stay with the unit for another deployment or ship off to the Maneuver Captain's Career Course and prepare for company command. Staying with the unit left me the option to exit the service. However, it did not offer the optimal career course. The other option required more years of active-duty service. If I chose to go the career course, I probably would end up on multiple deployments, making it more difficult to transition to civilian life. There was no light at the end of the tunnel.

My guess was that a soldier could expect to be overseas half their time in service, unless they went to a nondeployable unit. The Army publicly stated that they would continue to do yearlong deployments. Meanwhile, the Bush administration had lost credibility with me because nothing they said came to fruition. We didn't come home when we thought, and the mission remained unclear. I imagined doing a year overseas and returning to my son, who would grow up without me. I couldn't bear it and submitted my paperwork to exit the service.

Within a month of submitting my paperwork, I was reassigned as a staff officer in a new brigade in the 3rd Infantry Division. Part of the Army's new initiative was the modular brigade unit of action. The concept was born prior to the invasion of Iraq. Brigade units, normally composed of approximately 4,000 troops, were to be redesigned to have the capabilities that higher echelons previously had at their disposal. As a part of the program, the 3rd Infantry Division created an entirely new brigade: the 4th Brigade. My life as a junior captain changed when I moved from an all-male infantry unit to a more diverse brigade staff that included women.

Major Ross Coffman, the brigade operations officer, became my new boss. My initial meeting with Coffman wasn't memorable, but his personality certainly was. He was a people person, energetic and always engaging soldiers while filling the room with energy. He was excited to take on the enormous challenge of launching a new brigade, knowing that he would eventually take them to combat in Iraq.

It was during morning physical training that I first became acquainted with the brigade commander, Colonel Ed Cardon. The "Old Man," as Coffman referred to him, was an introspective and humble engineer. To be an engineer officer put in charge of a maneuver brigade of over 4,000 soldiers was unheard of in recent times, because these commands typically went to infantry or armor officers. Among his unique qualities, Cardon had an even-keeled temperance and steady professionalism.

My first impression was formed during a staff meeting with the commander. The brigade XO had prepared a briefing for Colonel Cardon based on an order from higher command. The newly promoted lieutenant colonel had worked with Cardon before and demonstrated a focused intensity. Colonel Cardon patiently waited through the briefing and held all questions until the end, speaking only after careful thought—and sending the staff back to the drawing board to focus on key issues that would face the unit as it grew and reorganized.

A couple of weeks later, Colonel Cardon approached me while I was on staff duty with a letter he had written to his contact at the Pentagon. He did not know me but asked for my thoughts. That night on duty, I read through his thoughts and echoed some themes and added some of my own in a white paper draft. In early spring 2004, it remained unclear to me how Iraq would progress. However, I saw the insurgency as an enormous obstacle. So many aspects of the insurgency were tied to our lack of knowledge of the culture. We should have prepared more for stability operations, and we needed to know the language. After I shared my additions, Cardon probed a few of my ideas further and built some planning around them.

Under this leadership team, Cardon and Coffman, I began to reconsider my decision to leave the Army. Their commitment to soldiers and the mission was inspiring.

Some weeks later, the brigade coordinated a "hail and farewell" party for its officers. Just as I said goodbye to 2-7 Infantry, I would be welcomed to a new unit—because the engineer brigade staff would become the new 4th Brigade. Engineers were leaving, and more combat arms officers were coming into the unit.

Unfortunately, we couldn't find a babysitter, so Lucy had to stay home with Brandon. I got home late from work to prepare for the event. Lucy and I scrambled to get ready. At one point, she began to iron one of my shirts as I searched for my pants. It was a recipe for disaster.

Within the blink of an eye, Brandon got behind Lucy, where the iron was sitting on the counter. The next thing I knew, my baby boy was in shock. He had grabbed the iron handle with one hand and the hot surface with his other hand.

The adrenaline of combat returned. *What do I do? Holy shit!* I grabbed the iron out of his hands. Within seconds, his palm had turned pale white, and he screamed louder than I had ever heard a child scream. The swelling was instantaneous. We put ice on his hand, and I got him and Lucy in the Jetta and sped off to the hospital. I knew I could get my boy to medical treatment faster than they could to me.

My mind went back to Iraq and the little Iraqi boy. At one point in traffic, I bypassed an entire column of cars on the shoulder. I hoped to be stopped by a police officer so that I could get an escort, but that didn't happen. Within ten minutes, we were at the hospital.

When we first arrived at reception, the hospital personnel did not understand the severity of the burn. Once they did, the staff situated us in a room to be evaluated and gave Brandon morphine for his pain. Our fears were slowly confirmed: We would need to go to the burn center in Augusta. Thankfully, the morphine kicked in, and Brandon slept quietly on the drive, his hand wrapped up. When we arrived in Augusta, we were checked into a room overnight. I called Major Coffman as soon as we arrived. Coffman told me to take as much time as I needed.

Doctors in Augusta told us Brandon had third-degree burns, which meant that his skin was gone from most of his palm. As reality sank in, Lucy and I suffered an enormous blow to our confidence as parents. We had failed to protect our son. We replayed those moments, imagining what we could have done, but there is no turning back the clock. All we could do was deal with the situation at hand and hope for the best.

The doctor who treated Brandon had a gentle touch and showed such compassion as we discussed Brandon's treatment. First, the doctor cut off all the dead skin and applied pigskin to the wound. This provided the wound an opportunity to heal on its own. The next day, we headed home. A week later, we returned to Augusta for a follow-up. It turned out that Brandon needed a skin graft, since much of his palm remained unhealed.

Trips to Augusta became a weekend routine for us during that spring and early summer. The next trip was for Brandon's skin-graft operation. We had two choices: The skin would come from his leg or his butt. The thigh was the obvious choice because he was still not potty-trained. When the doctors took him into the operating room, I prayed to God for his recovery as I fought to restrain my emotions.

The way it was explained to me was that the doctors would take an apparatus not very different from a cheese slicer and cut a thin layer of skin from his thigh. The doctors would then process it for placement on the hand. We wouldn't see his hand for several weeks. In the meantime, Brandon gained another wound. The spot on his thigh proved to be difficult to manage. The nurses applied some special material to help with the healing, but it still irritated him.

This traumatic experience brought us together as a family. Until that point, work had been my focus, not family. Thankfully, Brandon's wound healed about as quickly as my confidence did as a parent. Then, one day, he just took off the cast on his own. He was healed, albeit with severe scarring. Our doctor had prepared us for the worst: Brandon's hand might have constrictive skin tissue and cup his hand. However, his hand healed up fine over time and remains just as functional as his other hand.

Lucy and I lived a relatively normal life following the ordeal with Brandon's hand. We made a habit of playing a board game after putting our son to bed, and in the mornings, I was gone before they woke up. However, it was tough managing the transition home. First, we still had debt to pay off. It strained our relationship as we failed to communicate our mutual objectives.

I planned for the future, and Lucy lived in the moment. I believed that both aspects were weaknesses as individuals but that together we balanced each other out. Lucy forced me to "smell the roses," while I kept our family on track for the long term.

One weekend in July 2004, on my initiative, we took a spontaneous family trip up to Dahlonega, Georgia. Normally, Lucy was the one who got us out the door with no plan.

Driving to Dahlonega, we initially took the same highways we had taken to Augusta. On such trips we often talked of the future. Lucy dreamed of living in the country but also wanted the conveniences of a small city. Winter Park was one of her favorite places to dream about. North of Orlando and home to the beautiful Rollins College campus as well as several parks, the town also has a street with many small boutiques and diners. Lucy and I saw a bright future ahead but had not figured out how to get there.

When we arrived in Dahlonega, we found a Best Western just outside of the town square. It was just like during our courtship, when we would meet up and find a place to stay on the spur of the moment. While hiking on the mountain, Brandon climbed a massive staircase on his own. It was amazing to see him scale each step, making it the majority of the climb to the waterfall with little assistance. That little guy had determination in him that I could not explain. When we got to the top, we gazed with pride at the stairs we had just conquered. Our familial bond felt stronger than ever.

On the drive home, we stopped and grabbed some drinks and snacks. I was a fan of pork rinds and soda on road trips. By the time we got back home, I had finished a large bag of rinds and was exhausted. I went to bed almost immediately. That night, I had the worst nightmare of my life, which I added to my journal.

"The Nightmare"

I was underwater, or so I muse. I tried to swim to the air, beyond the darkness,

But had no limbs to use. Somehow, I wiggled my way to the surface,

Overcome with the sickness of the scenery. My stomach churned as I was in a sea,

The putrid stench of the pit of despair. Sulfur and vileness filled the air.

Ghouls vomiting in every direction, consuming one another without discretion.

Heat, fire, and everything of pain, among the maladies this pool did contain.

Unavoidable scene as my eyes froze, realizing I had no eyelids to close.

My claustrophobia and the ghoulish cries caused me to seek refuge.

There was no land in sight, only a deluge. Lost souls and demons tormenting,

Devouring one another, despite the smell. Those dominating earning time,

To live the agony of Hell. There was no water, only the sulfuric slime,

Lathered on the souls tossed into the lake of fire, no reprieve from the torment.

The only escape from this crisis so dire, relent, and sink into the dark acidic solution,

Concede my spirit is spent, damning my soul to its final dissolution.

I woke up gasping for air, thankful that it was only a nightmare. "Holy shit," I said out loud. "I'm never eating pork rinds ever again."

While I slowly reintegrated with my family at home, I continued to feel more engaged at work in my new unit. I had as much as if not more combat experience than any of the officers on the staff and found a role in helping coach the staff in hand-to-hand training. We practiced against one another, with rank not precluding a fight.

In one of my fights, I went up against Colonel Cardon. At the time, I was a twenty-five-year-old infantryman and in prime condition, while he was in his forties. We went back and forth, until I eventually put him into an arm bar. He did not relent. It surprised me because I didn't want to hurt my senior rater. One of the younger captains I had fought earlier charged that I had broken his ribs while I had him wrapped up with my stocky legs. Still, I did not let up on the commander.

Colonel Cardon was fiercer up close. He put up an enormous fight and broke the hold despite my resistance. In another bout, he had a rough bout with a junior staffer. Cardon was bleeding from his head but just stood up, slightly winded, as if nothing had happened. His steady leadership allowed the brigade combat team to meet its aggressive milestones and eventually be fully prepared for another deployment to Iraq.

In the late summer of 2004, I was informed that I would be put into the command queue prior to going to the advanced course. This reality, combined with a coming addition to my family and lingering wounds from my first deployment, forced me to evaluate whether I was prepared to leave my family behind and command soldiers in combat again.

CHAPTER 23

Rear Detachment

FORT STEWART AND SAVANNAH, GA

January–April 2005

While the war continued overseas, other battles on the home front required just as much dedication and resolve. Throughout 2004, I served as an assistant brigade operations officer for the newly formed 4th Brigade. I planned the unit's major training events, including a rotation to the Joint Readiness Training Center. Sometime in the summer of 2004, Lucy became pregnant with our second child, another boy. Having already declined to attend the career course, I volunteered to serve as a rear detachment commander when the brigade deployed in January 2005. Fortunately, one of the newly formed units within 4th Brigade, 6-8 Cavalry Squadron, needed someone to fill that position. I began in January 2005, shortly before the brigade deployed to Iraq and as Lucy entered her third trimester of pregnancy.

As the rear detachment commander for 6-8 Cavalry, I was responsible for all stateside equipment and unit issues. More importantly, I was the commander's representative in all family-related matters, including casualty affairs. My new boss was Lieutenant Colonel Mike Harris, whom I had become acquainted with during my time on brigade staff, but he deployed within a month of my arrival. I effectively worked for his wife, Angie Harris, who was responsible for the family readiness group, or FRG.

After the unit deployed, I hoped for the best and that my job on rear detachment would be uneventful. Unfortunately, it did not take long for the squadron to take casualties.

It was late February, just a few weeks into deployment. I was at home when I got the notification from the forward unit. "Six-Eight Cav just lost one soldier, and another is in critical condition," the voice said from a world away. "Just want to give you a heads-up, but go ahead and contact the casualty center."

"What is it, honey?" Lucy asked. "Did someone die?"

I nodded, but it was not my authority to tell anyone else. "Don't tell anyone," I instructed Lucy. "If any spouses call, don't answer. No one can know."

I found out that the soldier killed in action was Min Soo Choi, a young soldier with family in New Jersey. The other critically injured soldier, Landon Giles, also had no immediate family in the area. This meant that the notification officer would not come from Fort Stewart, but I still had to manage information flow to families.

By the time I got to the office, I was informed that Landon, too, had died of his wounds. Their names rang a bell, but I did not remember their faces. I had helped secure the photographs of all soldiers before they left and completed their deployment orders.

My unit had an established information policy. On the other side of the world, the soldiers were in a communications blackout until the next of kin (NOK) were notified. Once the notification to the NOK was made, the name could not be released for a prescribed period. To keep families informed, we organized a negative notification for the unaffected units. We called units who were not involved while the affected unit was left in the dark until the next of kin was notified. As Lieutenant Colonel Harris held a memorial service for the troopers in Baghdad, Angie and I made plans to receive the families of Landon and Min Soo.

Lucy gave birth to our son William in early March 2005, just before I welcomed the parents of our heroes, Landon and Min Soo, to Fort Stewart.

The garrison command at Fort Stewart had a formal plan to memorialize the heroes of the 3rd Infantry Division. For each soldier killed in Iraq, a tree was planted along two paths surrounding the parade field and bordering the post golf course, along with a plaque commemorating the soldier's sacrifice.

The process of planting the trees was an operation in itself, with an entire staff dedicated to requisitioning and planting the trees. When this deployment began, there was a relatively short line of trees planted from the 2003 deployment.

Landon's mother and sister came for the ceremony. Angie, compassionate and caring, handled most of the consoling duties, but I remained available to offer the uniformed soldiers compassion for their losses. I hugged Landon's mom as she cried in my arms. I imagined her holding Landon as a baby, as I had just held my William. My eyes swelled with tears, but I focused on keeping my sympathetic military bearing.

"Landon is a hero. I will always remember him," I said to her with a simple promise I have kept.

Min Soo's father attended the event, but his mother remained at home, devastated by the loss of her son. He was stoic. Both sets of parents desired to hear more, in person, concerning the circumstances of their children's deaths.

At the ceremony, two of my assigned soldiers stood at the position of attention in front of the trees planted for Landon and Min Soo. One by one, the master of ceremonies named the soldiers for which the previous trees had been planted. Then came the soldiers of 6-8 Cavalry.

"Private First Class Landon S. Giles, Sixth Squadron, Eighth Cavalry Regiment."

"Private First Class Min Soo Choi, Sixth Squadron, Eighth Cavalry Regiment."

A bugler played "Taps." Following the tree ceremony, we held an informal gathering at the squadron building. Lieutenant Colonel Harris pulled me aside.

"Ryan, I want you to tell these parents what happened to their children." He proceeded to give me more information. He had taken the loss to heart and was passionate about apprehending the insurgents who took his troopers' lives. "Tell them when I get back, I will address them in person."

When the parents visited our company headquarters, I provided the details they asked for: "Min Soo and Landon were riding in the back of a Humvee on this road." I pointed to a satellite image of the road we had available from our planning sessions. "At this point here on the map, a bomb exploded along the road and impacted the rear of the vehicle where your sons were sitting."

It was difficult, but I did my best to maintain composure. Both sets of parents cried as I shared the full story, offering them closure. We hugged again. They could now better picture where their children had completed their journeys on earth.

Tragically, the tree ceremonies became a monthly routine. In the first months, the ceremonies ran no more than thirty minutes. However, there were months when the casualty lists swelled. It became an effort to stand at attention in tight formation and last through the heat. By the end of the year, the trees lined the pathway from one end of the parade field to the other and beyond its boundaries.

The master of ceremonies commented to me one day, "I hope people stop dying. We're running out of room for trees." It was an awkward but sincere comment, given that each tree signified a life sacrificed for the country. The master of ceremonies was a simple man. Never did we think we would lose so many heroes in Iraq. What began as an open field meant for celebratory marches slowly transitioned into a forest—hallowed ground for mourning and remembrance.

The constant awareness of death overseas gradually took its toll on me, and my nightmares greatly influenced my decision to leave the Army for good. In one nightmare, I was at the site of the IED attack on Giles and Choi, with some of my former comrades playing other roles. Major Kelly was on the scene, even though he now worked for the division commander. I saw the action as an invisible soldier.

A soldier I had known, Private Bradley, was also injured, awaiting evacuation. Major Kelly moved out of the area with the two wounded soldiers. In my nightmare, the scene changed focus, and I watched a sergeant tend to Private Bradley, who had bleeding in his ears but had to wait for the next vehicle. Bradley tried to get the sergeant's attention, "Hey, Sergeant. Is everyone okay? Fuckin' A! I can't hear shit."

The sergeant tried to calm the young soldier. "I don't know, Bradley. Just sit still, man. Don't need you going into shock or anything."

Bradley, who was deafened by the explosion, yelled as he grabbed onto his ears, "Huh?! I can't hear you!" He held his hand in front of him to see the blood. "Goddamn ears are bleeding . . ."

The sergeant tried to shush Bradley, but the private began talking to himself. "I can't fucking believe this. We're trying to help these people, and they're fuckin' killing us."

The sergeant looked up at a crowd of Iraqi civilians gathering around. "Which one of you motherfuckers did this?"

The crowd stared on with apathy. The Iraqis didn't feel the loss of an American soldier. They rarely felt the loss of their own people, unless they were family.

"Stop fuckin' staring. Get the fuck away. Why do you people do this shit? Fucking cowards. We're trying to help you!"

In another nightmare, I was blown up by an IED. I had felt guilty about wanting to leave the Army, but that vision left me believing that if I deployed again, I would end up dead, leaving my children fatherless.

In 2005, approximately 846 US military personnel died in Iraq, 669 of which were uniformed US Army service members. The men and women of the 3rd Infantry Division returned in January 2006 and marched onto a parade field newly surrounded by trees marking the sacrifices of soldiers killed in action.

With their return, I no longer had to worry about casualty affairs calls. My friends who had deployed were home safe, reunited with their families. I eagerly sought to reconnect with the leaders I used to wrestle during physical training a year and a half prior. I caught up with Major Coffman in the hallway one day, and it was clear he had spent a good amount of time bulking up in the gym. His bonds with the staff officers who deployed overseas were stronger, evidenced by interactions in my presence, but he offered encouragement for my future as a civilian.

In February, I ran into Colonel Cardon in the headquarters hallway and chatted for a moment. The optimistic "Old Man" with a soft smile was gone, hardened by the losses in our brigade. No longer unassuming, the colonel filled out a far more commanding presence.

On my last day in the Army, I met with Angie Harris and her husband. They gave me a farewell and wished me luck in my new life. I shook Lieutenant Colonel Harris's hand and gave Angie a hug. As we separated, she simply told me, "I know you won't ever forget the sacrifice of our troopers. Never forget." Those words would haunt me as I ventured out into a world that had long ago detached from the wars it so eagerly embraced in the aftermath of 9/11.

CHAPTER 24

Fateful Decision

CHARLOTTESVILLE, VA

August–December 2006

Life is often defined by choices that seem small at first but go on to change everything. During the summer of 2006, Lucy and I transitioned from our life in Savannah and the Army to a new path in Charlottesville, Virginia, at the University of Virginia's Darden School of Business, where I would be pursuing my master of business administration degree in anticipation of a career in corporate finance.

Lucy was pregnant with our third child and well into her third trimester when we arrived, and the summer was memorably hot, so we spent much of the time indoors, settling into our rental home at Lake Monticello, approximately forty minutes from campus. The gated community offered a country lifestyle with minimal streetlights and spacious yards between the homes.

My aspirations were for a career in investment banking on Wall Street. I felt that if I didn't like the Wall Street experience, I could make a jump to corporate finance. I kept my family life and career separate in terms of decision-making since Lucy was a stay-at-home mother. Wall Street seemed like just the sort of challenge I needed in my career. By the time we settled into our home, though, Lucy and I were readying the house to welcome a girl into the world, and I began reconsidering my career decisions. At a minimum, I felt it necessary to delay committing to a specific career path while adapting to a household full of children and completing a full-time MBA program.

The University of Virginia (UVA) and Charlottesville are almost as synonymous as the United States Military Academy and West Point. The campus extends across nearly half of the city, and the architecture uniquely defines the learning environment. It is a beautiful campus all seasons of the year. West Point and UVA also claim Thomas Jefferson as their progenitor and Edgar Allen Poe as a failed student.

Darden was established in the middle of the twentieth century, and several of the original faculty remained on staff. The MBA program had churned out many Fortune 500 CEOs and successful entrepreneurs. I began classes in mid-August and quickly became known as the guy with a baby on the way. My phone rang one day in class, and I got called out by the professor. "Oh, a phone. Who is it?" the professor asked with a grin.

"I apologize; we're expecting a baby soon," I replied. My face heated as I saw all the attention in the room shift to my seat. I was barely acquainted with anyone yet, and the first thing they learned about me was something very personal. The professor's expression became less annoyed.

"Oh, congratulations. Just keep it on vibrate from now on."

Most of my MBA peers were a few years younger and single. Furthermore, the military culture was more conducive to and encouraging of young families than corporate America, where young professionals typically wait until their thirties to have children. For most young professionals, business school was a second chance to party. I merely hoped to have a mid-career break as I retooled for the next chapter.

One young classmate of mine, Steve Lowery, was only a year out of undergrad and sat beside me in class. He had youthful energy, having yet to go out and "conquer the world." Steve had been a social chair in college and was genuinely interested in making as many friends as possible, even guys like me in the parent crowd. During a coffee break between classes, he leaned over to me.

"I feel like I'm still a kid, and you're having a baby. That's pretty cool."

I had to laugh. "Can you believe I have two more at home?"

"Whoa!" Lowery said in disbelief. "You're like a real adult. Man, I couldn't see myself doing that for a long time."

I hoped to reduce a potential social barrier by explaining. "I was in the Army, and, well, I guess it's the culture, but a lot of guys get married and have kids young, although I'm probably young even in the Army."

"You were in the Army?" Lowery asked. "Did you go to Iraq?"

I already knew where the conversation was going. So far there had been a variety of responses to learning I was in the Army, but I knew what question he would ask next when I said, "Yes, I was there in 2003."

"Whoa," he said with increasing interest. "Did you kill anyone?" I credit him that he said it with reservation and did not make me feel obliged to answer.

"Well, Steve . . ." I smirked and thought about how to respond but eventually gave him a rain check. "How about we save that story for another time, maybe over a beer."

The tension broke when our coffee break ended and class resumed. I tried to push the memories of war out of my mind, as I had other things to think about. My hope was to minimize the amount of class I missed when my daughter was born.

After Julia was born in September, Lucy and I began to live increasingly separate and distinct lives. She cared for our three young children at home, thirty miles away from Darden, making friends with our neighbors and establishing a social network close to home. I focused my attention on coursework and got to know my classmates, mostly younger professionals. My classmates who had children lived closer to campus. Lucy and I began to grow apart as a result.

During the first semester, I did not spend nearly enough time with my family. The pressure to get top grades was intense because the companies that recruited at Darden used them as a benchmark for top talent. There was little time for television, but on Sundays I watched *60 Minutes* and football. The news allowed me to stay connected with the war, and football offered escapism. One night, I saw a familiar face from Baghdad in 2003. It was the "godfather" I had met in Iraq, Ziad Cattan.

During the *60 Minutes* exposé, I learned that Ziad had capitalized on his credibility gained from selling phone services and food to become the defense minister of Iraq. While in charge of the Ministry of Defense, Ziad supposedly stole over a half billion dollars. As audacious as ever, Ziad talked directly with reporters and gave the same circular answers he used to give us. He hid behind a pretend language barrier and played off every tough question.

"How the fuck?" I said aloud in our living room. "I always knew that guy was corrupt." I turned to Lucy. "This guy was a snake oil salesman. Unbelievable what he could do, though—what he could get ahold of. He knew everyone."

"Really? You knew him?" Lucy asked. "Why did you guys use him if you didn't trust him?"

I took a minute to think about her question before responding.

"I don't know, but I wouldn't have been able to call you at home if we didn't use him," I said. "Sometimes salesmen have all the power. You know, he seemed to know all the generals well, and maybe he knew where to buy weapons, so people became reliant on him. They must have given him unchecked power, for him to steal this money."

"Well, I wouldn't have trusted him," Lucy said. "He looks crooked. I don't care if he gave me a phone or not. Unless it was the only way you could call me." She smiled as she remembered talking on the phone with me in Iraq. There was a point to Lucy's idealistic view, but that would have meant going without the comforts that helped us survive the deployment.

"I agree. Once you give someone like that power, and you don't put a check in place, you're asking for them to take."

It was around this time that I weighed whether I wanted to put in the hours in investment banking or if I could be content with a job in corporate finance. My idealism was being tested. We had a comfortable life in the Lake Monticello community, but we had no income. I financed our lifestyle with student loans. The only way I could finance the second year of school was to get a high-paying internship and pray for a sizable signing bonus to carry us through.

This reasoning was a slippery slope to becoming a salesman. And once I embarked on the journey to the dark side, there was no going back.

CHAPTER 25

Becoming an Investment Banker

CHARLOTTESVILLE, VA

December 2006

In the fall of 2006, US financial markets were roaring, as was the job market in investment banking. Investment banking offered its employees unfathomable amounts of money, albeit with less family time, while corporate finance jobs paid less and afforded more family time. I only committed to investment banking when a person from Lehman Brothers sent me an email inviting me to attend a cocktail party.

"With your military background, you'll have a lot of recruiters' attention," the email said. This email tipped the scales, but my decision came late in the process. The recruiters from companies on Wall Street had already gotten to know many of my classmates well.

The bulge bracket investment banks were at the apex of prestige and desirability for MBA candidates seeking to embark on lucrative finance careers. Goldman Sachs, Lehman Brothers, Bear Stearns, JP Morgan, and Morgan Stanley were arguably the big five. Each firm attracted MBA candidates from across the country seeking to join their associate classes. Internally, the investment banks offered paths for their entry-level analysts to advance to associate, but the attrition was high. Many analysts went into banking to get the experience necessary to work at a hedge fund or private equity firm. Also, the burnout rate for analysts and associates was high given the long hours and stress.

Associate classes at the bulge bracket firms were recruited in the same cycle during the year, allowing candidates and firms to match. The firms limited the number of schools they considered for internships as a way of narrowing their search. The banks began their recruiting efforts as soon as the business school class matriculated, sending their recruiting teams to various campuses to identify talent. In December, the banks would host Week on Wall Street where candidates congregated in New York City to tour offices and meet bankers in their element. Interviews, held in January, were often perfunctory based on interactions and informal interviews that had already taken place.

When I arrived at the cocktail party, I met up with my Lehman Brothers contact and learned that the process was more focused on appearances and social interaction than anything of substance.

"This is a sales business. We sell our services to clients, so it requires a sales mentality and ability to build relationships and trust," my contact confided in me. The banker and I talked only briefly, and he encouraged me to meet other Lehman staff. It was a different environment from anything I had known in the Army in terms of networking for a business purpose. The Army was not without its own social networking, and drinking was certainly part of the culture, but the values were different. To alleviate the pressure, I socialized as much with my classmates as I did the Lehman bankers.

"McDermott, it's good to see you out. How are the wife and kids?" Lowery greeted me along with two other classmates in the group.

"Fine, thanks," I replied. "This is a new game for me. How many people should I be meeting?" Barely used to wearing business suits, I struggled to decode the process.

"Just go with the flow, buddy. That's what I do," Lowery said as he took a swig of beer. "I'm headed for the bar for another drink. You want anything?"

"Sure, I'll head over with you."

Lowery motioned over to the bartenders and put up two fingers. "Two vodka tonics, please." He turned and said, "So, McDermott, you don't think it's a little late to join the game? I thought you were going for a corporate finance job. We've been at this recruiting game for two months."

"Well, I gave it a lot of thought, and this is what I want to do. I figure it gives me options going forward," I justified. "You know, I can always do something else after the summer, but the pay is great. This is the best thing in town for the summer."

Lowery paused and then said, "So, we got our drinks. Do you want to tell your war story?"

"This wasn't exactly the drinking environment I was talking about; after all, we're here to network for a job," I confessed, reluctant to recount a story that might make me emotional and also define me in a new way to my classmates.

"True, true." Lowery pointed out another classmate. "Whatever you do, don't be like that. That guy has been clinging to Jessica all night." The classmate had cornered the recruiter and was preventing her from talking to other candidates. She was clearly put off by the intensity.

"So, where else are you looking, Lowery?"

He leaned in and lowered his voice. "Well, I feel good about DB and these guys. Maybe JP and B of A. We'll see." He was referring to Deutsche Bank, JP Morgan, and the Bank of America. "What about you?"

"This is it, Lehman Brothers," I said openly. "I talked to someone at Bear Stearns, but no one on the recruiting team. I'm going to cast a wide net and try to see if I catch anyone biting, then try to get in on the interview."

Lowery's expression said it all: I was well behind in the race.

"Good luck," he said with some sarcasm. "Are you going up to Week on Wall Street?"

"Yeah, I guess I have to, don't I?" It dawned on me that our conversation was taking up valuable recruiting time. "I'd better get back in the game and talk to some more people. I'll see you in class tomorrow."

One advantage I had was that there were not a lot of combat veterans seeking banking careers. I was among the first waves of post-9/11 veterans entering the corporate world. As I talked to other bankers that night, I operated methodically: Initiate contact, get the banker talking about whatever they wanted to, make sure they remembered me as the Army infantry guy, and then ask for their card so I could follow up with an email later. It was impersonal, but the art of interaction could make it feel personal. Getting the business card was critical because it allowed for continued engagement.

One night out, and I was becoming a salesman. The experience was all new to me coming from an Army culture devoid of superficial politics—although maybe I just never noticed. After a few hours of trivial conversation, I went home to finish up my assignments for the next day.

MANHATTAN, NY

January 2007

In January 2006, after finishing semester exams, I traveled up to New York City and stayed with Lucy's brother Jimmy, who rented an apartment in the Upper West Side. I spent the week touring the various investment banks hosting my classmates. They all wined and dined us, and I was further enticed by the career prospects in the industry. By interview time in January 2007, I realized I had to go all out for Lehman Brothers. My interviews went well, and I got an internship offer for the following summer.

Lehman Brothers flew all of six Darden offerees up to NYC in February for a "sell day" event. Steve Lowery was among the other candidates. We were put up in a nice hotel in the heart of Midtown and invited to dinner the night before sell day. At the dinner with senior bankers, conversation eventually turned to the topic of when the bull market was going to end.

"I think it ends whenever the housing market collapses—there just seems to be a big bubble," I proposed to the table.

"Everyone would probably agree with that, but when will that happen?" one senior banker responded. Everyone could see the market boom tied to housing. It was sort of like predicting we are all going to die; it's only useful information if we know when. "There is more liquidity in the market today than the market can handle. We have tons of deals in the pipeline."

"I'm not so concerned about where the market is now but where it will be this summer and when I come back full-time in 2008, hopefully," I admitted.

"I wouldn't worry about it," the same banker said. "It is all part of the cycle of Wall Street. We live it up most years, then struggle in down times." The banker proceeded to finish his glass of wine and looked to the waiter for a refill. Table conversation continued for another hour as the senior bankers gauged the incoming class of summer interns. By the end of dinner, I felt more buzzed than I should have been with such senior people at the table. However, the bankers excused themselves before my buzz was obvious.

"Where are we headed tonight, fellas?" Lowery asked the junior bankers and incoming interns. Our recruiter proposed a nightclub nearby, and we followed her out the door. We drank the night away on the corporate card. Lucy and the kids became an afterthought as I engaged in this new world. The temptations were limitless and immediate. We had all made it through the door most people don't know exists: the door to endless financial opportunity and wealth accumulation. We might all become millionaires someday, and this moment defined the beginning of that journey.

"Tonight's a night for celebration, McDermott," Lowery said. "Let's see what you can do."

He continued to deliver drinks to the group and encouraged a second change of venue. As long as we had the corporate card and Lehman escort, we were going to be drinking. The next stop was the

Whiskey Bar in the W Hotel. The first thing we drank contained Red Bull. I had not been out much to bars since the stuff became a staple mixer. It got my energy up, and I got more drunk.

The night became a blur as I walked back to the hotel with a more responsible peer. I blacked out. The next thing I knew, I was getting a phone call the following morning. *Oh, shit.* I was close to being late for the sell-day events and meetings with bankers. I jumped in the shower and threw on my suit.

I met up with my peers in the lobby and tried to make sense of the evening and how I got back into my room. "Thanks for getting me home," I told my friend.

We all looked like hell as we received a briefing from a senior Lehman banker and ate breakfast.

"We represented last night, didn't we?" Lowery said proudly. "You can do more for your career in a night drinking than you can in a year's worth of output." He understood from the beginning that the business was client-facing and sales oriented. The ability to build relationships over the course of a night of drinking was an invaluable skill.

During breakfast, I drank soda and tried to regain my focus. I rarely drank alcohol, so I was hit hard by the night of indulgence. The series of meetings were essentially useless; I just wanted to get home. By the last meeting, I was eager to head back to Jimmy's apartment for a quick nap before heading to the airport. I flew home and took the rest of the semester off from heavy drinking.

My career ambition was being fulfilled beyond my wildest dreams. I was going to be working at one of the most prestigious investment banks in the world. But I didn't think about what life would be like for Lucy and the kids while I was away. It was justified in my mind because we needed the money. I defined my role as a father increasingly narrowly—to that of provider only. I was present at holidays and other family celebrations, but my mind was always somewhere else. The future seemed clear to me: I would go to work at Lehman Brothers, advance up the corporate ladder, make a lot of money, and accumulate wealth and power, and my family would love me for it.

Investment banking was not a path I chose for my family but a path I came to lust for with selfish ambition. The childhood fantasy of becoming Luke Skywalker was erased from my mind. I readily gave in to the temptation of the dark side.

CHAPTER 26

Golden Handcuffs

MANHATTAN, NY

June–August 2007

The summer of 2007 marked the peak of a boom cycle for investment banking. From the end of the recession in 2001 through 2007, increasing financial activity and deals allowed banks to grow their staffs to record sizes. Liquidity was readily available as companies sought to expand, and globalization and the internet allowed them to expand rapidly into new markets around the world. Nearly everyone in my business school class had a Facebook account and at least one iPod. The original iPhone was released. Credit flowed freely, facilitating new capital deals and investment products. New investment products created assets few understood, but it didn't matter. Everyone was getting richer, though some in our society benefited far more than others. Those professions closest to the spigot of flowing capital captured the most gains—professions such as investment bankers.

The bulge bracket investment banks were on a roll, piling up increasing profits and realizing higher share prices along with massive market capitalizations that encouraged increased risk-taking. Each year, they hired more new associates to fill their growing ranks. The associate class of 2008, which received their offers at the end of the summer in 2007, was forecasted to become the largest in Wall Street history. Needless to say, I was excited about my professional and financial prospects when I went to New York City in June.

That summer, I stayed with Dave Chen, an old Army buddy, at his parents' house in Washington Heights. The upper-middle-class neighborhood sits just north of Morningside Heights and Harlem. Staying with Dave and his family supplemented some sense of family while I was separated from my own.

Each morning, I woke up around 5 a.m. and at 6 walked to the subway station at 181st Street, where I got on the blue line A express train. New Yorkers mind their own business on the subway. It was not uncommon to see a homeless man sleeping in a subway car, and that seemed fitting for the city. After a relatively short trip and a few stops, I took the subway exit at Columbus Circle and walked from Fifty-Ninth Street over to the Lehman Brothers building in Times Square. My path to the office took me down Broadway, where I could appreciate the smells and bright lights of the city. I felt its energy resonating around me, but in the morning, it was at its lowest volume. In those moments, I anticipated the activity of the day—the hustle and bustle of investment banking.

During the first week of orientation at Lehman Brothers, the new associates participated in many social events. Most revolved around alcohol. We seemed to drink more than we worked in this business. But we also sat through plenty of presentations. Lehman Brothers was proud of its heritage, and the summer process required indoctrination into the organization.

One briefing was provided by the chief administrative officer (CAO), a relatively young man to be so senior in such a large company. However, when he began to speak, I saw how he had risen through the ranks. He was energetic, confident, and brilliant. Plus, he was obviously a great salesman.

After filling in some points about how they intended to build the business, the CAO talked about the brain trust that helped make strategic recommendations. "We have the smartest people running strategy—ex-

BCG and ex-McKinsey types." His presentation was impressive, and I was sold on Lehman Brothers' prospects going forward. How could some of the smartest people in the world go wrong?

After the week of activities and briefings, my associate class was placed in various groups across the investment banking division. For the summer, I was placed in Equity Capital Markets in Natural Resources, which mostly covered the oil and gas industry. The capital markets business focuses on gauging the appetite of equity investors for new issuances and having a pulse on the stock market in specific sectors. In the summer of 2007, business was booming in the oil and gas sector, as were the equity markets in general. Times could not be better.

"How many deals are we working on?" I asked one experienced associate on the team.

"Dude, I don't even keep count," the associate replied. "Just take your time and try to get on board, but it's like an assembly line. You just have to jump in and start working."

All the work I did in some way supported the senior bankers' ability to counsel clients on their proposed stock transactions. IPOs, block trades, secondary offerings, and anything equity-related in Natural Resources, this group did it.

The managing director of the group, Bill Burnett, was a respected analyst and powerful force in the oil and gas sector across Wall Street. Top executives personally relied on Bill for his knowledge of related equity markets.

He rarely made social gestures to anyone at work during trading hours, which I respected. At heart, Bill was an equity trader, which is a competitive profession within the bank. It's zero-sum; you either win or lose in every transaction. Bill had been a college football quarterback and thrived on the competition of executing deals and winning. The computers at his desk often had several charts running all at once, and a litany of stock quotes to accompany them. He stared at them intently to make sense of it all, like in *The Matrix* when the operators watch the green streaming code.

It was customary for the junior bankers to listen in on client calls so they would be prepared to react with information for the senior bankers' use, if necessary. It was during these calls that I gauged Bill's influence.

"What's happening with our stock, Bill?" a CEO might ask.

A typical answer sounded like this: "We're seeing a lot of deleveraging in the sector. You are trading well above your peers." Deleveraging refers to the fact that many funds hold equity positions with the use of debt instruments. As the market deteriorates, a fund might need to "deleverage" in order to meet its maximum ratio of debt to equity.

When I met Bill for the first time, it was for but a minute. We exchanged introductions, and he asked where I went to undergrad and what I did before school.

"I went to West Point and served six years in the Army," I told him, seeing recognition in his expression.

"My father and grandfather went to West Point," he said. "I have a lot of respect for those who serve." Then he was pulled onto a call, and that was all I heard from Bill for three weeks, even though I sat less than eight feet from him.

Although it was the shortest introduction I received at the firm, I appreciated that he acknowledged my military service. It was refreshing to know someone cared.

Throughout the summer, the recruiting office set up events to facilitate bonding between the summer associates. I believe it was also a way to sell the firm to us. In boom years, the competition for talent was fierce. All across Wall Street firms threw similar events and were equally if not more lavish in their tactics.

Midsummer, Bill took me out to lunch across the street from Lehman Brothers at Bobby Van's. The conversation spanned from the war in Iraq to Secretary Rumsfeld to my career considerations. I sensed that Bill did not think his group was a good place for a newly minted MBA to start in the business, although I doubt he thought about it much. Bill joined Lehman in 1989 after graduating from Amherst and spent time as an equity trader before eventually moving to the capital markets division. I didn't think about the career path that way. I just needed the job for the money and would figure out a career later.

At the end of the summer, I received an offer to return to Lehman Brothers and a signing bonus of $60,000. *Where do I sign?!*

Including the $20,000 salary I received during the summer, ten weeks of work had just paid me $80,000. Before signing, I savored the opportunity with the other summer associates who had received offers. The Lehman recruiting team arranged another night of drinking, this time atop a "posh" spot in Midtown. I still don't have a clue what posh means.

After the official function, the Lehman corporate recruiting team had a senior banker host more drinks on a corporate credit card. *This would never happen in the Army*, I thought. We drank in the Army, a lot, but we paid for alcohol ourselves. It was absolutely ridiculous. I thought back TO a time when I thought a new contractor food facility in Kuwait was extravagant. The food was good in Kuwait, but nothing like this excess. I imagined this was the type of partying I missed experiencing at a normal college.

As the drinking intensified, a few bankers dipped their fingers in a liquor and lit them on fire and had to down a shot before the pain became intolerable. Once the shot was finished, they put out the flame by licking it with their tongue. That was not for me. I stuck with beer for most of the night and tried to avoid hard liquor. Then the senior banker started handing shots out to people like it was his job. He pushed several shots on me, and I accepted, knowing the results would be coming shortly.

"The Golden Handcuffs"

Blindly following a euphoric crowd, donning the banker's shroud.

A tear slowly rolls down my cheek. My body begins to quiver.

Is this the path I truly seek? No turning back, this will stand forever.

To no avail, each hand I try to rinse. For I have just lost my innocence.

My boundless ambition, unrestrained, put me on a path that's quite rough.

Each hand, now forever stained, bound by a golden handcuff.

By the end of the night, I was pals with the managing director because I was still standing. Unfortunately, he was too drunk to remember me afterward. The next morning, I felt a significant hangover when I went in to sign my offer. I had briefly consulted Lucy, and she was on board. Without hesitation, I signed my life away under the terms that Lehman set forth and returned to Charlottesville as a future full-time employee of the Brothers. My golden handcuffs bound our future to the *Titanic* of Wall Street.

CHAPTER 27

Financial Crisis of 2008

MANHATTAN, NY

June–October 2008

By the time my family left Lake Monticello for New York City in June 2008, we were ready for the next chapter of our lives. Lucy and I had grown further apart after the Lehman offer, but we resolved to go to NYC together for the sake of the kids. We drove up as a family in our Honda Odyssey and stayed in a hotel north of the city. It was an ideal location for us to link up with the owner to get the keys to the apartment and plan our move-in. Lucy offered some thoughts on my plan.

"Ryan, how are we going to get all this stuff in there? We can't do it ourselves. Why don't we get someone to help?"

I conceded Lucy's point and sent out a request on Craigslist for help. I picked a helper who seemed trustworthy: an actor who had a Myspace page. The next day, our truck arrived in front of the apartment early, and earlier than our helper, so Lucy and I began the process of unloading the truck ourselves. We worked together while her sister Shannon watched the children in the new apartment. By the time our helper showed up, Lucy was at her wit's end.

"Ryan, how much money did your company pay you to move here? Why are we doing this ourselves? I'm never letting you do this to me again," she complained.

"We don't have the money right now," I said, holding back my annoyance because I had done all the planning and managed the finances. "This will be the last time we will need to do it this cheaply. Believe me, I'm never doing this again."

Within a few hours, we were fully unloaded and in the apartment with our stuff. Lucy's brother Jimmy came over and helped organize the living room, making it presentable. When it was done, I was proud to call it home. We officially became New Yorkers.

Lehman's stock had a wild run that week. At one point, I wondered if we would still have jobs before orientation. I just wanted to get that first paycheck. It was stressful. We had moved into the city and were stuck waiting to start work for a company teetering on the verge of bankruptcy.

Things seemed to stabilize, relatively, by the time I had to show up on the first day. It was early August, and we had six weeks of training to complete before starting our rotations.

During our first week, in early August 2008, I saw a familiar face: the CAO who had briefed us the year before. Much of what he said was simply regurgitated from the speech he gave a year prior. Only this time, I noticed a different tone. He was less believable, but outwardly he seemed more eager to convey the confidence he had a year before. The CAO even told the same story about Lehman CEO Dick Fuld. It was strange to hear it told the same way given how drastically the market had changed.

The CAO eventually took questions from the new associates. One of my colleagues asked the obvious question of the day: "What do you think about strategic alternatives?" In other words, what did he think about selling the company to another bank or raising more capital?

Clearly masking his annoyance, the CAO replied, "That's a great question," as he had with all the other questions. "We believe the market is not valuing our assets properly."

Right after that, he spilled his entire cup of coffee on the computer at the podium.

"Oh well," he said with no remorse. "I just destroyed this computer." He gestured to a technician in the back of the auditorium, then continued cockily, "I'm in favor of doing a management buyout. I think it'd be a lot of fun and a chance to make a lot of money."

I seriously began to worry about my future, tethered as it was to the fate of Lehman Brothers.

The bulk of training for new associates was conducted across the Hudson River in Jersey City, far away from the drama playing out within the Lehman headquarters. My associate class comprised people from around the world. People from the UK and Asia offices also trained with us. Together we learned the common fundamentals of investment banking, valuation, accounting, and tax considerations. Most of the material was review, but it served to certify the class as a whole.

Along with the training, the firm again offered a full schedule of social events to facilitate cohesion. At such events, we might mingle around the bar for a couple of hours. We continued to be courted with extravagance—free food, drinks, and alcohol. It was surreal given the company's situation.

New associate training was not without stresses. The financial strain the company was under meant there was zero toleration for subpar performance. There were several training requirements to complete. First, we had to pass an accountancy exam. Second, we had to pass the Series 7 and Series 63 exams. Failing meant you were fired, and it wasn't clear to me whether I would owe back the signing bonus. The accounting exam was particularly stressful. Each answer had to match the answer sheet exactly—no missing decimals or misreading of information allowed. The standard to pass was high.

Ahead of the exam, I studied intensely and felt the pressure of the world on my shoulders. If I screwed it up, I wouldn't be able to support my family. As I prepared my last study review, I felt breathless.

The anxiety swept over me, and I could hear my pulse as I tried to concentrate. The guy sitting next to me must have thought I was hyperventilating. Perhaps I was.

That's when I discreetly said a prayer. I cleared my mind of the pressures and took time to review the material with my thoughts in focus. At test time, I performed well enough to pass comfortably.

With the accounting exam complete, we said goodbye to our international colleagues. They were all preplaced and ready to start work abroad. Everyone in the US still had to pass the Series 7 and Series 63 exams. The Series 7 took place on September 11, with my testing location right next to the World Trade Center site. We had our prep classes in the area as well. They were long and boring but necessary for quickly learning the material.

During the week of the test, Lehman's stock teetered again. Until this point, I hadn't taken the prospect of bankruptcy seriously because allowing a large bank to fail seemed akin to allowing a nuclear bomb detonation in the credit markets. Our government simply wouldn't allow a nuclear bomb to go off—would it?

That assumption changed the first week of September, when Lehman's bankruptcy seemed imminent, with a salvage deal its only potential saving grace. My associate class still had to take the Series 7 amid that anticipation. I passed easily and walked back through the crowds commemorating the September 11 tragedy.

That next day, we celebrated the end of training at a cooking and wine-tasting event that Lehman recruiting had prepaid for. Tension was in the air as we drank fine wine and Lehman's stock tanked. On Saturday, September 13, emails from bankers in my first rotational group began to pour into my BlackBerry. Everyone expected there to be no more work at the 745 Building in Times Square and began boxing their personal items. People sent their contact information, while others were more enthusiastic about "sticking together." I realized that I might not be receiving my paychecks from Mr. Fuld and Lehman Brothers for much longer.

On Monday, September 15, 2008, Lehman Brothers filed for bankruptcy and set off a global equity sell-off and credit crisis. I went into work that morning as instructed, directly to the twenty-third floor, which the industrial group occupied, but it was immediately apparent that the new hires were not a priority. Everyone was plotting their next career move.

As a junior banker with zero experience, I had nowhere to go for sanctuary in a collapsing industry. So I tried to get as much information as possible. Few people offered more than their own speculation about the firm's destiny. Would another firm buy the broker-dealer out of bankruptcy? Rumors indicated that it was possible.

On the night of September 15, as I walked away from the Lehman Brothers headquarters building, I stared back at the sign, knowing it might not be illuminated a day later. Everything I had worked for seemed to be falling apart. I choked up as I considered what I had invested in the pursuit of my career.

Despite our marital troubles, thoughts of Lucy and my children kept me from losing hope.

Lucy sought to understand the situation. "What does this mean? Are you out of a job?"

"For now, it looks like that may be the case," I replied. "I don't know. We can't really do anything yet, except see what happens."

The next day, we were still allowed into the building, and there was a hint of optimism in the air. In the cafeteria, I met up with several friends who were in on the gossip. A friend rotating in the Financial Institutions Group laid out what was already in the news: that Lehman could sell, and we might have our jobs spared.

Behind closed doors, Barclays was negotiating the purchase of Lehman Brothers. Most of the bankers I talked to wanted Barclays to buy the firm because it meant fewer layoffs and less change in the investment banking division. It seemed too good to be true, but on

Tuesday, we held out hope that an offer would be announced within the next few days. If the bank failed to achieve a deal quickly, it would result in a mass exodus—quickly devaluing what little of Lehman remained. There likely would be nothing to salvage.

Fortunately for us, Barclays made an acceptable offer and acquired Lehman Brothers. When the deal was finally announced, we cheered our leadership as they paraded in and out of the packed auditorium to outline the sale. What was amazing, though, was how quickly the attitude went from "Please rescue us" to "Let us run things." Our lexicon would soon include terms like "legacy Lehman" and "Barclays guy" or "gal."

In the immediate aftermath of the acquisition, tensions rose as employees from Barclays moved into old Lehman offices. The industrial group was the one place of significant overlap in the investment banking business, and everyone knew what was coming: integration cuts.

In the short run, people played nice.

"We need to start working as a team. We will sort out who works where, but in the meantime, this is our team," the former Lehman group head told us. He would share the title of group head with someone from the Barclays side.

The group knew it had cuts coming and were on the watch for signs of when they would happen. The sign would appear through the conference-room booking system, which was always all booked up on days when layoffs were done. This one happened to be a Tuesday. One guy I had become well acquainted with got laid off. He had been with Lehman for just one year. The layoffs in the group came on both sides in a ratio that maintained the balance of power between employees of Barclays and legacy Lehman Brothers. Needless to say, office politics intensified, turning into battles fought behind closed doors—little wars that determined who remained employed and who did not.

CHAPTER 28

Post-Traumatic Stress

In Iraq, my body grew accustomed to intense combat stress and running on adrenaline for days on end. At Lehman, stress eroded my ability to function well in any aspect of my life. In the aftermath of the bankruptcy, my hands began to shake uncontrollably at work. I was too proud to admit there was something wrong. I spent my limited time at home resting from the onslaught at work and didn't try to connect with my family. They were living a different life, and my mind was preoccupied by the future. Would I be laid off? Would I have money to provide for my family? These were not the sorts of questions I wrestled with in the Army.

I felt more isolated than I'd ever felt in my life, facing the abyss. In banking I felt none of the sense of purpose that had driven me into and through my Army career.

My only connection with the world I left behind was through the news, on TV and over the internet. I became engrossed with the political season and watched political debates across the campaign of 2008.

During one such debate, within the discussion on Iraq, I heard mention of a name: Patriquin. It was not a common last name, and I knew they must be referring to Travis. Hearing his name triggered a memory of the man who had huddled close with me in the Georgia lowlands to keep warm. Though we did not stay in touch, I felt connected to him. As I refocused on the TV, one candidate cited the Army captain's efforts in Iraq to turn the Sunni tide against Al Qaeda. Apparently, Patriquin played a key role in initiating the Anbar awakening, and the surge merely reinforced what was already happening.

I was not surprised that Travis had made such an impact. Patriquin spoke Arabic, could think outside the box, and was fearless in his pursuit of the warrior ethos. He would have done everything in his power to make the mission succeed. I looked up Travis Patriquin online and quickly learned the rest of the story.

True to form, Patriquin had designed a slideshow for soldiers to understand how to turn the Sunnis against Al Qaeda. It was a brilliant albeit simple presentation. In response, Al Qaeda targeted Patriquin, and he was killed in Iraq in December 2006.

Until that moment, Travis Patriquin had remained a living presence in my mind. For years I had tracked the daily casualty rosters to see if anyone I knew had been killed, but I stopped once I got to business school. I felt ashamed. I had let go and stopped paying attention to the sacrifice. It was easier to join my civilian counterparts in ignorance.

I broke down that night, as if I had lost a loved one. I had been interviewing in NYC the day he was killed, totally oblivious to the ultimate sacrifice he made. Some consider Patriquin a martyr, and his death helped bring about peace for a while. As I read stories about him, I regretted that I had not stayed in touch. But I was enormously proud of what my former battle buddy had accomplished.

The next day, I opened up to my officemate about the loss. "I found out last night that a friend of mine died—two years ago." I hoped for some acknowledgment of the sacrifice my friend made.

She said, "Oh, I'm sorry to hear that."

I couldn't blame her for not empathizing more. Who in the banking world mourns someone who has been dead for two years? The only thing mourned in the banking world is your career, and even then, you mourn alone. But my officemate and I connected better on the election.

None of my colleagues shared my war experience, and my political views sharpened. I supported Barack Obama because of one issue: the Iraq War. Obama's opposition in 2001 later drew my attention as I watched casualties add up while the rest of the country seemed to ignore the sacrifices. His personal story also attracted my attention. Like me, Barack barely knew his father, and he made similar decisions to search for closure. The energy of the Obama campaign captivated the nation.

"Hope & Change"

Few resisted the "dumb war" we fought. Now I live in a world that forgot.

My battle buddy, you did not die in vain, but I cannot stand idle with this pain.

Is this the dream our forefathers sought? Why should it matter whether they did or not?

Give me my life. Free my soul. Sound the fife and give us control.

End the war that seems like a stain. Bring back hope with a monsoon rain.

Wash away the sins of our past. Bring us change and prosperity that lasts.

Impossible as it may seem. Together, we'll fulfill the American Dream!

Afforded by all, though some say it is a trope, victory is within range,

So answer the call! Come join with hope, become the change!

Every woman, every man, stand together. Yes, we can! Yes, we can!

On Election Night, work was relatively slow, so I went to the Rockefeller Center to watch the results before the tally projected a winner and president-elect. As the results came in favoring Obama, I felt relief. I saw Obama's campaign success as validation of his position of supporting the troops but opposing the war. I was proud of my service but dismayed by how the war was handled. Obama's campaign also showed that a man who grew up without a father active in his life could overcome those adversities.

The crowd in Rockefeller Plaza expanded substantially in the minutes before the election results from California were called. The atmosphere was uniquely tense in anticipation of a historic moment. I stood amid an enormous, diverse crowd who cheered as the waves of results came in. At the top of the hour, the call was finally made, and broadcasters projected that Barack Hussein Obama would win the 2008 election and become president-elect.

The stress and frustration I felt in my daily life dissipated for a moment. Surrounded by the lights of the Rockefeller Center and the celebrations, I sensed what this meant for the people around me. A Black man standing nearby cried tears of elation. An older White woman smiled wide with pride. For me, the election marked a new beginning, but it was also time to get back to work. I returned to the Lehman office to finish my tasks for the day, my enthusiasm subsiding. Hope was not enough. I still had my job to keep and family to provide for. The time for celebrating was over.

Barack Obama's election did not change the course of the economy or the state of the capital markets. More proximate to my situation, the banks that survived the financial crisis continued to complete post-merger integrations, which meant layoffs. The banks had already discarded workforces from the post-boom cycle but also had to eliminate duplicative staff as firms were combined. It was not a good market to be looking for an investment banking job and challenging to keep a job if you were lucky enough to have one.

The election and market volatility distracted me from my job in the industrials group. My undiagnosed PTSD left me feeling isolated; even the veterans I knew in banking did not share the same wounds of war. Near the end of my rotation in industrials, I had a bad feeling about where things were headed. There were lots of closed-door conversations and politicking. Everyone was positioning themselves.

With three days until Christmas, I found myself at work and wondering if my efforts would produce fruit. There was no Christmas tree and no presents. Here I was six years into my marriage, with my oldest son now the same age, and this would be our tightest Christmas ever. Would Brandon notice? Would it matter to William and Julia? I recalled the night Mom raced us out to the department stores on Christmas Eve only to find the stores all closed. I decided to take an extended lunch break at work to visit Toys "R" Us and bought a load for the kids. The magic was dim for me, but I hoped that my kids would still see it.

We got a tree two days before Christmas and decorated it with ornaments purchased the same day. Lucy and I wrapped presents that night. On Christmas morning, our children were delighted. "Santa came!" My kids gave that cheer every Christmas, and this year did not disappoint. I felt relieved not to miss that moment but also empty. Any joy was a short-lived reprieve from the realities at work.

Everyone at Lehman knew that additional layoffs were coming after the winter break, likely targeted at the recent Lehman associate class. The 2008 class was allowed to complete group rotations before taking any cuts. Any new associates who were unable to find a spot in a group would be laid off. In the rotational process, I made a fatal error at the outset. I should have sought a position in Equity Capital Markets, where I had interned the summer before. My original logic was that there would be fewer spots there than in the industry coverage groups. But I was at a distinct disadvantage because I knew no one in the industry groups, while other associates had established relationships across them.

But I didn't give up. There was value in getting job experience by passing the Series 63 exam. It was only sixty questions and required a 70 percent to pass. For me, though, it was a challenge to focus, given the financial pressures at home and the career pressures at work. And I could potentially secure a spot in the last rotation in the Financial Institutions Group.

Otherwise known as FIG, the Financial Institutions Group still had a considerable workload as various financial institutions and insurance companies sought to expedite deals through the credit crisis. My exposure to bankers was more limited, and I only worked on one major project during my rotation. Rich Costello was head of the group and the leading managing director on a sale process involving a multibillion-dollar insurance company. Our interactions were limited, but he did take time to get to know me.

"Where are you from?" Rich asked.

"I'm from Orlando." I proceeded to provide a little about my background and the fact that I had three children. He looked at me with concern.

"That's a lot of pressure," Rich told me. I saw empathy in his eyes and knowledge that it was likely my fate to be out of work in the not-so-distant future.

"Yeah, well, I've been to combat," I began, but then realized this might be more pressure. I conceded, "I guess it is a lot of pressure."

Rich said, "That's a different type of pressure. You have a lot of pressure."

I could tell he was trying to gauge how I was handling the situation. It was a bit out of character for a senior banker to show such empathy. If you knew someone was a dead man walking, would you inquire on their state of mind or keep your distance?

Our dialogue continued into more personal areas. Rich had mentioned previously that his son got into the college of his choice. I imagined Rich nurturing his boy into a man. He had pictures all over his office of his family. At one point, he mentioned having to leave a vacation early in order to complete a deal, leaving his wife and kids on an island.

"That sounds like a good woman."

The conversation took a turn then. "I've been divorced for quite some time."

In those words, I saw the truth. Rich put his family second to his career. Sure, the money he made provided for his kids, but it camc at a price. He lost his family. Yet who was I to judge? What value did I have as father to my children? But with the Series 63 exam days away, soul searching had to wait.

Later that night, I called Lucy and told her I would be late. I had no time to talk. "Lucy, I need to get the studying done. I will certainly lose my job if I fail this test. Even if I pass, I could still lose my job, but at least I'll have the certification done."

"Okay, honey, do what you need to do," Lucy said with resignation. "I hope we can spend time together and go to Central Park with the kids soon."

I felt her distance in our conversations as I continued to fail her in ways that mattered. I was not there for her—physically or emotionally.

I hung up the phone, quickly dismissed the conversation, and continued with test preparations. I read through the test materials, but the words did not make sense. All I could think about was that my kids might not be provided for and would think less of me.

I couldn't help showing my anxiety at work. When one of my coworkers asked for help on a work assignment, I felt helpless and pushed back. My colleague didn't have to take the test; all my associate classmates had taken the exam earlier in the fall.

"I need to fucking pass this test, or it won't matter."

He left me alone, but I felt more isolated in the process.

The day before the test, I failed to pass three out of five practice exams. I was also trying to work on an assigned project. The decision was simple: *Do I blow off this project and potentially fail my exam? Or do I blow off the exam and focus on the project?*

There was no winning.

Later that night, I finally got comfortable with the exam material. I showed up to the exam site early the next morning and knocked out the sixty questions. There were so many I had never seen before, and I prayed right before submitting my answers. Then popped up the score: 78 percent. I passed the exam, though not with a large margin. And passing the test offered little relief. I went back into work still feeling like a dead man walking. I was no longer in the game for a spot in FIG. My enthusiasm had been sidetracked by the test, while many of my peers were focused on other projects.

Decisions were being made by each group regarding which associates they would take full-time and, by extension, who would be laid off. Feeling increasing desperation, I called upon the group I thought I had the best shot at making.

"How's it going?" the banker greeted me as I walked into his office. His demeanor seemed much more distant than when we had worked with each other just weeks prior.

"I'm doing fine. Just checking in and wanting to express my interest in the group. I'd like to come back," I told him.

His eyes held the truth while his lips equivocated: "You did a great job. I told them that. Why don't we grab a beer sometime next week?"

I approached the group staffer's office and found him busy on the phone. He signaled to me that he would call, so I went back down to my desk. As soon as I returned to my desk, six floors below, I got the ring from his desk and answered the phone. "How's it going, Ben?"

"Good, what's up?" Ben replied.

I got straight to the point. "I'd like to go on the record and just say I'd like to come back to your group. I had a great experience."

Ben was direct: "Just to be up front, you should not expect to come back to this group full-time."

I was somewhat shocked, since this guy had loaded me up with a bunch of assignments while many of my peers went home early.

"You didn't show any interest," he told me.

"Really? I emailed you a couple weeks ago. I didn't think it was appropriate to just barge in."

Ben took a minute to look through his email. "Oh yeah, you did email me. Well, I'm sorry, it's too late. We feel good about who we're going to get. We have a lot of people from our summer group. Just to be transparent, I don't think you should expect to come back."

"Well, I'm not sure if it was my performance or lack of interest, but I just wanted to let you know that I enjoyed the work," I said. "I took on whatever you gave me to try to support you, but I guess I should have expressed my interest sooner."

Ben thanked me and we concluded the conversation. That's when I knew I would be laid off. I didn't play the game, impress the right people, or play politics with a group. My breathing deepened as I returned to that place of anxiety. *How will I care for my family? Will I end up homeless? Of course not, but how do I get by without damaging my credit? Can I keep my sanity if they lay me off?* My thoughts raced.

Back at my desk, I stiffened my back and squinted at my computer screen as my eyes began to swell. I sighed. *Time to take action.* Immediately, I fired off a few emails to see if I could find another avenue. There was something therapeutic about communicating concern. But I didn't get any assurance.

Even Bill Burnett, my boss from the summer before, thought it was "good to be realistic." That confirmed that there were no alternatives. After I was done writing notes to several outside mentors, I found peace. *The game is over; checkmate.* The cuts were coming. We didn't know when they would come, but everyone knew the signs.

That following Monday, I knew I was going to be laid off but could not know when it would happen or prepare for my reaction. Monday was a normal day. After our morning project meetings, I did not sense doom in the air. When the clock struck 11 a.m. and no one had been laid off, it seemed that the axe would fall another day.

On Tuesday, a conference was held at the firm, and it seemed logical that such an occasion might be sufficient reason to further delay layoffs. No one was cut by 11 a.m., and I decided to head home early. When Wednesday came, I knew going into work that it would likely be my last day. Rumors and reports of layoffs began circulating across my networks. One of my friends sat on the floor where Human Resources was preparing severance-package folders for the unfortunate employees.

WHAT'S THE WORD? I texted a few people at approximately 9 a.m. through our internal system.

NOTHING YET, one of my friends replied. Another texted in response, THE HR PEOPLE LOOK DRESSED UP TODAY AND ARE RUNNING AROUND. IT LOOKS LIKE IT IS TODAY.

There was nothing I could do to control the outcome at this point. So I went to Rich Costello's office with my project team for a conference call. I felt like a ghost. The expressions from the senior bankers suggested it was business as usual. They discussed the structuring of a transaction.

At one point, my BlackBerry vibrated. I checked it, assuming it could be my assistant. Instead, it was a standard email notification from the corporation. As I stood there, I wondered if people were being laid off on the floor. In between glances at my phone, I listened to the bankers on the call discussing the transaction. 'We should do this . . . blah, blah, blah . . . The $7.5 billion case . . . the $9.5 billion case . . .'

Here I was worrying about my $95,000 a year job, with a wife and three kids in an expensive Manhattan apartment, barely able to afford the expenses, and the bankers were casually discussing the difference between scenarios valued in billions of dollars. I felt small and insignificant.

Just as I lowered my guard to focus on the call, my BlackBerry vibrated again. This time I had more hope that it might be merely another notification, but there it was—game over.

Message from Shannon Smith: LAUREN CALLED FOR YOU.

My eyes fell from the BlackBerry to my West Point ring, and I remembered the importance of the one-word class motto—"Perseverance"—etched into the gold. I resolved to carry myself with dignity.

I stood and told a member of my team I had to go. As I walked to the elevator, I thought back to my role as casualty notification officer. This was different, but I imagined it might be difficult to tell someone they're being laid off. I sympathized with Lauren's position. As I passed by the office, she called me over from another.

"Is this it? Am I done?" I asked.

"Ryan, as you know, these are unprecedented times," Lauren said, sticking to the script.

I cut her off to spare her the trouble. She seemed to appreciate not having to recite the whole thing.

"You've been a friend, Lauren. I'm just concerned with severance."

The Human Resource representative from Barclays had a British accent. "Ryan, it is important that you pay attention to three points . . . Blah, blah, blah . . . Are you paying attention?" My mind was elsewhere, focused on exiting gracefully. The severance package was generous, but I couldn't easily control my emotions. I was just trying to get through the meeting with my packet and leave.

"I'm sorry. I'll pay attention; it's just kind of sudden here."

She continued, "I understand. There are three things you need to take from this . . ."

I turned over my BlackBerry and remote-access password device and collected my things from my office. Within minutes, I had been sent on my way. Before leaving the building, I decided to send out farewell emails to several groups. I was gracious in all my correspondence.

"It's a crapshoot. Sorry to hear," one of my colleagues wrote me back. Others expressed compassion concerning the randomness of the process, but I was more realistic. I did not play the game well, and I was now unemployed.

I walked out of the building that day with a naive sense of relief that it was over with; I was still in denial of the implications. My job was gone, and I had only three months of income funding me to find a new one. Furthermore, I did not have the savings to make a move without lining up a new job. These facts slowly became clear over the following days. No one in the market was hiring. Layoffs were accelerating. There was nowhere to go.

Prior to being laid off, it never occurred to me that I would have to wake up without the pride of knowing that I could provide for my children. Getting laid off was the biggest blow to my confidence I have ever experienced. Brandon would innocently ask whether I could "afford" something because even at his young age he understood that

I was no longer working. He told people, "My daddy lost his job."

Dealing with the change was difficult. I had made a habit of running during the tough times in high school, as if I could exert enough energy to wear out the negative feelings. It worked on most occasions. Two days after losing my job, I decided to get back into shape. I embarked on a run around Inwood Hill Park on a freezing-cold morning. I had taken this route, located near our apartment in the northernmost tip of Manhattan, several times before. The park was still layered with snow. I had to be careful on the icy paths. As I crunched up the hill overlooking both the park and the Palisades in New Jersey, my chest felt cold and numb. I regretted not wearing more layers, but I continued running.

I pushed through the weather conditions by running faster and took my run down the west side of the hill to a park on the river. From there, I ran to the high ground of the Cloisters and on to 181st Street, where I had stayed with Dave Chen and his family during my internship. I briefly thought about brighter and warmer times in the summer of 2007. And I tried to imagine a new future. Where would I work? How would I provide for my family?

I had done the same thing while training for the pole vault. Daydreams kept me going. But this run was different. The job market was tanking, and the future remained hazy at best. Just months before, I'd dreamed of a future for my children, imagining their senior years and creating holiday memories to last a lifetime. Now I could not see where my family would be in three months.

Anxiety intensified as I ran to the George Washington Bridge. When I crossed the bridge the previous summer, the sky had been bright, the weather warm, and others were also venturing out on runs. Now I was alone, barely able to see New Jersey through the fog over the Hudson. I wanted to cross to the other side to test my fortitude. Negative thoughts overtook me as I reached the middle of the span. Somewhere in those thoughts was the memory of the bridge over the Euphrates River in Iraq.

I could see the carnage in and around Objective Peach: the dead Iraqi soldier, whose face was missing eyes. I couldn't see the future. All of a sudden, I was overwhelmed by fear of the future this journey across the bridge somehow represented. I thought of people who might have reached the edge and taken the plunge over the railing. It looked almost inviting. How easy it would be to jump. But I could go no further. Overcome by vertigo, I turned around and raced home.

When I finally got back to the apartment, I was shivering from the wet cold and jumped into a hot bath.

"Ryan, it's going to be alright," Lucy comforted me as I tried to gather my composure. I was disoriented, neither depressed nor energized.

"I hope so." I looked up at her with a stoic face and realized how fortunate I was to have her love. "I know so."

"You are going to get another job, a better job, and you'll always have us," Lucy said. "That's all that matters."

"You're right," I said. Eventually, my body heat returned to normal, and I was inspired to give a special person a call—someone who always knew how to cheer me up.

When I got dressed, I grabbed my phone and dialed a familiar number. A gentle voice greeted me. "Hi, Ryan! How are you?"

"Hi, Mom. I lost my job, but I'm doing alright. How are you doing?"

"Oh." Mom didn't continue immediately. Then "I am sorry to hear that." She paused again. "Everything is going to be okay. You can do anything you can dream of; I know it. Just hang in there."

Patty was ever the optimist when I was in need. Mom told me she had secured free tickets to Disney World through a family friend and offered me two of them. Lucy agreed that it would be a good idea for me to take a trip to Orlando and recover from the Lehman ordeal. She also thought it would be good for Julia to go with me. It was a wonderful idea; I had not been home in over a decade.

CHAPTER 29

Survival of an American Dream

The American dream is as much about supporting our families and communities as it is attaining success individually. On a cold morning in January 2009, Julia and I woke up early to prepare for our trip on planes, trains, and automobiles from New York City to Orlando.

Lucy walked us out to the A train, and after a few connecting rides, we were at Newark Airport, with Julia excited to be on an excursion. It was her first time flying. I was mindful of the pressures I felt and compared them to Mom's experience years before. Being a parent responsible for the lives of others was far different from being a kid depending on a parent who struggled. I related to my mom's situation in 1996 in a different way—in that feeling of hopelessness balanced by my optimism for my children.

On the flight, I decided that Mom and I needed to talk about the events surrounding my senior year, including some sensitive moments. For twelve years, a lot had gone unsaid. We needed to clear the air about the trauma of losing our home, our family, and the closeness we felt in my youth.

After a nearly three-hour flight, Mom picked us up and took us back to her apartment. I spent the next couple of days at her home, enjoying quality time with Mom and Julia. Patty let me borrow her car, so I dropped her off and picked her up from work every day. We visited my sister Laura, who was now at Rollins College. Julia got to see a little bit of Laura's sorority life and toured the campus.

I was curious to see my old neighborhood, so I took Julia on a drive to Casselberry, wandering ever closer to the home on Sandpiper Drive. The closer I drove to the old home, the more intrigued I was to see its current condition. Before long, I spotted it around a turn. It looked completely abandoned, with leaves from the previous autumn still on the ground. The fence was in disrepair, and a beer bottle lay on the lawn. I continued past the house and back out of the neighborhood.

After stopping for lunch, I took Julia to a local Chuck E. Cheese only a few miles from my mom's office. Then I picked Mom up and we headed to her house. Julia fell fast asleep, so I prepared her for bed. That was when I found my opportunity to open a conversation.

"Hey, Mom, how was work today?" I asked.

"Fine, it was really productive," Patty began. "I had a client who didn't understand their benefit structure, and I was able to solve a problem another agent couldn't figure out." She was always keen to get into the minutia of her work, going into details that made it difficult to follow. Not long into her monologue, though, she turned to other topics.

"What did you guys do today?" she asked.

"We went to the old house on Sandpiper Drive. It is completely run-down."

Mom looked guarded. "You know that's painful for me, Ryan," she warned.

I was well aware of her bad memories from that time. She lost her marriage, her home, and her children. Still, I attempted to reengage. "Mom, one of the reasons I came down here was I realized that we haven't talked about what happened back then."

"Okay, I understand," Mom said. "What would you like to discuss? I'm past all that now and would be happy to discuss it, but the house just . . ." She paused to collect her thoughts and finished, "It is still painful for me."

"I know Mom, but . . . okay," I said as I struggled to reapproach the issue. One of the things I've realized with age is that we all see the world differently, and those differences in perceptions often prevent us from coming together. In some cases, we might have a totally different memory or interpretation of an event. In others, we might agree on what happened but not empathize with others' reactions. After weighing what to say next, I asked, "What do you remember about how everything ended at the house?"

She took a few moments to think, gazing up, then to either side of the room, before reengaging eye contact. "I don't remember too much, Ryan, because it was really a painful time."

"I know. It was for me too. We've come such a long way since then, and I think we have to discuss this. I mean, I had to keep my distance for a long time. But you—and we—have come a long way."

Buried beneath that statement was an acknowledgment that our relationship had not been the same since I left the house on Sandpiper Drive in 1996. We came together for graduations, holidays, and other family events, but our foundation was unstable.

"I know, Ryan. I don't blame you for doing what you did," Mom replied. "I've learned a lot from you, and you had help from others."

Her response confused me. I couldn't fathom why she would blame me for anything.

"Mom, what do you remember happening back then?"

As we looked each other in the eyes, I saw her finally return to the pain.

"I remember that I had a choice between sending you to the prom or having the electricity on. I wanted you to have your senior moment."

"Do you remember what happened on my prom night?" I asked as I evaluated the integrity of my own memory. I thought about the moments preceding that day and the argument on prom night that sent me on a different path.

"You left. I don't blame you for leaving," Mom said. She regarded me compassionately and said, "For a long time, I thought you simply headed for greener pastures. Now I'm glad you did what you had to."

I realized at that moment that she was blocking out a key moment.

"Mom, do you remember your delusions?"

There it was: I ripped off the Band-Aid and scab all at once.

I moved closer and came out with it. "Do you remember that you told me you didn't love me anymore when I tried to point out your sickness? You actually threatened me, Mom."

After a long pause, she acknowledged, "No, I don't remember that, Ryan, but if that's what you remember, then that explains a lot." We both grew emotional and tearfully embraced in a hug. "I didn't realize I forced you out like that."

"I think you did it because you knew that was the only way," I comforted her. "The only way for me to move on. It was tough for you. We both know that. The marriage, the job, the house, the girls." I paused. "You dealt with a lot and had no one there for you. Anyone would break under that."

I saw the pain in her eyes. "You might be right, Ryan. I might have done it to force you . . ."

Then she began to weep as she described what happened after I left.

"Grandma and Rick called the police on me and had me taken out of the house. I was humiliated."

As I tried to comfort the woman who had comforted me as a child, I cried too. I implored her to continue. "Mom, let it out. I need to know what happened." I realized that my own perception of reality was skewed. While I was focused on school and pole-vaulting, she was in the fight of her life. How could I have been so cold? I felt ashamed that I wasn't there for her, as well as a new admiration for her, for simply having survived.

"They had me in the hospital for a few days and left me with no way home. I wasn't going to call Grandma after what she did. I had to hitchhike back to our house." She took a moment to regain her voice. "It was the most humiliating moment of my life, and I wanted to die."

Mom had no family to rely on and was left alone to beg a stranger for a ride. She had no home, none of her kids, and on top of all that, I had been taken in by another family to finish out my senior year. My crying intensified as I realized my failure as a son and felt the pain that Patty felt. Thirteen years ago, I had detached from her when she needed me, and it took me thirteen years to recognize that her trauma was greater than mine. In that moment, we finally broke those barriers that had separated us for so long.

"Ryan, you've made it through, and that makes me as proud as any parent could be." Mom's tears gave way to a smile. "Julia and Brandon and William are wonderful. You're doing a great job."

"Mom, you did a great job, and I think you are amazing," I sobbed.

Eventually the tears gave way to smiles of relief. We had survived the agony of opening the old wound and understood each other's decisions.

We have to go back to the house, Mom," I proposed. "I think that we need to go back there to get closure."

Mom contemplated the idea. Laura had broached it with her earlier that day. She finally said, "Okay, let's do it! First thing tomorrow." She smiled and hugged me, then went to bed. I checked on Julia, who was still resting easy, and headed to bed as well.

The next morning, Mom, Julia, and I ate breakfast and headed off to Rollins College to pick up Laura, who was always up for an adventure. Her uplifting mood was incongruent with mine and Mom's more thoughtful state. She didn't have the same negative associations with the house since she was so young when she was last there. To her, it was a long-faded memory. She'd probably lived a dozen other places throughout her childhood.

As we approached the house, we stopped by to see our old neighbors, the Gonzalez family. Mr. Gonzalez greeted us at the door with a big smile and welcome.

"Hello, so good to see you!"

"We did not know what happened. If we would have known back then," Mr. Gonzalez began in broken English, "then we would have tried to help, with something. No one has lived in that house since you left, I think."

It was difficult for the El Salvador immigrant to communicate his thoughts, but I sensed a connection. He too had a difficult ordeal, though he had family to help him out. Mr. Gonzalez shared his memories of us in the neighborhood. We eventually excused ourselves and thanked him and his wife for their hospitality.

Meeting with the neighbors helped settle Mom into the moment because she realized other people actually cared. She and I walked ahead as Laura watched over Julia. We stared at the overgrown front lawn.

"What do you think, Mom?" I asked as I watched her eyes weigh the past.

"I'm glad I don't live there anymore," she laughed.

We headed toward the backyard, where a fence had been torn down. It seemed open for public viewing, and it still felt like our home. Around back, Mom pointed out plants from thirteen years ago. It surprised me that a potted plant could survive on its own for that long. It was as if we were time traveling.

"Hey, Ryan," Laura called out, handing Julia to my mom. "I think this window is open." She reached up to my parents' old bathroom window with a devious grin, and I immediately knew what she was thinking.

"Lift me up," she said.

I obliged and got her into the small opening over the shower. Within a minute, she came around to open the sliding glass door.

"This is amazing," Mom cried with excitement. "We're like explorers going into some old cavern."

In the kitchen, it was evident that no new tiling had ever been emplaced. The floor was still bare from when we stripped it. However, the carpet was relatively new, and there had been some construction activity, but the bottled water on the counter was expired. We found it impossible to date the last time anyone had been in the home. I found a piece of mail from the previous fall thrown just inside the front door. We quickly discovered more items from thirteen years ago. When I opened the door to the garage, it was like opening a door to the past.

"Holy shit, this is our stuff," I exclaimed. "What the . . .?" I saw the old stereo shelf I'd built when I was a teenager. Most of our old furniture lined the sides of the garage. In the laundry bins, Mom found my sisters' old clothing. Among the various items, she also found an old high school yearbook, which she immediately reclaimed.

Laura asked me to look for old toys in the attic, so I ventured up into the hot storage area beneath our roof. There was nothing. Some things must have been either sold, lost, or thrown out. As I rummaged through various items in the garage that seemed organized for a yard sale, I heard Laura call out from her old room.

"Oh my God," she seemed to scream. "It's my teeth."

I was puzzled and made my way to her room.

Up until this point, Laura had seemed to appreciate the novelty, more than anything, of investigating a place she knew as if from a dream. Now she was facing reality.

"I remembered that I used to bite down on this window blind." She pointed at the markings and began to laugh. "This is my bite mark."

Mom was in the old bathroom looking for anything we might have missed. There was no electricity, but I found a flashlight. We discovered various personal items, some of which belonged to us. Memories came back as I opened drawers. "I remember this," I would say. "I don't know what it does, but it was here before."

I found a ruler with the initials LH on it. "Laura, look at this."

"Whoa, that's cool," she said. I asked if she wanted to keep it, and she simply put it back.

Patty seemed excited to explore the old home but became uneasy about being in there uninvited. So we put everything back as it was, except for my mom's high school yearbook. Thirteen years ago, circumstances had dictated what we took with us. This time, we got to choose what effects were left behind. And we reclaimed some happy memories.

As we drove away, we reflected on the house. Mom expressed feeling closure on leaving it behind and contentment with the home she had recently purchased. She had what mattered most to her: Her children were healthy and achieving their dreams. I believe Laura finally remembered that we once had a normal family life. And I realized that it wasn't the house or yard that completed my American dream; the dream was our family there.

CHAPTER 30

Counseling—Session 4

WASHINGTON, DC

May 14, 2011

In recalling my journey to Wall Street, I began to see the root causes of my failures and felt shame. When I arrived at Paul Rubin's office, I sensed he knew the answers, but I would have to find them on my own.

"How are you today, Ryan?"

I had emailed him a few times during the week and probably exhausted his attention.

"I've been better, but I'm still breathing," I said. "I feel like the answers are just beneath the surface, and you can see them clearly. What do you think of me?"

"That's not my role here," Paul reminded me. "I think you are a mensch."

I didn't know what that meant but brushed past it. "I have three kids who are a two-hour flight away, but I haven't seen them in over a month." I teared up as I considered the significance of my absence. "I used to think my biological father was heartless for being absent in my life, and now I'm the absent father. How did that happen? For years, I suppressed the fact that he owed it to me to be my father. He should have acknowledged me years before I entered West Point. He only cared about me when it reflected well on his stature—when it fed his ego."

"Keep going, Ryan," Paul encouraged me. "Pull on that thread more."

And then the epiphany hit me like a punch to the gut. "All the years of running, of trying to protect them from the worst parts of me, and yet here I'm doing the very thing I loathed most about my father. It is the trauma of my life I'm passing on to my children. What kind of father does that?" I considered what I had endured and what my parents had endured. They were connected. "How do I break the cycle? Is it even possible?"

Part of me didn't believe it was—like trauma was something you couldn't escape, something that became part of your being. But Paul's words lingered, giving me hope. *Maybe there is a way out.* Maybe I could be the father I never had.

"That's a hard thing," Paul acknowledged. "I have a colleague whose client is the daughter of a successful financier. Her father lost his father when he was young, and that trauma fueled him to become successful in finance. Some people falter under such circumstances; others escape into their work. Yet he was not able to keep his family together. His children endure a different sort of trauma. You see, your resilience makes you incredibly capable in your career, but that has not always helped you manage adult relationships."

"That makes sense," I said. "And not being balanced with my family caused the support that I need to fall apart." I thought for a moment. "I wonder what my kids will think of me. Opening those old wounds is hard, but I can see how it is necessary to healing. I've been stuck in these patterns I adopted from childhood, and each successive trauma put me further down the rabbit hole. I have felt as if my life is a tragedy at times, and now that I share it with you, I can see the absurdity of it all." My eyes grew watery again. "Can people change? Can I change, or am I doomed to fall in the same traps and imprint that trauma on my own children?"

"Ryan, you've learned a great deal in a short time, and we are all flawed in our own ways," Paul encouraged me. "It is not my place to diagnose you clinically, but I would recommend you consider getting evaluated for PTSD from your combat experiences. This is not an easy journey. I'm here as a guide, but I cannot walk it for you."

I held on to the hope that maybe—just maybe—this didn't need to be the end of the story. In that moment, I saw a glimpse of my future; it was in my children and being the father they deserved. Keeping that realization to myself, I closed our last session.

"It looks like our time's up and maybe a little bit past it. Thank you, Paul."

"You are a mensch, Ryan," Paul said again with a smile.

"Thanks, but I don't know what that means," I laughed and shrugged.

"It means you are a good guy, Ryan," Paul said as we shook hands. "Good luck. You'll be fine. Just keep breathing. And take one step at a time. You know what to do."

"One step at a time," I said. And I set out on my journey home.

Counseling provided perspective and lessons I couldn't have gained on my own. I learned that most of the dysfunctional behavior patterns in my life were rooted in trauma. Through reflection and cathartic writing, iterating certain passages countless times, I found similar closure as I find when a poem comes to completion. But I also learned that I need to take long breaks from my catharsis, sometimes years, so that I remain focused on what really matters: the present, with my family.

EPILOGUE

Downriver to a New Horizon

The world breaks everyone, and afterward, some are strong at the broke places. But those that will not break it kills. It kills the very good and the gentle and the very brave impartially. If you are none of these you can be sure it will kill you too but there will be no special hurry.

—ERNEST HEMINGWAY,
A FAREWELL TO ARMS

This story ends shortly after I reconciled my childhood trauma because it filled a key void. I had to stop dwelling on the past and focus on my children. For well over a decade, I've done that while periodically revisiting my manuscript. There wasn't a good ending worth sharing. I just needed to be a father.

For years, I was focused on my dreams, my goals, and my career. But none of that matters in the long run. Rather, our lives as parents are prologue to the stories our children live out. Their dreams and their futures are most important. The American dream isn't just about what we accomplish in our own lives; it's about passing down the hope and resilience needed for the next generation to thrive.

In the quiet moments that followed the home invasion in April 2011, I pieced together meaning from the struggles that had shaped my life. Hitting rock bottom forced me to reassess my trajectory. I could have easily been killed, my short life assessed as a tragedy. My family had fractured as I struggled to cope with undiagnosed PTSD and provide for a family of five. Staring into the abyss offered clarity. I drafted this poem for Lucy in the aftermath of the home invasion and refined it over the years.

April 2011

"Downriver"

We're divided by a river. I'm up here. You're down there,

And it seems like forever since we've been together.

I can hear you, and it may seem that the river that now divides has shallows.

The water is deep and it's a lonely walk downstream beyond the gallows.

Walking home, I realize how alone I feel. The dream of a past life before my eyes,

Gone now, with the nightmare now real, and my lonely heart cries.

My eyes shed a tear and my mind takes a break. Crossing back to this lonely town,

I have nothing to feel but heartache. So, I walk faster before I break down.

As I walk through the door, I wonder how long the hurt will last.

Our life together is no more but I still hold on to the past.

I realize spring and summer are long gone. And last season's leaves finally fall.

Those memories that remain begin to wash away like autumn leaves in the rain.

Why did they fall? And is this all? When did you know? You could no longer grow.

And why did I go down that winding road that took me to the end of the world?

The walls are crashing in. Where did it all begin? Was it the war?

I return to my place of solitude and remember the days we made love.

Creating children. Gifts from above. Treasures from heaven.

When push came to shove, we wanted the same thing from life.

Family of our own. We'd never be alone. We could make it if we try.

And now, I remember. To kiss you and Bran goodbye, facing the unknown,

Not knowing if I'd die, I began to let go. Little did I know,

That it would be such a long road home from that forsaken war.

No, I am not lost, but I'm still gone, and don't know if I'm ever coming home.

Do you remember the parade? Promises that I made. Wanted to give you a great life.

You wanted to be a good wife. Looking into your eyes. So full of surprise.

We didn't see the road before us and would get caught at a swerve.

And then the crash. Love turns to ash. And I don't know if there's any going home.

Why did we fall? Where did our love go? When did we know

We could no longer grow? And why did we go down that treacherous highway,

Leading to this lonely dark abyss in the city?

Walls are crashing in. When does it end? Will I ever get home?

Perhaps we went in too soon. But that night as I walked with you,

We thought of the moon. Was that too far to aim for a star?

We have to admit we couldn't make it without our love.

Aiming for the stars above, without changing the tires ever,

We were bound to plunge into the river that now divides us.

You on one side, me on the other. Maybe we'll get to meet back downriver.

Realized I wasn't good enough when I saw you dance.

Everyone loved seeing you and I only took a glance.

I should have done more of what you asked me to do.

I should have loved you more and danced with you.

But I was stuck in a place and couldn't get out.

Now I'm going back downriver but it's a lonely route.

It was the only way. I cannot see day. And I cannot make it right.

Without going through the night. And go insane and feel the pain.

Before I reach the shallows, a walk to the gallows.

With a lonely heart that this distance makes me feel.

Heart feels empty. It needs plenty. I am coming home.

So, I keep on walking downriver for a place to cross the water.

Promises that I still need to deliver, and most of all, I need to be a father.

Unfortunately, there was no simple happy ending for me and Lucy, at least not for another decade. Lucy and I separated in 2010, and after a year of trying to reconcile in 2012, we amicably divorced in March 2013. Later that year, I sought help from a former West Point roommate who worked in Veterans Affairs, got assessed, and was eventually diagnosed with PTSD. Only then did I begin to truly address my traumas and grow from those experiences to be able to live a happier life.

My focus shifted from my career and past to spending time with my children as often as possible. Over the years, we did weekend trips to Disney World and other area theme parks. Most of the time, we just relaxed at my mom's house, and I helped my kids with schoolwork. My mother, who had previously lost everything, provided me a safe place to stay when I visited. In those trying years, she became my greatest supporter and my rock once again. My mom, Patty McDermott, is the ultimate hero of my story.

Her grit and perseverance through her adversities continues to inspire me. It was impossible to see just how amazing she was when I was younger. It wasn't until I endured my own hardships in adulthood that I recognized the strength of her spirit. When Mom lost everything in 1996 and was placed in a women's shelter, she worked to rebuild her life. She bought a home and now spends leisure time improving it, anticipating family during holiday celebrations. My mother's journey and the bonds she shares with me, my family, and siblings represent the survival of her American dream.

Throughout my young adult life, my focus was driven by my professional ambition. The logic was that if I became the best provider possible, then being a good father and husband would follow. But the reality is that I was not a present father, nor a good husband. I lost touch with my childhood ambition to build a strong family.

Since my epiphany in therapy, I have tried to live in the moment while remaining mindful of the burdens of the past. I committed to building and sustaining relationships with my children. In addition to repairing my bond with Mom, I improved other relationships in my family. Rick was not the parent I wanted as a child, but he was the dad I needed. Rick was generous in those years when I struggled to rebound, hosting our family for weekend getaways and Christmas mornings. He and I built a loving relationship, along with Jessica, Laura, and their significant others. Rick is my dad, and I would not be the man I am today without him in my life.

I also developed a close relationship with my biological father, Bill Carder, in the aftermath of the 2011 home invasion. He welcomed me to Roanoke shortly after, and we went sailing with my brother, Dane. It is a memory I will forever treasure. Bill Carder became an invaluable mentor, and friend. He died in 2017 from cancer, but a part of him still lives in me—the poet. My sister Lauren, who was at his bedside in Costa Rica, afforded me an opportunity to say my goodbye minutes before he passed. Months later, she asked me and Dane to walk her down the aisle at her wedding. I felt my father's presence as Dane and I escorted Lauren to her groom in 2018.

Lucy and I restored a strong coparenting relationship in the aftermath of divorce. I realized I had not done enough to support Lucy and took her love for granted when we were together. But I tried to make up for that. In 2012, I helped Lucy apply to nursing school as we sought to reconcile. Following our amicable divorce in 2013, she and I provided our kids the best lives possible. We built greater respect for one another than we ever did when we were married.

Lucy graduated from the University of Central Florida with a bachelor's degree and became a registered nurse in 2017. She purchased a nice townhome north of Orlando that same year, just before Brandon entered high school. My chaotic senior year came to mind when Lucy was considering her home-buying options, and I helped her through the buying process. I wanted my kids to have stability throughout their high school years. And I wanted to fulfill my promise to Lucy.

In March 2020, I was visiting Florida during my kids' spring break when the coronavirus pandemic forced lockdowns and upended our lives. The home provided a foundation for success, but the pandemic presented a unique challenge for our family. As a registered nurse,

Lucy had to care for patients, but she could not do that and manage a household alone. At the time, Brandon was finishing up his junior year and aiming for a West Point appointment. William and Julia, too, were at critical points in their education and social development. I needed to be with them.

Lucy welcomed me to stay at her home. We spent nearly every day of the lockdown living together as a family. Lucy and I eventually reconciled and recommitted to a relationship founded upon shared goals, a sense of family, and love.

I wrote the following poem on Valentine's Day 2023.

"One True Love"

There's a place in my heart, where time stands still,

Eternal, with no end or start. Forever, our love always will.

Before we were born, our souls formed as one.

In life, that fabric is torn, until our journey is done.

When I look into your eyes, I can feel your heart beating.

They've brought me to life since our first meeting.

How many lifetimes has it been since we found each other?

How many hearts were broken, for us to finally come together?

And now that we are one, our hearts gravitate to each other's pull.

As the warmth of a rising sun, my love for you will always be full.

Brandon was admitted to the West Point class of 2025. Coincidently, Colonel Todd Kelly, my commander in Iraq, is currently serving as deputy commandant at West Point and greets Brandon whenever they cross paths. William and Julia, who are younger, struggled during the pandemic but continue to grow and mature into kind people. William enrolled at UCF just years after Lucy's graduation. Our children's stories are just beginning.

Lucy continues caring for patients at the hospital at night and making a wonderful home for our family by day. My hope is that Lucy and I will write a story that continues as one, and with hard work and commitment, perhaps we can continue to bind old wounds and sustain an everlasting love.

WEST POINT, NY

August 2024

On a beautiful summer day, Lucy and I drove up to West Point from Northern Virginia to celebrate Brandon's class of 2025 Ring Weekend. Just three years before, we had dropped Brandon off for his Reception Day during the pandemic. Two days after that, Brandon and his classmates executed their first parade on the Plain at West Point. That summer morning was uncharacteristically cold, the sky a bright blue without a cloud to be seen. When I identified my son in the crowd, my eyes filled with tears of pride.

Over three years later, I felt a similar sense of pride as Brandon and his classmates received their West Point class rings. The sky was again bright blue as the cadets marched onto the Plain in their summer formal attire—the India White uniform.

Following the ceremony, Lucy and I found Brandon amid the sea of cadets and their families. We hugged our son. We took pictures. We admired his class ring. Brandon had selected a modest stone, black onyx, reflecting his humble nature and desire to honor the school colors of black and gold. The motto for his class—"Together We Thrive"—was clearly etched on one side of the ring, while the West Point motto of "Duty, Honor, Country" and the crest was sculpted on the other. Lucy gazed at him in sheer admiration.

I pulled Brandon aside to convey my sentiments, looking up at him, as he was now three inches taller than me.

"Brandon, we are unbelievably proud of you. You, William, and Julia are just incredible, and I wish I had been a better father to deserve to feel the pride I feel right now. You have become a better man than I could have ever aspired to become."

There was a pause as my son smiled back. "Dad, I think you did a great job with all of us and deserve to be proud." Brandon then looked at his mother. "You and Mom did everything to make this happen, and I appreciate everything you've both sacrificed to do so. I hope to someday be the kind of father you've been for me."

My eyes burning with unshed tears, I excused myself so Lucy could have one-on-one time with our firstborn.

As a cadet, I had often walked alone along Flirtation Walk, a path skirting the banks of the Hudson River. Now I returned to my place of solitude to reflect.

As I stand by the banks of the Hudson River at West Point, admiring its serene, steady flow, I am reminded of the journey that brought me here and where it took me after. I am reminded of those who preceded me to West Point and beyond, who served our country in peace and in war. My gratitude is strengthened by the bonds with those ghosts whose legacies live on, forever etched onto the landscape of the Academy grounds and into the fabric of our nation, just as the river has shaped West Point's shores.

Looking downstream, the Hudson reminds me of my past. I see not just the battles and hardships but the resilience and growth that emerged from them. I see generations who have sacrificed and formed a bedrock for our Army and our country. I see my friends and brothers and sisters in arms, and my pride could not be stronger to know so many great Americans.

As I look upstream toward Newburgh, the ripples of the river flow toward West Point, where the water makes its inevitable turn around the bend, and I think about the future. While the composition of cadets has changed, the path that brings new generations to West Point has remained the same since the US Military Academy was conceived. This generation grew up after 9/11 and witnessed the nation's military fight for twenty-plus years. They were guided to West Point by the same values, sense of patriotism, and commitment as those who preceded them. I could not be prouder of my son and those of his generation who have answered the call to service.

My relationship with my children is my anchor. They are my purpose and have kept me going through dark times. Brandon's arrival at West Point in the summer of 2021 represented more than his personal achievement, though it was that above all; it was a testament to our collective family strength. Lucy and I found a way to coparent with mutual respect and understanding. Our love was restored. We are not the same people we once were, but our shared history binds us, as does a profound sense of purpose and commitment. The same can be said of our extended family, who helped Brandon along the way—grandparents, aunts, uncles, and friends.

Looking forward, I am filled with hope and determination. I have new goals: reinforcing a norm of mental health awareness and proactive treatment among our military and veteran communities and helping the broader public better understand how traumatic experiences can be transformed into personal growth—the crucible of every warrior poet. My professional journey continues to evolve, driven by a deep desire to contribute meaningfully to support our warfighters and ultimately our national security. Through it all, poetry remains my solace and voice. It captures the essence of experience and emotion. Each poem provides me closure and perspective—and readiness to embrace the future:

"New Horizon"

Walking the banks of the river to the sea

Where waves climb upon the shore,

There is a well-beaten path to a jetty

That dives deep where it meets the ocean floor.

Far too long have I dwelled on traumas of the past.

My warrior heart now seems healed at last.

Embracing the path before me, I look forward to swimming in the ocean.

Gripping hands with those before me, I embrace the promise of a new horizon.

In the quiet of the night, I finally understand that my journey wasn't about returning home—it was about discovering who I'd become, forgiving myself, letting go of the past, and focusing on the future. This is not the end but rather the beginning. The river flows, and so do we, ever steady, ever winding through life's terrain, shaping the landscape, until one day we return to the ocean and reach the horizon. For the first time, I am not fighting the current. I'm letting it carry me forward.

Ryan McDermott
USMA, Class of 2000
"With Honor in Hand"

AFTERWORD

If you carefully consider the story my father has told, taking time to understand the path he took, you may draw your own conclusions, some positive and some that are not. He is a warrior, both humble and accomplished. He has demonstrated great service to our family and to this country. My father has spent his life seeking redemption, as many of us do. I share this afterword not to judge him but to honor the lessons we both learned—about sacrifice and faith.

Some may scrutinize his decision to leave the military and pursue a career on Wall Street, seeing it as an about-face from his service in Iraq. But I believe he did this out of love for our family and a commitment to honor his marriage to my mother before God. The Army does its best to accommodate families, but no salary or benefits can replace lost time together. That was the choice my father faced when considering a commitment to more combat deployments or transitioning to civilian life.

I was raised in a home built on Christian-inspired love and structure. As a child, there was no greater joy to me than being generous to others. When our family was whole, it felt like paradise—my own Garden of Eden. That stability was shattered during the 2008 recession. The financial pressures forced my mother, my siblings, and me to move to Florida, where life was cheaper. What may have been meant as a temporary adjustment became permanent, as my parents decided to remain apart—perhaps a failure on both their parts.

People often talk about divorce rates and statistics, but they rarely acknowledge the real, human consequences of growing up in a broken home. Let me tell you what it did to me. I had social capital in Virginia and New York. I had friends, adults spoke highly of me, and I thrived. But Florida was different. In second grade, I had many friends, but I never saw them outside of school. By third grade, I had few friends. By fourth grade, I had more bullies than friends, and my life took a turn for the worse.

Without a father I could reliably turn to, I felt lost. I was not strong enough to endure the trespasses against me, and so I became what I despised. I don't think it's a coincidence that, during this time, I lost my faith in God.

I know my father believed he was serving us by providing from afar. I have no doubt that he loved me deeply, but perhaps he forgot that he was more than a provider; he was my dad. And I loved him very much. Some may say, "This seems like a very compromising assessment of your father in his own memoir." But let me make this clear: The decision to stay on the other side of the river, so to speak, was not simple. He had to let go of the past and forgive himself. As I read his poem "Downriver" and the epilogue that follows, I see my father's redemption in his renewed relationship with God. I believe my dad finally embraced God's mercy, forgiveness, and unconditional love.

In 2011, my father was brutally attacked by two men who showed up at his door. He was already at rock bottom. Divorced, alone, and broken, he had spent his life trying to do the right thing—only to endure suffering beyond measure. But the experience marked a point when my father was reborn. He kept going and eventually made it home.

No one escapes life without hardship. But we do have a choice: to let it define us or to rise above it. For years, I held on to resentment, certain that my father could have crossed the river sooner. Over time I realized the most important thing: He never stopped trying to come home.

The pandemic was a blessing because it allowed my dad to live with us. Reconnecting with my father made me feel like I had returned to the Garden of Eden. He helped me prepare for admission to West

Point by training me for the physical tests and explaining the mental and emotional challenges I would endure. I read an earlier manuscript of his story. When I reported to West Point, along with my mom and dad and my family, I carried his lessons with me, not just as his son but as a future leader. His journey shaped my own as I experienced the crucibles he had written about—and I grew in my faith. I look forward to serving in the Army with great anticipation of building a family within the warrior community.

My father struggled after he left the Army for a civilian world he didn't relate to. I see that my father lost his way and shame undermined his relationship with God, but he never lost his faith. His story provides an invaluable lesson: What matters is not the path we've taken but whether we find our way to the river crossing home—and still have the courage to venture over it when we get there.

My father carried the weight of his war, and whether I wanted to or not, I have carried it too. But now, I choose to carry his lessons instead.

Brandon McDermott
USMA, Class of 2025
"Together We Thrive"

ACKNOWLEDGMENTS

This book represents over twenty-five years of writing and over fifteen years of soul-searching. Writing it has been an act of reflection, and my sincere hope is that my journey helps others facing their own battles. That said, I could not have transformed my personal catharsis into a coherent narrative without the support and guidance of many.

This story is a personal one, but it is also part of a much larger narrative—the story of my fellow soldiers. The experiences of those who fought in Iraq in 2003, and the broader Global War on Terror, are forever intertwined. The men and women who served multiple tours inspired me to tell my story in a way that respects the integrity of their service. I sought feedback from the soldiers and commanders I served with in combat, and I deeply appreciate their support and understanding.

MILITARY MENTORS AND BROTHERS-IN-ARMS

I began writing the war chapters in the immediate aftermath of the 2003 Iraq campaign, at a time when my chain of command encouraged me to reconsider an Army career. Several of my commanders continued serving for over a decade beyond my departure in 2006:

- LTG (Ret.) Edward Cardon, who went on to command a division, Army Cyber Command, and later laid the foundation for Army Futures Command.
- LTG (Ret.) Ross Coffman, who later served as deputy commander, Army Futures Command.

- COL (Ret.) Michael Harris and his wife, Angie, who continue to honor the sacrifices of the troopers of 6-8 Cav to this day.
- LTC (Ret.) Rock Marcone, my commander in 3-69 Armor, who retired a few years after our combat tour and later became an executive at General Dynamics. Today, he coaches high school football, continuing to lead and mentor young men.
- LTC (Ret.) Scott Rutter, my battalion commander in 2-7 Infantry, who retired in 2003 and later found success in business and health care. He also served as a war correspondent and remains a steadfast supporter of the soldiers he once led. While not mentioned in this book, Scott was a superb commander and has become a great friend and supporter.
- COL Todd Kelly, former commander of Charlie Company, 2-7 Infantry, who remained in the Army through 2024 and eventually returned to West Point as deputy commandant, where he has mentored many cadets—including my son, Brandon.

To my fellow platoon leaders and soldiers, I am grateful for our shared experiences.

- Steve Gleason, who exited the Army in 2006 and served a career in federal law enforcement. He and his wife, Meg, have two daughters, and they eventually treated me to that amazing Italian dinner he bragged about in Iraq.
- Justin Morseth, who transitioned into medical device sales and faced challenges with PTSD and traumatic brain injury. He has found healing from starting a woodworking business selling his handcrafted wooden footballs and flags. Justin is also a public speaker and determined veteran advocate focusing on combat trauma, overcoming adversity, leadership, and resilience.
- Mike Pecina, Michael Keirstead, and Joshua Van Etten with whom I was honored to serve.
- SSG (Ret.) Luis Rosa, my driver in Iraq, who later deployed again as a squad leader and suffered severe injuries from an IED attack, losing three limbs. Reconnecting with Luis after my rock bottom in 2011 was a powerful moment. His unwavering spirit continues to inspire me. Through his painting, he embodies the essence of a warrior poet.
- Soldiers of the Black Sheep platoon: Edward Verdun (my reliable gunner and battle buddy in our Bradley turret), Cordell Gailliard (my first platoon sergeant), Brett Creeley (my platoon sergeant in Iraq), Andrew Sorenson, Randell Scott, Corey Anderson, Pat Dove, Troy Faver, Jon Barfield, Jason Chase, DeAndre Tyler, Joe Hester, Jason Mason, Richard Krum, Stan Dombrowski, John Lewis, Darrell Foster, Cory Heustis, Tony Childs, Jack Sullivan, Anthony Ramos, Christopher McGuire, Josh Robinson, Nathan Bennett, Aaron Marne, Dan Watson, Perrin, Perry, and Rivera.
- Tankers of the Steel platoon: James Currence, Charles Hall, Ross Carlson, Matthew Graff, Matt Heydon, John Woods, Jacob Arriaga, and Silvers.

- My fellow rear detachment commanders: Dave Chen, Keith Zieber, Eric Hooper, and Becca Elliot, who endured with me the losses of our units in 2005, cementing a bond that lasts to this day.

ACADEMIC INFLUENCES

My storytelling evolved while attending the Darden Graduate School of Business, and I owe much to my professors and mentors:

- Professor Jim Clawson, who taught leadership at Darden, emphasized self-assessment and personal growth, shaping how I processed my thoughts through writing. He was one of the first to read my manuscript and encouraged me to refine it, even during my darkest moments.
- Professor Ed Freeman, who taught ethics and leadership through theater, helped develop my artistic expression as I collaborated on a play about a casualty notification officer. His encouragement over the years was invaluable.
- Professor Alec Horniman, an Army veteran, who encouraged my storytelling.
- Professor James Rubin (now passed), who encouraged me to explore writing creatively, emphasizing the musical rhythm of prose and inspiring me to incorporate poetry into this book.

To my Darden classmates and faculty, and to the class of 2008, thank you for the experiences and friendships that have enriched my life.

FRIENDS WHO MADE A DIFFERENCE

I could not possibly list everyone who has played a role in my journey, but I want to acknowledge a few who have had a profound impact:

- The Frank family, especially Terri and Allen, who welcomed me into their home when I had no place to go.

- My best friend, Cory Frank, who provided feedback on my manuscript.
- My high school coach, Bill Cashman, who inspired me to believe in my dreams and coached my sons, Brandon and William, many years later to do so as well.
- My dear friends Brian Clarke and Kathy Johnson Clarke, who helped connect me to Charlotte Rogan, author of *The Lifeboat*. Charlotte's guidance on my manuscript was instrumental in how I ultimately shaped this memoir.
- Eric Chewning, Phil Dickinson, and Chris Ix, Army veterans at Darden, who helped me transition into civilian life.
- Saul Yeaton, who worked with me to bring a play to life in theater class, embracing the role of a casualty notification officer.
- USMA classmates Mike Cahill and Steve Dunaway.

COLLEAGUES AND MENTORS IN THE CIVILIAN WORLD

- Dick Beattie and Roger Altman, who provided safe harbor during the Great Recession.
- Warren Kohm, an amazing former boss who helped me get back home.
- Elizabeth Cheever, a great colleague and friend, who encouraged my writing.
- I also thank my former Pentagon colleagues—COL (Ret.) Ari McSherry, the Hon. Shawn Skelly, and Lucas Schleusener—for their friendship over the years.

MY FAMILY: MY GREATEST INSPIRATION

Finally, to my family, who have shaped me in ways I cannot fully express:

- I am deeply grateful to my mother, Patricia McDermott, for allowing me to share part of her story. Her strength, resilience, and transformation continue to inspire me.
- I also extend my heartfelt appreciation to Lucy, the mother of my children, for her enduring love and support through so many challenges.
- Lucy and I owe much to her parents, Paul and Kathy McGinnis, for their enduring support.
- I thank my dad, Rick Hardwicke, and my siblings—Jessica, Laura, Lauren, and Dane—for their unwavering love.
- To my children, Brandon, William, and Julia: You are my greatest motivation. My story represents only the prologue to yours, and while I wish it could have been different, I'm enormously proud of who you've become. May your lives be filled with purpose, love, and adventure.